Roger Sessions and His Music

Studies in Musicology, No. 81

George Buelow, Series Editor

Professor of Music
Indiana University

Other Titles in This Series

Roger Sessions and His Music

by
Andrea Olmstead
Head of the Department of Music History
The Boston Conservatory

UMI RESEARCH PRESS
Ann Arbor, Michigan

Produced and distributed by
UMI Research Press
an imprint of
University Microfilms International
A Xerox Information Resources Company
Ann Arbor, Michigan 48106

Library of Congress Cataloging in Publication Data

Olmstead, Andrea.
 Roger Sessions and his music.

   (Studies in musicology ; no. 81)
   Bibliography: p.
   Includes index.
   1. Sessions, Roger, 1896- . 2. Sessions,
Roger, 1896- . Works. 3. Composers—United States—
Biography. I. Title. II. Series.
ML410.S47304   1985   780'.92'4 [B]   84-28110
ISBN 0-8357-1633-3 (alk. paper)

To Burton Kaplan

Contents

List of Figures

Preface

An oral history generates its own primary source material. From 1974 to 1980 Roger Sessions and I discussed his life and music for an hour weekly at The Juilliard School in New York where we both taught. These interviews were recorded and transcriptions dot the landscape of this book, which attempts to portray the composer's own view of his life and music, as well as others' views about him. Sessions cooperated fully. In addition to participating in more than six years of interviews, he read the entire manuscript. While a composer's thoughts during and after the creation of a work represent a unique perspective, it is not the only view. Included here are other's reactions to Sessions's music—quotations from scholarly articles and newspaper reviews. Particularly illuminating were articles by Andrew Imbrie, Edward T. Cone, and Elliott Carter.

Interviews were also held with many of Sessions's well-known students and associates. I am grateful to all of them, named in the text, for their cooperation. Performers Beveridge Webster, Tossy Spivakovsky, and Louis Krasner were especially generous in contributing material on Sessions's piano music and his Violin Concerto. Suzanne Bloch provided insight into her father's relationship with Sessions. Others were helpful with regard to the text and deserve special thanks. Andrew Imbrie read the manuscript and made valuable suggestions. Martin Anderson and Edward T. Cone advised in the overall organization. Susan Saslow edited an early version and provided technical assistance. I would particularly like to thank Mary H. Smith for her practical help.

The libraries of The Juilliard School, the Oral History Collection at Columbia University, Princeton University, the Library of Congress, and the American Academy in Rome were invaluable. Institutional assistance was provided by the Sinfonia Foundation of Phi Mu Alpha Fraternity, which honored me with their 1980 grant for Research in American Music. Particular thanks are extended to the Edward B. Marks Music Company and to Merion Music for permission to reprint examples of Sessions's music for which they own the copyright.

Portions of this book have appeared, or will appear, in somewhat different forms in articles in *Tempo, Perspectives of New Music,* and *The New Grove Dictionary of Music in the United States.* Permission to republish is gratefully acknowledged. The John Simon Guggenheim Memorial Foundation and the American Academy in Rome indirectly assisted work on this book by granting Fellowships to my husband, composer Larry Bell. They did not realize they were aiding two endeavors at once—he helped prepare the musical examples.

Words of gratitude to Roger Sessions cannot adequately convey his unflagging patience, his generosity and graciousness, and the enormous amount I learned from him. In many ways this book was written for my students at The Juilliard School and at The Boston Conservatory, and for all performers approaching Sessions's music. As Sessions says, "It's the teacher who learns."

Andrea Olmstead
Boston
August 1984

Introduction

The development of Sessions's music through his eight symphonies, his opera *Montezuma*, . . . and his chamber music, has remained constantly interesting to me for its opulence of sound and imagination. His orchestral works, like those of so many more elaborate moderns, have suffered from inadequate performance and will certainly become an important part of the American repertory when conductors bother to make the effort to find out what is in them. . . . Sessions's music has been one long confrontation with the musical materials of our time. . . . The profound faith in ordered processes of musical thought and expression that go into the making of a work of art as it was conceived by the masters of the eighteenth, nineteenth, and early twentieth centuries, and still is by most of those interested in music, makes Sessions's music very satisfying to follow—full of musical substance and . . . rich in expression and idea.[1]

Thus Elliott Carter describes the music of Roger Sessions. The breadth and quality of his musical and prose output, as well as his influence on his many students, make Sessions an American composer of considerable stature. However, his music is not performed frequently, nor has there been significant investigation into his life and work that encompasses biography, analyses, and bibliography. Sessions's uncompromising approach to composition helps to account for the maintenance of his intensely personal musical style. His integrity is unshakable. Such a composer, committed to high artistic achievement, cannot accommodate public taste or prevailing musical fashion if they contradict the dictates of his own art. A greater familiarity with Roger Sessions and his work will certainly enlarge the devoted circle already convinced of his significance.

Next to his music, Sessions's greatest influence on the musical life of this century has undoubtedly been his teaching. That no Sessions School exists can be easily demonstrated by considering the diverse music of some of the composers who studied with him: Leon Kirchner, Andrew Imbrie, Milton Babbitt, David Diamond, Frederic Rzewski, Earl Kim, Miriam Gideon, Donald Martino, Edward T. Cone, Ellen Taaffe Zwilich, and Peter Maxwell Davies. Sessions's teaching encouraged in each his or her own artistic vision.

Sessions influenced a larger audience through three books of essays: *The Musical Experience of Composer, Performer, Listener,* six lectures delivered in 1949 at the Juilliard School of Music; *Questions About Music,* the lectures he gave as Charles Eliot Norton Professor at Harvard in 1968–1969; and *Roger Sessions: Collected*

Essays, published in 1979. Music students throughout the United States have been raised on his textbook, *Harmonic Practice.*

Sessions is generally considered an orchestral composer, and his nine symphonies, two concertos, Double Concerto, Concertino, Rhapsody, Divertimento, and Concerto for Orchestra amply support such a notion. Indeed, the orchestra has been described as his instrument. One might also regard Sessions as an instrumental composer. Three piano sonatas and two sets for piano, a Solo Violin Sonata and Duo for Violin and Piano, two string quartets and a String Quintet, Organ Preludes and a Chorale for Organ, and the Six Pieces for Violoncello represent a significant addition to solo and chamber music literature.

However, future generations may well view Sessions as primarily a vocal composer. Although Sessions has written almost as much music for vocal compositions as he has for instrumental ones, several circumstances explain why his vocal music is not as well known. One is its sheer difficulty. Those brave vocalists who attempt his angular lines must struggle to maintain their prominence over a thick, but essentially supportive, accompaniment. The soprano in the *Idyll of Theocritus,* for example, sings almost continuously for 42 minutes against a full orchestra. Boldness must be combined with technique and musical insight to give this music successful performance. Another circumstance is the nonavailability of scores and recordings. Sessions's opera *The Trial of Lucullus* and the orchestral version of *Psalm 140* for soprano are not published. The *Three Choruses on Biblical Texts, Romualdo's Song* (from *The Black Maskers*), *Turn, O Libertad, The Trial of Lucullus, Montezuma,* the *Mass,* and *Psalm 140* are not recorded. Commercial recordings of only three of Sessions's ten vocal works are available—*On the Beach at Fontana,* the *Idyll of Theocritus,* and *When Lilacs Last in the Dooryard Bloom'd.* The third reason, and the most damaging, has been infrequent performances of Sessions's vocal music. For example, Sessions's largest work, his opera *Montezuma,* languished twelve years awaiting its American premiere and has been performed only twice here.

It is not usually wise to generalize about any composer, especially one whose musical productivity has spanned almost 75 years. Nevertheless, a stylistic uniformity has been evident in Sessions's music since *The Black Maskers* (1923), although his output can be divided at five places for the purposes of periodization. This unity reflects Sessions's consistency of outlook and persists despite changes in technical procedure.

Sessions was affected by other composers. The influences of Stravinsky, Dallapiccola, Bloch, and Schoenberg are found in his music, but they are not powerful enough to erase Sessions's own strong individualism. He incorporated the contribution of others to distinctly personal ends. Certain identifying features characterize Sessions's style. One is the much-discussed "long line." Sessions's long phrases arch gracefully and participate in a highly complex contrapuntal texture. Another characteristic is rhythmic flexibility achieved by frequent shifts of time signatures and the use of polyrhythms. Third is his colorful orchestration.

Such dense, active, "complicated" music has proved difficult to grasp and has often been considered too difficult to play. However, both performers' capabilities and audiencess' willingness to listen have caught up with such music. The level of technical ability has gradually risen to meet the occasion. Having had wider exposure to the intricacies of contemporary music, audiences can now assimilate Sessions's music, providing they present what he calls a "willing ear." Sessions has waited years, in some cases decades, for his music to receive accurate performances and recognition.

The fact that he writes twelve-tone music has provided critics a "filing cabinet" in which to dispose of Sessions. Initially, he ardently opposed serialism. His music evolved very gradually from tonality through so-called atonality to twelve-tone procedures. However, he feels any procedure is subordinate to the music.

> The series is a point of departure for me always. It's certainly organized, but very freely organized, because I don't ever let myself be bamboozled by it. . . . The row is one's own possession; one is not possessed by the row. . . . A row evolves from working out of an original musical idea in which the role of the ear cannot be underestimated, but in the final analysis, organization of a piece of music is in the music itself.[2]

Popularity has never been among Sessions's goals. He pursued the same course he charted at age thirteen, when he abruptly informed his mother, "I'm going to be a composer." Acceptance of his music by audiences and even by musicians has been slow in coming. Sessions's remarkable patience has been supported by his awareness of how great music is often misunderstood in its own time. He believes that his music will endure.

Notes

1. Allen Edwards, *Flawed Words and Stubborn Sounds; A Conversation with Elliott Carter* (New York: W.W. Norton & Co., 1971), p. 64.

2. Taped interview 21 April 1976.

1

Early Biography

Forty Acres

Driving north up the Connecticut River on Route 47 from Hadley, Massachusetts, one is led by signs to the local historic site, Forty Acres, or the Porter-Phelps-Huntington House. During summer months a dollar buys a guided tour of the museum-house built in 1752 and the possessions of six generations of families who lived there. With its deeds and diaries dating from the French and Indian Wars, a 185-year-old grandfather clock that keeps perfect time, former slaves' quarters, a Southern veranda (the "Stoop") looking out onto the river, a secret staircase, tales of a ghost, antique furniture, and portraits of ancestors who entered the clergy, taught at Harvard, or fought in the Revolution, Forty Acres radiates continuity with the past. Ruth Huntington, daughter of one of its best-known residents, Frederic Dan Huntington, met her future husband—her second cousin Archibald Sessions—at Forty Acres. Research on the biography of their son Roger leads to this house.

Sessions's ancestors, the Phelpses, Porters, Huntingtons, Pitkins, and Cookes, emigrated to America from England seeking religious freedom.[1] In 1659 Samuel Porter was among the first settlers of Hadley, on the Connecticut River, a town surrounded by a stockade built for defense against the Indians. Outside this stockade four tracts of land were commonly owned. The tract north of the village was used by the owners of the northwest corner of the town, one of whom was Samuel Porter. His great grandson, Moses Porter, built the first house outside the stockade in 1752 and named it Forty Acres. Three elms still standing were planted by Moses Porter; each represented a member of his family.

Charles Phelps, Sr., who married Moses's daughter, Elizabeth, enlarged the 500-acre estate to a plantation of over 1,000 acres and built the huge barn that is now the Farm Museum in Hadley.[2] The Reverend Dan Huntington, Roger Sessions's great grandfather, married Elizabeth Phelps, and they had eleven children, all raised at Forty Acres. Their eldest daughter, also named Elizabeth, was Archibald Sessions's grandmother. Their youngest son, Frederic Dan, who became Bishop of Central New York, was Roger's maternal grandfather. Therefore, Archibald Sessions and Ruth Huntington, Roger's parents, were second cousins once removed

Figure 1.1. Forty Acres, or the Porter-Phelps-Huntington House, Hadley, Massachusetts. Built in 1752.

(see appendix 1). Roger Sessions later married a woman named Elizabeth and named his daughter Elizabeth.

Sessions's mother, Ruth (see fig. 1.2), was one of the Huntington's five children. Ruth's mother, Hannah Dane Sargent, was descended from William Sargent (see appendix 1). Hannah's mother, Mary Otis Lincoln, was the granddaughter of Major General Benjamin Lincoln, an associate of John Adams, John Hancock, and Paul Revere, and the first Secretary of War under George Washington. Sessions adored Hannah Sargent Huntington: "I always told people I had a grandmother complex."[3] To have known his maternal grandfather, Bishop Frederic Dan Huntington,[4] "who lived at a time when Beethoven was the greatest living composer and James Monroe was President of the United States," amuses Sessions.[5] A family tradition began with the celebration of the Bishop and Hannah Sargent's fortieth wedding anniversary. Photographs of the clan on the east porch of Forty Acres were taken every ten years from 1883 until 1913. In the 1903 photograph of their sixtieth anniversary (see fig. 1.3) Roger can be seen with his parents, Archibald Lowery Sessions and Ruth Huntington Sessions.

One of the few sources of information we have of Roger's fraternal grandparents is a description of his grandmother by Ruth Huntington Sessions:

> She and her brothers and sister had been educated abroad; there was an element of cosmopolitan tolerance in their outlook and a breadth of view that counterbalanced the Puritan inheritance she shared with her generation. This broad-mindedness she owed, as we did, to the grandmother who left Calvinism for Unitarianism. Her likeness to our Grandmother Huntington [born 1779] was pronounced, and her face had the same strong lines which we had seen in Aunt Bethia's face and in the pictures of Elizabeth Phelps—the long upper lip and delicate nostrils, severity softened by sweetness of Character.[6]

Roger's father, Archibald, had three sisters, Clara, Adeline, and Grace. Adeline, five years older than Archibald, and her brother were friendly with the conductor of the New York Philharmonic, Theodore Thomas. Archibald sang in Thomas's chorus. Adeline began as a soloist in Thomas's chorus but gave up her career because of stage fright. Berlioz gave her the baton with which he had conducted the Wagner Festival, and Sessions treasures this gift from his aunt. Not only did she exert a musical influence on him in his youth, but she also aided Roger financially in the 1930s.

It was during a visit to Forty Acres to meet his second cousins that Archibald Sessions met Ruth Huntington. They discovered common interests in music and religion, and an immediate bond was formed between the two. They were married, years later, in Forty Acres's Long Room, the very room in which they had met.

Archibald had brown eyes, was prematurely bald, and sported a handlebar mustache (his son shared these characteristics). He lived in New York most of his life and is remembered by Sessions as a "real New Yorker—not really happy anywhere else."

Figure 1.2. Sessions's mother, Ruth Huntington, in 1885.

Figure 1.3.   The Sixtieth Wedding Anniversary of Bishop and Hannah Huntington on 4 September 1903. The Bishop and his wife are seated on the right. The Sessionses are on the left: Archibald (standing), Ruth (sitting), John (left), and Roger (right). Hannah Sargent Sessions sits on the ground next to the Bishop. The scene is the east porch of Forty Acres.

He had been educated at Harvard, and he entered the field of law possibly because his father, also a lawyer, wished it. However, when John Sessions died in 1899, Archibald left law and pursued a literary career, editing *Ainslee's Magazine* at the firm of Street and Smith on Seventh Avenue in New York. Like his son Roger, he was interested in politics and ran for public office.

Archibald's success in his literary career is hard to assess; perhaps the lack of evidence is silent testimony. However, he associated with successful writers. In the first decade of this century, he and O. Henry together visited bowling alleys and shooting galleries on Sixth Avenue. In a note preceding O. Henry's *The Voice of the City: Further Stories of the Four Million,* Archibald writes of him:

> I have always thought that the dominant trait in O. Henry was his sensitiveness. By that I mean his extraordinary perception of delicate and subtle shadings of character in other people and the instantaneous reaction they produced in his own mind.[7]

He lists three "rebuffs" that O. Henry met with in trying to get his stories published, although he notes that "it is perfectly true that he escaped most of the discouragements experienced by the average run of young authors."[8] Perhaps Archibald was referring to his own experience in the literary world. His wife blamed his lack of success on a "false friend" who stole and sold Archibald's play.[9]

We have a clearer picture of Ruth Sessions than we do of Archibald. This is due in part to the scarcity of published prose by Archibald compared with the abundance of information contained in Ruth Sessions's autobiography and in the books by her family members. In addition, Ruth outlived her husband by nearly twenty years.

Her interest in music was evident from an early age. Exposed to the "gentle influence" of music on the Chickering piano as a child, she studied piano and taught Indian children how to play the instrument. Eventually, she decided to travel to Leipzig by herself to study music—something quite unusual for a woman at that time. Ruth's fascination with music is evident in this account, which she wrote from Leipzig to her future husband:

> We tip-toed softly down to the further end of the Hall [of the Gewandhaus] and opened the door just a wee crack to peep in. The concertroom is always dark in the morning for the few windows are closed and barred so the whole [room] has a mysterious appearance. There before the grand piano sat Clara Schumann, all alone—a dear old lady, large, with such a pleasant face, and soft grey hair. Dora and I were transfixed. She was playing the Beethoven Sonata which was to come in the evening, practicing it all in utter unconsciousness of listeners, and we were afraid to move for fear of breaking the charm . . . we stole up a back stairway, and came out in a corner of the gallery which looked *straight* down at her as she sat just under us at the piano. We meant not to be seen but the music and especially one beautiful run that she was playing over and over drew us nearer, and we got close to the edges, inching each other most fearfully to keep ourselves from screaming with delight, for we hardly knew what we were doing. Presently, however, she looked up and saw us, and smiled—just think of two girls having such a treasure to themselves as a smile from Clara Schumann! and we felt as if we could almost have sprung over the rail-

ing. . . . We waited until she was gone and then *didn't* we rush about and embrace each other in perfect ecstasy.

She certainly is, as the paper afterward said, the queen of piano players. Every note is so clear and perfect and comes from her finger ends with such absolute ease and exactness that you can nowhere find a fault. At the last she played some of her husband's little pieces, ever so many one after the other and we listened entranced.[10]

Ruth Sessions was an accomplished writer. She published *The Ups and Downs of Emily*,[11] a children's book, and stories in *Munsey's Magazine* and *St. Nicholas Magazine*. From her autobiography, *Sixty-Odd; A Personal History,* comes most of the information we have about Roger's background. Ruth was also active in politics. She led an unconventional life, working for liberal causes, including the women's suffrage movement. Her autobiography leaves the impression of an intelligent person who, on the surface at least, was free from bigotry. In describing his mother, "a highly complex woman," Sessions comments: "As bigotry went in those days my mother wasn't bigoted at all, but there were certain prejudices that were universal, and she couldn't escape that."[12]

Archibald and Ruth Sessions, married on 16 November 1887, had four children. In 1889 Sessions's sister, Hannah (named after Hannah Dane Sargent), was born. A second child, Mary, was born in 1892 but died of what is now called crib death. Their third child, Roger, was born on 28 December (Holy Innocents Day) 1896 in Brooklyn, where his mother was busy gathering signatures for a "white list" of companies in New York that provided adequate working conditions for their employees. She wrote about her "serious baby":

And on the morning of the twenty-seventh [*sic*], just in time to be welcomed by daylight, our oldest son appeared; a funny little baby, all mouth, as the nurse observed, and with eyes as dark as the proverbial fruit of the blackthorn.

. . . The cold throve apace. My sister Arria came to stay with me, and was godmother at his baptism. We had settled on naming him Roger—Roger Pitkin, I had planned to call him, after a collateral ancestor in England. I was ashamed to give him a purely arbitrary fancy name. The other two saw no sense in bringing in the Pitkin, so they made a plan of their own, and at the service, when Arria was asked to "name this child" as she handed him to the clergy-man, I was somewhat amazed to hear her say, quite positively, "Roger Huntington." I had no chance to protest, and we promised with mutual stoutness that he would fight manfully against the world, the flesh and the devil, name or no name. [Sessions was later to drop the use of Huntington.]

He was a strong young fellow, very sleepy and hungry, but awakened suddenly one cold night when the tinny jangle of a hurdy-gurdy started up under our window, ground out by a forlorn man who appeared to have been moved by desperation to attempt an out-of-season performance. I have never been able to remember the melody he produced, probably some rattling jig, for the baby claimed our attention. His eyes opened wide, his face grew pink, his hands moved excitedly. Evidently he was listening.

"That child's going to be musical," cried the nurse. "Look at him; he's all stirred up."

We rewarded the hurdy-gurdy man lavishly, and suggested politely that he should move on, the instrument not being suited for a lullaby, but he insisted on giving us an encore, which Roger quite appreciated. The incident was duly recorded and we found our surmise was correct; the infant's diminutive ear was sensitive to tonal vibrations, and his whole nerve-system responded to them.[13]

Roger's brother was born in 1899. His mother describes him:

> He was a merry little person, with an equable nerve-outfit, and even in his early babyhood made few demands on the attention of his elders. We named him John, after Archie's father, who had died a few weeks before. Roger greeted him with broad smiles, and settled himself into the big-brother attitude.[14]

Roger Sessions recalls the following incident here recounted in *Sixty-Odd*.

> Walter Damrosch was then conducting a series of young people's matinees, one of the most important moves in the history of American music. I took Roger to one of those; he was three now, and more musical than ever, always wanting to be at the piano, where he touched one note at a time, prolonging it and listening to its last vibration, and then perhaps playing a chord, stretching his small fingers apart and striking the keys almost timidly, with a smile to himself. He never attempted tunes. . . .
>
> We sat in a proscenium box, the second tier, and the concert began with the *Pilgrims' Chorus* from *Tannhäuser*. Listening so intently that I had forgotten the small figure beside my knee, in white kilts which made him look particularly infantile, I happened to turn my head toward the audience once, and noticed that people were looking toward the box and smiling. Roger was standing there with one hand in the air, following Damrosch's baton with absolute fidelity, beat by beat, a broad grin on his countenance. He kept it up unconsciously until the very last notes of the overture, for I hated to interrupt him; then he climbed up in my lap, still smiling but saying not a word.[15]

When Archibald Sessions's law firm closed its New York branch, financial prospects looked rather dismal for the struggling young family. Ruth Sessions attempted to resolve this difficult situation; she felt that if she could help give her husband a year or longer in which to make his way in the literary world, the talent she was certain he had could be developed. She searched for a way to make a home for her children and at the same time provide for the family expenses.[16]

> In spite of all the preconceived, traditional views of the essence of matrimonial responsibility, all the ordinances of social life which made a wife a dependent under the law, it was an absolutely clear conviction in my mind, growing with each year of marital experience that the mother's obligation for the support of her children was as great as the father's. Her share of the work for the household might with equal propriety consist in wage-earning.[17]

President Seelye of Smith College and Bishop Huntington discussed the idea of Ruth Sessions opening a house off-campus for students. The Sessionses agreed to accept this offer, one which meant separation. She describes the difficulty of the decision:

> It was not easy to make, and yet the very fact that we loved one another deeply, and wanted the best for our two selves and for our children, kept it from being a tragedy. For each one a door of opportunity was offered; freedom with its inescapable price of isolation, sacrifice

Figure 1.4. Ruth Huntington Sessions in 1901.
With Roger and her youngest son, John.

that would be keen and possibly bitter; hard work; a complete readjustment of our plan of living. Things we could not face all at once, nor even work out with the imagination which set itself to appreciate them.[18]

This supposedly temporary situation—Ruth Sessions living in Northampton and her husband residing in New York—lasted for 25 years. Although Archibald visited Northampton in the summers, it took Roger years to reconcile his parents' unconventional living arrangement. "I don't know what went on, it was always a puzzle; it didn't simplify life for the children."[19] He dismisses, however, any notion of disharmony between the two. "I think they were always very attached to each other, you see."[20]

Sessions began taking piano lessons at the age of four with a Mr. Edwards. In the fall of 1901 he studied with the organist of the St. John's Church of Northampton, with whom he "wasn't trained to listen to a phrase."[21] In 1906 Sessions entered the Cloyne School in Newport, Rhode Island, where his piano lessons were discontinued. At this age the tunes in head were the Intermezzo from *Cavalleria Rusticana* and the Spanish tune *La Sorella*.

Sessions still recalls the Cloyne School with a certain amount of bitterness. Although ranking high scholastically, Sessions quickly ran up against their Dickensian discipline. He was required to wear a yellow ribbon for misbehaving, which meant that no one was allowed to talk with him. He was once made to memorize Longfellow's *Evangeline*, "rather awful doggerel,"[22] as punishment for some misbehavior. Sessions, who cried easily, had difficulties with the headmaster, who shook his fist at the boy, reminding him of the school motto, "Prompt and silent obedience is the first duty of the soldier and the schoolboy," and admonished him not to cry.

By Christmas his mother and father realized their error in sending him to Cloyne.

We had not realized, however, that a child who is more or less precocious and uneven in development cannot be thrust into a crowd of average youngsters, without some of the martyrdom of the misfit. He came home at Christmas time a bundle of nervous terrors, and we felt we must find a new school at once, where a moderate, sympathetic headmaster would handle those fears by quietly carring confidence with him. . . . But we found the best possible conditions in the Campbell [*sic*: Kingsley] school at Essex Falls, New Jersey, whose principal combined the very qualities we sought.[23]

Kingsley was a kind of military school at which the students wore blue-gray military uniforms, drilled with guns, and exercised with a former major in the Spanish-American War. There Sessions "lived a much more rough and tumble life" and discovered that he was ahead of his class.

He resumed piano lessons in the summer of 1908 studying, among other things, Bach preludes and the Soldiers' Chorus from *Faust*—"a dreadful, absolutely awful piece, although at the time I liked the Soldiers' Chorus."[24] Later that year, at the Kent School in Kent, Connecticut, he continued piano study with the English teacher,

Mr. Whittingham. "I kept it up more or less, but I didn't practice. It [the piano lessons] paid no attention to one's ear, only to one's fingers."[25]

From age eleven to thirteen Sessions studied at the Kent School. Father Sill, the headmaster, was a monk of the Order of the Holy Cross, the order founded by Sessions's uncle, James Huntington. At Kent Sessions read piano music at sight. Again he got into trouble. For making a derisive comment about the headmaster he was not allowed to play the piano for two weeks. However, Sessions feels none of the bitterness towards Kent that he still feels for Cloyne: "I didn't have any really bad memories of Kent, although I was impatient and always a rebel there."[26] Sessions later sent his own son, John, to the Kent School.

Sessions began writing music in the summer of 1909 and continued to do so throughout his second year at Kent. Terrified of being ridiculed because of his experience at Cloyne, he waited until the fall of 1910 to announce to his parents that he wanted to be a composer. "The fact that I loved music was just a picturesque, peculiar trait" to his parents, although his mother boasted about it.[27] In 1910 Archibald Sessions asked the opinion of several musicians about the musical prospects of his thirteen-year-old son. Engelbert Humperdinck, in New York for the Metropolitan Opera premiere of his *Koenigskinder,* was consulted, as was Puccini, whose opera *La Fanciulla del West* was also being presented. Later, Dallapiccola told Sessions that Puccini had paced the floor all night over advice to some young composer and finally had decided he could not make a decision of that importance for someone else. He was probably referring to Roger, since that was what Puccini told Archibald.

Often having visited Forty Acres as a child, Sessions feels "like one of the trees." Partly because of his family's New England traditions and preoccupation with ancestry, but also because he studied and wrote music in this country until he was twenty-seven, Sessions did not find it necessary to prove himself "American" in style. Years later, Sessions reflected on how his upbringing affected his music.

> I come from an old family and that is *undoubtedly* part of my life, because I realized that with this background I always had a basic sense of social security; I mean a security in American society. Anything I did and put my whole self into must have something American about it. I don't believe in being self-conscious about these things; then the music becomes essentially contrived.[28]

His formal training as a composer began at the age of fourteen, when he entered Harvard University.

Apprenticeship

Ruth Sessions recalls her son starting his college education:

> Roger entered Harvard in the fall of 1911; at fourteen he was large and strong, with the appearance of a sixteen-year-old. But he was mortally afraid of being recognized for the youngster

he really was, and had a nervous terror of publicity. He and Nan, therefore, were quartered for two winters in a little apartment on [*sic*: off] Brattle Street, with an elderly maid to look after them. Roger had definitely decided on a musical career, and had written, two years before, a miniature opera scored quite correctly for an orchestra of twenty instruments. [Not quite correctly: Sessions did not know orchestration well and mistakenly used a violino piccolo, an obsolete instrument.] It was composed in the manner of Wagner, and contained various motives. He named it *Lancelot and Elaine;* I recollect that he made the Guinevere motive, as he told me with all the earnestness of a romantic twelve-year-old, the most attractive one of all but with less *meaning,* because, though very beautiful, she had no soul. He was never especially willing to play his productions, always asserting that he could hear them just as well without; and they were not taken with him to Harvard; he already felt them to be childish.[29]

Sessions did not feel that music courses at Harvard were directed toward people planning to become serious musicians. "Few people knew what a really good music education involved."[30] Sessions's musical education gained more from his regular attendance at the Boston Symphony Orchestra than from classwork. Sessions retained the sound of this orchestra as his model—its principal oboist, Georges Longy, produced the ideal oboe sound for Sessions, who himself played oboe for a year at Harvard. The orchestra's frequent performances of Wagner, under Karl Muck, also influenced Sessions, who knew *Tannhäuser, Lohengrin,* and *Die Meistersinger.*

At Harvard Sessions took courses in counterpoint and in canon and fugue from Archibald Davison. For the fugue class Sessions wrote a "monstrous fugue with all sorts of modulations."[31] He studied orchestration with Edward Burlingame Hill; he liked this course so much he repeated it. He wrote several pieces for a course in vocal and choral writing, taught by Spalding. Hill suggested that Sessions go to France to study with Ravel. Sessions was extremely enthusiastic about this idea, but the year was 1914 and the First World War frustrated these plans.

Before Sessions had gone to Harvard, he met Arnold Dolmetsch, the English music antiquarian. He advised the young composer not to bother with harmony but to study counterpoint. Harvard, however, had a harmony prerequisite, and Sessions took the required six-week course with George Vieh, a pianist and pupil of Bruckner, in order to enter Harvard's counterpoint classes.

Sessions joined the staff of the monthly *Harvard Musical Review,* "a completely quixotic enterprise" begun in October 1912 by members of the 1914 class. Sixteen-year-old Sessions published his first article, "Wagner's Opinions of Other Composers," for its Wagner centenary issue. With the April 1914 issue Sessions became the head of the Board of Editors. He edited the journal through January 1915. In March 1916 the *Harvard Musical Review* folded. Generally, Sessions's opinions about critics, program music, and "American music," and his fundamental attitudes about music, were already formed at this young age and did not significantly alter over the next seven decades.

Between May 1913 and December 1915 Sessions contributed thirteen articles to the *Harvard Musical Review.* His writing is characterized by strongly held opinions and an ability to fix upon the core of an issue. For example, in his first article about Wagner,[32] Sessions reveals his wide knowledge of Wagner's writings and perspicaciously concludes that Wagner was "a man who was governed by his aversions rather than by his sympathies."

Sessions criticized music critics. In "The Case Against Professional Musical Criticism" he condemns critics for spoiling good causes, as for example Brahms's disciples did, and for making personal remarks against composers. Although he mentions Bernard Shaw, Olin Downes, and Ernest Newman in a positive light, he concludes that "problems in artistic appreciation should be discussed as if they were problems in morality. But we must guard against the great danger of taking professional criticism too seriously, for as it now exists it is utterly useless—nay, harmful, except when considered purely as a means of making a living."[33] Discussing the subject of critics who cannot find form or melody in revolutionary modern music, Sessions writes:

> Music requires, perhaps more than any other art, logical statement of ideas, but it is first of all an expression of emotion or thought, and as our emotions and thoughts are not of the type that are readily coerced and measured out according to the prescription of others; neither can their physical expression be fitted into the mould which others make for them, no matter how competent those may be.[34]

In "Our Attitude Towards Contemporary Musical Tendencies" Sessions is incensed by his contemporaries' attitudes. Responding to an article about ragtime that appeared in the same issue of the *Review,* Sessions comments: "Not till the advent of a genius, who shall, as a genius, be unhampered by prejudice of this kind can we have a true American music; and the sooner we realize this, the better."[35] He also attacks Ernest Newman for viewing Elgar and Holbrooke as greater composers than Debussy and Strauss.

In 1914 Sessions was taken with *Parsifal:* "As for the music of *Parsifal,* too much can scarcely be said in its praise."[36]

One of the most intriguing episodes in Sessions's early prose career begins with his three-part series entitled "Fifty Years of Richard Strauss." He reveals his familiarity with virtually all of Strauss's important music to date. Again, he cannot refrain from stating his beliefs firmly. His praise of Strauss is absolute: "The most striking characteristic of *Don Juan* is its absolute perfection of form."[37] "It is difficult to praise *Tod und Verklärung* too highly."[38] *Feuersnot* contains "one of the greatest love scenes in music."[39]

He opines about Brahms, Tchaikovsky, Mahler, humor, and program music. "In reality the sonata form is Brahms's master." He cites the first movement of the Fourth Symphony and the Violin Concerto, but rejoins: "Those who find nothing but form in Brahms are surely beyond help!"[40] Tchaikovsky "can never really move us; he gives us a sensation of acute physical pain rather than spiritual conflict or sorrow."[41]

Strauss's nearest competition in modern times is probably Mahler. Mahler's canvas was gigantic, his emotion profound; but he was incapable of the refinement of a Strauss; beside those of Strauss, his melodies and harmonies seem almost absurd in their obviousness. And Mahler's spirit was narrow; he was the musical metaphysician. Strauss is the more universal artist, the painter of human emotions and destinies.[42]

Sessions feels *Till Eulenspiegel* should be regarded as absolute music rather than as program music, and here he examines the ingredients of comedy. "The truly humorous man is on intimate terms with humanity, and is able to appreciate more deeply its sorrows as well as its joys and its follies."[43] And finally, about program music: "Strict program music is just a source of amusement for people who do not understand music."[44]

A little more than a year later Sessions's opinions about Strauss had changed drastically. In a second set of three articles, published after a year's hiatus in his contributions to the *Harvard Musical Review,* Sessions qualifies his appraisal of each of Strauss's works. Already, in 1915, Sessions issued a post mortem on Strauss, announcing that Strauss is "of the past." Strauss's music tended toward what "Wagner termed *Kapellmeistermusik*—in the vernacular of our time, 'hack-work.'"[45] Sessions analyzes Strauss's technical failures, particularly those in his harmony. The tone of these articles contrasts sharply with the earlier series. Presumably, Sessions's disappointment stemmed from his impression that Strauss did not continue to turn out masterpieces. Here Sessions concentrates on the defects, rather than the strengths, of Strauss's music. Sessions feels Strauss has lost his "self-assurance." "We feel that he is now no longer a conqueror, but a slave of his success."[46] This essay was written just prior to the first performance of the Alpine Symphony. As if to justify Sessions's assertion that "Strauss is no longer a creative force in music," a negative review of the European premiere is reprinted without comment at the conclusion of Sessions's article. One can speculate on what influence this acquaintance with Strauss's career later had on Sessions.

Sessions was later to compare Harvard to Princeton: "Princeton is liberal, but Harvard is free." For Sessions Yale of 1915 was neither as "free" nor as liberal as Harvard, but the musical life was better. Sessions undertook a Bachelor of Music degree at Yale, where he studied exclusively, although not privately, with Horatio Parker; with him he took classes in music history, composition, advanced orchestration, and conducting. Sessions studied piano only during his first year. Sessions comments about Horatio Parker:

He was a very sad man, really; this is the way I always think of him, as a very sad man, a very good musician, but very lonely. . . .

I think he was discouraged and disillusioned; he had never been able to give the students what he wanted to give, and he'd sort of given up trying. He taught in an extremely traditional, con-ventional way, which wasn't always accepted very wholeheartedly by his students.[47]

Sessions characterized Parker as "a very shy man. I was really very fond of him, but I never felt that I knew him."[48]

Figure 1.5. Sessions House at Smith College, Northampton, Massachusetts. Ruth Sessions first ran this residency house for Smith students, still known as Sessions House.

Sessions had been rejected by the American armed forces because of his poor eyesight. He initially opposed the war, but later his conscience bothered him. When news of the Armistice reached Sessions House in Northampton, he was asked to play something on the piano. In response, he played part of the Beethoven Ninth—the work he felt most appropriate for the occasion.

After graduating from Yale in 1918, 22-year-old Sessions obtained a job teaching at Smith College, where his mother still ran the off-campus dormitory, Sessions House (see fig. 1.5). He was hired on the strength of having won the Steinert Prize at Yale for the first movement of his D-major Symphonic Prelude. William Alan Neilson, President of Smith, was "always a very good friend of mine who gave tacit support to me."[49] Other friends and faculty members included Roy Dickinson Welch in the music department, Arthur Locke, and Raffaello Piccoli, Professor of literature, whom Sessions felt understood him better than anybody else. Sessions fondly remembers a performance of the Mozart Requiem given by Gorokhoff, the former assistant choirmaster of the Moscow Cathedral.

At Smith Sessions first tasted the problems nearly always present among members of a college faculty. During an argument about teaching methods, he was called "a young upstart" by Henry Dyke Sleeper, the unpopular head of the Music Department. Despite the fact that Sleeper was subsequently voted out of his position as Chairman, Sessions's problems at Smith did not end. He felt misunderstood and "wasn't really among musicians at all in my sense of the word. It was not a real musical life."[50] He felt constrained academically as well: "I was supposed to ask the students to write little pieces about the snow on the campus and that sort of thing instead of teaching them harmony and counterpoint."[51] Sessions was so disenchanted that when he left Smith he swore off university teaching.

One project at Smith was a group undertaking in which members of the class of 1920 composed music for Shakespeare's *Merchant of Venice*.[52] It was also at Smith that Sessions met and became engaged to Barbara Foster, a junior from Claremont, New Hampshire. Sessions's mother describes Barbara, who later became an art historian, and their wedding on 3 June 1920:

> In June came Roger's marriage to a brilliant and fascinating student with whom he had been in love ever since the beginning of the war. They had been engaged for eighteen months, and Barbara had been living in a little annex to our old house, with five other girls, during her senior year. The two had studied together evenings, in our library, taken long walks, and heard concerts. Barbara played the violin very well and their mutual enjoyment of music was intense. They planned a honeymoon at the farm [Forty Acres], where they could be alone for a week before I moved there for the summer, and decided to have their wedding the day after examinations closed, escaping from commencement ceremonies. My husband and sister and I, with John and Nan [Sessions's brother and sister] made a quick trip to New Hampshire, where Barbara's parents lived; it was a home wedding in their lovely house, and we all enjoyed meeting them and beginning a new friendship.
>
> They were sure they could live on the small salary of an instructor, and they were eager to work together. They had picked out a tiny [*sic:* large] house in Hadley village. So we fathers and mothers stood by and heard them plight their troth to one another with the hope and pride and sympathy that had inspired our own parents. They went directly to the farm, but as com-

mencement approached, Barbara's teachers were dismayed at the idea of her being absent from the graduation ceremonies, because she had received high honors. We found it difficult to induce her to go there without breaking the news to her, but it was managed somehow by enlisting Roger's services, and in the end she was on hand to receive the *summa cum laude* which she had well earned.[53]

Fifty-six years later, Sessions commented simply: "My wife and I both married before we had any idea of what marriage was really like."

Barbara Foster (1899–1980) was the middle child of three sisters. The eldest, Eleanor, married a flautist, Merry Cohu, for whom Sessions wrote his uncatalogued Pastorale for Flute Solo. The youngest, Rosamond, who Sessions considered a "budding pianist," married Daniel Sayre, who founded the School of Aeronautical Engineering at Princeton. Sessions dedicated his First Piano Sonata to her. Rosamund Sayre was music librarian at Princeton for many years and was especially close to Sessions, particularly during the 1930s.

Sessions continued work on the Symphonic Prelude. Josef Stransky, conductor of the New York Philharmonic, had agreed to play it in Northampton and possibly in New York. At Smith Henry Dyke Sleeper added to this mounting pressure by his prodding. Sessions became bogged down in the second movement. He attempted to resolve the creative crisis by studying Cherubini's *Counterpoint* and Vincent d'Indy's *Cours de Composition*. He realized in November 1919, however, that he needed to discuss his musical problems with another composer. Sessions felt he could rely on Ernest Bloch's judgment. He describes his first meeting with the Swiss composer at his apartment on Lexington Avenue in New York:

> [Bloch] . . . treated me quite roughly. He sat me down at the piano and made me play the first movement of my symphony, and then stood behind me and shouted out the names of all the composers I was influenced by [d'Indy, Franck, Debussy, Wagner, and Strauss]. It happened that I knew that I was influenced by these composers so that, although I was a little disconcerted, I wasn't really fazed by it. It finally got so that I joined in with him just to show him what the situation really was.[54]

Bloch told Sessions years later that he did this only to see if Sessions could take it. This meeting marked the beginning of a profitable learning experience and a warm friendship.

Suzanne Bloch, her father's biographer, remembers his reactions to Sessions the first day they met:

> You know the story when he first played his music for my father and father kept yelling all the names of all the composers [he'd been influenced by] and Roger joined in after a while. This is a very good beginning, because they understood each other and my father at once realized this was a very serious student. He had many people who were more or less amateurs, but this was somebody he really believed in.[55]

Bloch urged Sessions to scrap the symphony and to work hard on elementary exercises, small pieces, and counterpoint in order to gain more facility. He promised that at the end of two years Sessions would be able to do anything he wanted to compositionally. They began that day with the first eight measures of Beethoven's F-minor Sonata, Op. 2, No. 1. Later, Bloch used Wagner's music as a model to teach form and Orlando di Lasso's to teach counterpoint. Sessions managed to save enough of his annual $1,500 salary at Smith to commute every six weeks to New York to study "musical anatomy" (as he called it) with Bloch.

In 1920 Ernest Bloch became the first director of the Cleveland Institute of Music. Sessions followed him to Cleveland in 1921. There Sessions felt among musicians—Theodore Chanler, Douglas Moore, and the composer Jean Binet, a disciple of Jaques-Dalcroze. Sessions taught theory, music history, and solfeggio, and he accompanied the chorus in which Suzanne Bloch sang. As she describes:

> [Roger] was teaching the Danhauser, and he was accompanying all the Danhauser pieces. He would also accompany in the chorus rehearsals, which were conducted by my father. And it was fascinating—there was Roger, anytime at the piano, for Palestrina to help with the pitch, he would be there to play. I remember always we did "Bonjour, mon coeur" by Orlando di Lasso, which was [she sings]. . . . He said, "Now Roger, how would Haydn harmonize that?" And he made it sound just like Haydn with a seventh dominant. He made it do different things, and he said, "Now listen what Orlando di Lasso does," which is very modal. . . .
>
> Now that summer of 1922, Father taught school and had Roger as his assistant. So right away, from the beginning, Roger became a very important part of the Institute as a teacher and as a friend, as a confidant to my father, and also to make up for the mentality that was in Cleveland at that time. Now Roger and my father had very much in common, and they also had the most wonderful Rabelaisian minds. And what went on in my father's office was something incredible. The stories that they told and the jokes they had!
>
> And the classes were absolutely wonderful, because Roger, though not devastatingly exciting, you know, he has a great sense of humor and knows music. Anything he can play. He doesn't have to give much explanation. He goes to the music and plays it for you and, with his sort of grunting way, brings out all the essence of it.[56]

Suzanne Bloch enjoyed telling another anecdote about Sessions and her father:

> . . . [Hubbard Hutchinson] and Roger were the two people teaching theory and ear training and so on. And Hubbard was very handsome, you know, with red hair and dressed fit to kill. Here comes Roger, you know, with soft collars, kind of a little bit lumpy. And [their patron] Mrs. Saunders said to my father, "I have to talk to you. There are complaints by parents saying Mr. Sessions goes and teaches with soft collars. He doesn't dress formally." And Father said, "Is that so?" Father next day only came wearing soft collars![57]

Ernest Bloch was a man with a complex and fascinating personality. Emerging from the relatively small city of Geneva, Bloch found success in cosmopolitan Paris with a performance of his opera *Macbeth*. However, he seemed often to be his own worst enemy, according to *Macbeth*'s librettist, Edmond Flegg. Bloch did much to destroy his Paris success. He flew from one emotional extreme to another. He dramatized his life, convinced that students, women, and friends were either completely for him or great betrayers. Feeling deceived at one point, Bloch took

Figure 1.6.   Roger Sessions with Ernest Bloch in 1923.

an overdose of barbiturates, went into a coma, and had extraordinary dreams. In one he went to heaven and met illustrious composers of the past. He asked Mozart why he wrote superficial last movements; Mozart said that he wanted to make people happy. This led Bloch to examine his conscience; he concluded that he had been a great egotist all his life. In another dream he met God, who communicated to Sessions the message, quite similar to Bloch's own, that Stravinsky was a nice man and a gifted composer, but on the wrong track. Later, at a performance, Bloch moved people to tears by making a half-hour speech, "a public confession of all his sins, an absolutely religious revival occasion."[58]

Sessions describes his problem with Bloch as

> simply that of a young man sort of prying himself loose. I was devoted to him, but there were certain things in his point of view about music which I just couldn't accept, and which I felt— well, accounted for things which I felt as weaknesses in the music itself. Bloch really in a sense belonged to a sort of Wagnerian tradition. In other words, he thought of himself as more than a musician, as a kind of prophet, which is a very hard thing to describe without making it sound very unsympathetic. . . . He felt that through his art, he was bringing a kind of spiritual message to people. The only trouble is that, Bloch being the kind of very complex character that he was, there was quite a bit of showmanship involved in this too. The thing that I objected to is that I felt—and I think I could certainly defend myself on this ground very well, by referring to the score[s]—I felt that this led to a good deal of shoddy workmanship in his music.[59]

Despite Bloch's warnings, Sessions continued to be influenced by Stravinsky's music, a situation probably furthered by his meeting Stravinsky. Nadia Boulanger introduced Sessions to Stravinsky when he came to Cleveland in 1925 to conduct the orchestra. Stravinsky invited the younger composer to ride with him on the train to Philadelphia for a rehearsal of his Piano Concerto—a piece which particularly interested Sessions. Although Stravinsky was friendly, Sessions did not follow up opportunities to talk further with the composer. Later, he regretted his shyness:

> After I'd been in Europe for a while I got used to the fact that older men, no matter how famous they are, like to have younger men around them, and are very cordial and friendly, instead of just feeling the younger men are a nuisance.[60]

During that same year Sessions wrote the unpublished incidental music to Karl Vollmüller's *Turandot, Princess of China* given at the Cleveland Playhouse. (Sessions's main mode of transportation to the Playhouse and elsewhere was his motorcycle with a sidecar. He still bears a scar resulting from an accident on that motorcycle.) Almost 40 years later Sessions discussed his view of Puccini as

> . . . a kind of operatic routineer, in the best sense of the word. I mean, I think that he turned the operas out, so to speak, and hunted around for a subject. But what I don't like about *Turandot*, I feel that in a sense Puccini is a little too sophisticated; the flavor of garlic has been sort of attenuated. Then, I detest the libretto. I think this is a sadistic story.[61]

In the meantime Bloch had problems at The Cleveland Institute for various reasons. One was his teaching fixed *do* solfège when the public schools taught moveable *do*. Also, he was apparently not effective as a fund raiser, nor did he frequent the social functions that the financially supportive society wished. When asked to resign, Bloch promptly refused, insisting that they kick him out. The Cleveland Institute did. In a gesture of support for his friend, Sessions resigned in protest. He felt that "it was bad enough [in Cleveland] with Bloch, without Bloch it would be impossible."[62]

After 1925 Bloch and Sessions saw each other infrequently. Sessions spent the next seven years in Europe, and Bloch continued to disapprove of the direction Sessions's music was taking. Bloch became ill in the late 1950s, and Suzanne urged Sessions to write to him. It would have meant much to the 79-year-old composer to hear from his most famous student, but Sessions, not a good correspondent, did not write. Bloch died in Oregon in 1959.

Notes

Material from the Roger Sessions oral history memoir in the Columbia University Oral History Collection is copyrighted by The Trustees of Columbia University of New York, 1975, and is used by permission.

1. A history of the family is outlined in James Lincoln Huntington's *Forty Acres: The Story of the Bishop Huntington House* (New York: Hastings House, 1949). See also appendix 1.

2. Elizabeth's diary, containing a record of events at Forty Acres and the histories of the families who lived there, is in the museum, along with other family documents and relics. One of these relics is Moses Porter's sword, with which he fought in the French and Indian War. Sessions likes to relate the bizarre tale of how news of Porter's death reached his wife: An Indian returned Moses's sword, spurs, and Elizabeth's unopened letters to her through an open window at Forty Acres.

3. Taped interview 2 October 1974.

4 The Huntington family and the family of this author are connected through the relationship between Reverend Frederic Dan Huntington and Reverend Charles Tyler Olmsted, who became Coadjutor Bishop of Central New York succeeding Bishop Huntington, who died 11 July 1904. Reverend Olmsted, my forebear, conducted the funeral service.

5. Taped interview 9 October 1974.

6. Ruth Huntington Sessions, *Sixty-Odd: A Personal History* (Brattleboro, Vt.: Stephen Daye Press, 1936), p. 336.

7. William Sydney Porter, *The Voice of the City: Further Stories of the Four Million*, with a note by Archibald Sessions (Garden City, N.Y.: Doubleday, Page & Co., 1925), pp. vii–viii.

8. Ibid., p. x.

9. Ruth Sessions, *Sixty-Odd*, p. 414.

10. Ruth Huntington, "Suddenly . . . music!" *The Christian Science Monitor* (12 November 1975). Letter dated Thursday in Holy Week, 1883.

11. Ruth Huntington Sessions, *The Ups and Downs of Emily,* illus. by Peter Larkin (New York: Dodd, Mead & Co., 1940).

12. Taped interview 13 November 1979.

13. Ruth Sessions, *Sixty-Odd,* pp. 331–32.

14. Ibid., p. 344.

15. Ibid., p. 346.

16. Ibid., p. 348.

17. Ibid., pp. 348–49.

18. Ibid., p. 350.

19. Taped interview 2 October 1974.

20. Taped interview 13 November 1979.

21. Untaped conversation 1 March 1978.

22. Taped interview 13 November 1979.

23. Ruth Sessions, *Sixty-Odd,* pp. 377–78.

24. Untaped conversation 1 March 1978.

25. Ibid.

26. Taped interview 13 November 1979.

27. Untaped conversation 1 March 1978.

28. Taped interview 23 April 1975.

29. Ruth Sessions, *Sixty-Odd,* p. 384.

30. Untaped conversation 14 March 1978.

31. Untaped conversation 14 March 1978.

32. Roger Sessions, "Wagner's Opinions of Other Composers," *Harvard Musical Review* 1, no. 8 (May 1913): 17.

33. Sessions, "The Case Against Professional Musical Criticism," *Harvard Musical Review* 2, no. 2 (November 1913): 6.

34. Sessions, "The Case Against," p. 4.

35. Sessions, "Our Attitude Towards Contemporary Musical Tendencies," *Harvard Musical Review* 2, no. 4 (January 1914): 5.

36. Sessions, "Parsifaliana," *Harvard Musical Review* 2, no. 6 (March 1914): 15.

37. Sessions, "Fifty Years of Richard Strauss—I," *Harvard Musical Review* 2, no. 8 (May 1914): 15.

38. Ibid.

39. Sessions, "Fifty Years of Richard Strauss—II," *Harvard Musical Review* 2, no. 9 (June 1914): 20.

40. Sessions, "Fifty Years—I," p. 15.

41. Sessions, "Fifty Years—I," p. 17.

42. Sessions, "Fifty Years of Richard Strauss—III," *Harvard Musical Review* 2, no. 10 (July 1914): 25.

43. Sessions, "Fifty Years—I," p. 17.

44. Sessions, "Fifty Years—I," p. 14.

45. Sessions, "Richard Strauss As a Tone Poet," *Harvard Musical Review* 4, no. 1 (October 1915): 4.

46. Sessions, "Richard Strauss As a Tone Poet—III," *Harvard Musical Review* 4, no. 3 (December 1915): 11.

47. Edward T. Cone, "Conversation with Roger Sessions," *Perspectives on American Composers,* ed. by Benjamin Boretz and Edward T. Cone (New York: W.W. Norton & Co., 1971), p. 92.

48. Frank Rounds and Edward T. Cone, "The Reminiscences of Roger Sessions," 2 vols., 13 March–24 October 1962, Columbia University Oral History Collection, p. 74.

49. Taped interview 4 April 1978.

50. Ibid.

51. Columbia University Oral History Collection, p. 96.

52. The music is at the Library of Congress.

53. Ruth Sessions, *Sixty-Odd,* pp. 411–12.

54. Cone, "Conversation with Roger Sessions," p. 93.

55. Taped interview with Suzanne Bloch 17 March 1977.

56. Ibid.

57. Ibid.

58. Columbia University Oral History Collection, p. 114.

59. Ibid., pp. 122, 128.

60. Ibid., p. 160.

61. Ibid., p. 64.

62. Ibid., p. 160.

2

Periodization and *The Black Maskers*

Periodization of Sessions's Music

Considering Sessions's aversion to "file cabinets," any discussion of periodization goes against the grain. Demarcations must be invoked, however, in order to view each piece in the context of Sessions's large output and long life and to note gradual shifts in style. No distinct boundaries exist among the periods presented here. Overlap, foreshadowing, and retrogression of style are natural occurrences in Sessions's development.

Sessions's 42 pieces can be divided at five places about a decade apart. Each period is delineated by a large, often vocal, composition either at its beginning or end. The first period (1910–1923) ends with the Incidental Music to *The Black Maskers;* the Concerto for Violin (1935) ends the second; the third culminates with *The Trial of Lucullus* (1947); the fourth ends in 1959, before the completion of *Montezuma;* the fifth concludes before his Cantata, *When Lilacs Last in the Dooryard Bloom'd* (1970); and the sixth includes all music written since the Cantata.

These demarcations often coincide with changes in Sessions's address or occupation. His first period culminates prior to his departure for Europe, and the second coincides with his return. The third concludes after his move from Princeton University to the University of California. The fourth is underlined throughout by the writing of *Montezuma* and includes his return to Princeton, where Sessions resided during his fifth period. In the late 1960s Sessions left Princeton for Juilliard, a move that roughly coincides with the beginning of his sixth.

Only two other authors have attempted to delineate Sessions's creative periods—Ronald Henderson in his dissertation[1] and Elliott Carter in his review of the Violin Concerto for *The Musical Quarterly*.[2] Their divisions and mine differ.

Henderson divides the "pre-serial" music into (1) 1923–1930 (the Incidental Music for *The Black Maskers* through the First Piano Sonata); (2) 1935–1940 (the Four Children's Pieces through Pages from a Diary); (3) 1942–1950 (Duo for Violin and Piano through the Second String Quartet). For Henderson, "the first period [1923–1930] features extended passages of clear tonal definition, consisting of obvious diatonicism, linear tonal stress, tertian harmonic identity, and prominent tonal cadences."[3] Henderson describes music of the second period as offering "a distinct contrast to that of the first period in increased contrapuntal complexity and more rapid harmonic rhythm, suggesting perhaps a neo-Baroque period."[4] He continues: "The tonal character of the second period involves instances of tonality which, on the average, are shorter in duration and more vague with less coordination of diatonicism, linear stress, harmony and cadence, than their counterparts in the earlier music."[5] Henderson describes further changes in the third period: "Compositions of the third period feature a free dissonant and chromatic contrapuntal style in which tonal organization, although still of fundamental importance to the composer, grows progressively less traditional and more vague as Sessions's style moves more in the direction of twelve-tone writing."[6] Henderson concludes that "throughout all periods, the movement of lines appears to take precedence over the progressions of chords."[7]

In search of "some illumination" concerning Roger Sessions's stylistic periods, Elliott Carter admits to doing "great violence to the facts . . . to talk of his Impressionist beginnings of around 1923, his neo-Classic period from about 1926 to 1937, and his Expressionist period from then until now [1959]."[8] Regarding the first period, Carter states:

> The devices of blurring, of crowding sonorities by figurational activity in "close position," the meaningful use of instrumental and registral tone-color, the shimmering backgrounds that in him have become contrapuntal—these are some of the marks of an Impressionism that was more prominent in his early works and that still can be glimpsed, although completely transformed, in such recent works as his Third Symphony.[9]

Of the "neo-Classic" period, Carter writes:

> It is true that his "neo-Classic" works are much more tonally centered than his more recent works. They also contain certain turns of phrase, figurations, rhythms that link them to other composers' works in this style . . . the sharply defined, vigorously incisive, rhythmic drive of primitivism and neo-Classicism as well as the intense, highly concentrated and characterized gestures of Expressionism furnished a springboard for the different techniques Sessions uses.[10]

Regarding the period up to 1959, Carter states: "The recent compositions, however, while approaching the 'atonal,' employ materials and methods very remotely related to any other composer's style."[11]

Although I agree with these musical observations, I disagree both with the terminology Carter employs and with the dates of divisions used by Henderson. While the last movement of *The Black Maskers* can be heard as impressionistic, the play and its music are decidedly expressionistic, and I feel that term does not apply to Sessions's later music. Carter concentrates on the Violin Concerto (1935) and extends Sessions's "neo-Classic" period beyond that piece to include the First String Quartet, while Henderson stretches past that to include the Chorale for Organ and Pages from a Diary. Chapter 3 will show that, for both personal and musical reasons, the Violin Concerto represents the culmination of Sessions's second period.

Carter groups all Sessions's music between the Chorale for Organ (1937) and the Divertimento (1959) into one period, while I divide that period near the point when Sessions adopts the twelve-tone method (ca. 1953). No other authors have attempted to categorize Sessions's music written since 1959.

Each of the following chapters treats a single period. Within these, catalogued works are examined individually. The date of composition, commissioner, dedicatee, publisher, location of manuscript, date of premiere and its performers, and movements are simply listed at the beginning of each piece. Discussion of the work may include biographical information, quotations from my interviews with Sessions, formal analyses, twelve-tone rows, performance history, scholarly opinion, and its reception in the press.

Even though the date of *The Black Maskers* Orchestral Suite (1928) places it in the second period (1924–1935), discussion of it will be logically combined with the Incidental Music (1923) in this chapter. The early uncatalogued works of the first period are not as important as *The Black Maskers* and appear in appendix 2, nos. 1–5.

The Black Maskers

Incidental Music 1923
Orchestral Suite 1928
(Score Marked Cleveland, Ohio, Hadley, Mass.,
February–June 1923)

Commission: Smith College
Dedication: "To Ernest Bloch"
Published by Cos Cob Press, 1932; New Enlarged Version, Edward B. Marks, 1960. Manuscripts at the Library of Congress, Princeton University Library, and the New York Public Library.
Incidental Music Premiere: June 1923, Smith College, Northampton, Massachusetts, Roger Sessions Conducting.
Orchestral Suite Premiere: 5 December 1930, Cincinnati, Ohio, Fritz Reiner Conducting.

Incidental Music Movements:
No. 1: Dance
No. 2: Wedding Music
No. 3: Romualdo's Song
No. 4: Close of Scene 1
Interlude
Scene 2
Interlude: Opening of Scene 3
No. 5: Music for Scene 3
No. 5a: Lorenzo's Song
No. 5b: Close of Scene 3
No. 6: Prelude to Scene 4
No. 7a: Romualdo's Song
No. 7: Lorenzo's Song
No. 7b: Lorenzo's Song
No. 8: Closing Scene

Orchestral Suite Movements:
I. Dance
Ia. Romualdo's Song
II. Scene
III. Dirge
IV. Finale

Expressionism in American music was still in its infancy in 1923 when Smith College requested Sessions to write music for a production of Leonid Andreyeff's 1908 play, *The Black Maskers,* a murky, confusing, and gruesome tale of insanity that was heavily influenced by Edgar Allan Poe's stories. Sessions had already read the play and felt drawn to it because it was "very striking—it had dramatic possibilities. *The Black Maskers* was quite ultramodern at that time."[12]

We learn about Andreyeff from his friend Maksim Gorki, who described his ability to extemporize:

> He was a wonderfully interesting talker, inexhaustible, witty. Although his mind always manifested a stubborn tendency to peer into the darkest corners of the soul—nevertheless his thought was so alert, so capriciously individual, that it readily took grotesque and humorous forms.[13]

Gorki also describes Andreyeff as an alcoholic, a painter, and a pessimist. "To Andreev man appeared poor in spirit, a creature interwoven of irreconcilable contradictions of instinct and intellect, for ever deprived of the possibility of attaining inner harmony." Gorki felt that Edgar Allan Poe was a "talent congenial to [Andreyeff's] spirit." He describes Andreyeff as a split personality, much like *The Black Maskers* protagonist Lorenzo.

> Strangely and to his own torment Leonid split into two: in one and the same week he could sing "Hosannah" to the world, and pronounce "Anathema" against it. . . . And one always felt as though he sensed the nearness of an invisible enemy, that he was arguing intensely with someone and wanted to subdue him.

The Black Maskers bears resemblances to Poe's *The Masque of the Red Death* and *William Wilson. The Masque* and the Andreyeff play share common features of a masked ball in a castle, an orchestra, and the presence of a terrifying guest whose mask proves unremovable. When William Wilson's *doppelgänger* appears the candles instantly become extinguished; similarly, the Black Maskers cause the lights to go out. At a Roman masquerade ball, where both William Wilsons wear a black silk mask, the evil character murders the good one, who tells him that in so doing, "thou has murdered thyself." In *The Black Maskers* one Lorenzo murders his duplicate.

In Andreyeff's two early plays, *The Life of Man* and *The Black Maskers,* the protagonists are victims, not of outward conditions, but of their own inner experiences. Andreyeff expounded a theory of theater called "panpsyche," literally "all thought," in which narrative action in drama was considered unnecessary. As a writer, he was compared in his lifetime (1871–1919) to Leo Tolstoy and to Maeterlinck.

Sessions describes the story of *The Black Maskers* in a 1974 interview: "It's a play about an Italian Renaissance [actually twelfth-century] nobleman, the son of a Crusader, supposedly. And he comes on a document [in scene 2] which convinces him that he is really the offspring of an affair that his mother had with a groom, probably. And that unhinges him, you see, as far as his sense of identity."

Figure 2.1.   Leonid Andreyeff.

Andreyeff gives us a clue to this play in his story "My Diary," related in the introduction to his *Plays*. "The castle is the soul; the lord of the castle is man, the master of the soul; the strange, black maskers are the powers whose field of action is the soul of man, and whose mysterious nature he can never fathom." Failing to understand the Black Maskers, representations of his own soul, Lorenzo splits into two, the one self slaying the other. This duality leads to his tragedy: insanity. At the same time, by killing the double and thereby renouncing the evil in his soul, Lorenzo has attained the knowledge of God and perishes in that same moment. In Andreyeff's expressionistic view man is entirely controlled by fate (which he curses in *The Life of Man*), while man in *The Black Maskers* attains perfection through suffering and calls upon us to worship God. Sessions admits he does not fully understand the play. The last scene, where Lorenzo is killed in the fire in his castle, is "not my idea of redemption exactly."

Elliott Carter cites Mittner's definition of the two main artistic procedures of expressionism, "the primordial utterance *(Urschrei)* and the imposition of an abstract structure, often specifically geometric, on reality."[14] We find that the *The Black Maskers* literally fulfills his definition. The climactic moment occurs in scene 3 when Lorenzo, completely overpowered by his own ravings, "utters a wild cry and falls." At that same instant the Black Maskers break into the castle; his primal scream has ushered in total chaos. Sessions's music mirrors this terrifying event in the Orchestral Suite two measures after no. 68.

An abstract structure is also present because the varied recurrence of the same events[15] makes it impossible to determine which scenes are "real" and which exist only in Lorenzo's crazed imagination. In addition to that obstacle to clear understanding, the play's action unfolds equally mysteriously. Plausible arguments could be advanced for at least four different chronological orderings of the five scenes. The play's structure is symmetrical, "geometric." Scenes 1, 3, and 5 take place at the ball where their similar action is varied. Scenes 2 and 4, away from the ball, are the only ones in which both Lorenzos appear simultaneously. Scene 3, where Lorenzo utters his primal cry, acts as the fulcrum of this palindromic structure.

Although Andreyeff's play readily lends itself to Carter's definition of expressionism, the musical portrayal of expressionism contradicted Sessions's philosophy, as he later stated. "I've always been in a sense anti-expressionistic. Because I think expressionism is a heightening of detail to the utmost. In *The Black Maskers,* what I was really striving for all the time was continuity. It was a problem for me. The detail can become so important that the line doesn't matter very much, relatively speaking."[16]

Although Sessions knew Schoenberg's music at this time, Stravinsky's influence was a temporarily stronger one. The orchestral scores of *Petrushka* and *Le Sacre du Printemps* were published in 1922, and those works influenced *The Black Maskers*. Sessions discusses this in a conversation with Edward T. Cone: "I do think that *The Black Maskers*, which I wrote the winter after my experience with the score of *Le Sacre du Printemps,* has a certain influence of Schoenberg, too. Of course, I was never quite totally sold on either Stravinsky or Schoenberg; but I felt for the moment that Stravinsky was the nearer to me of the two.''[17] Sessions elaborated on Stravinsky's influence: "The fact that Stravinsky was doing something of the same kind certainly helped give me the courage to do this.''[18]

Paul Rosenfeld's description of *The Black Maskers* could apply equally to *Le Sacre du Printemps.*

> . . . Musicians in the audience found themselves deceived as to the number and character of the components of the band. One, an expert, went behind the stage looking for bass-clarinets and contrabassoons; and found merely clarinets and fagots: the brilliant handling of the lower registers of these common instruments had caused the mistake.[19]

Nevertheless, in retrospect Sessions felt that he still had a long way to go.

> In writing *The Black Maskers* I felt there were certain things that I would have liked to do, but I simply hadn't learned *how* to do yet, especially in harmonic terms, because I could think of what in those days were "complex" harmonies. In the first movement of *The Black Maskers* they occur, of course. But I found it very hard to move them in the way I wanted. That was the main thing.[20]

When Sessions was asked to write the music for *The Black Maskers,* he began in his typical sketch fashion, penciling fragmentary ideas on one or two staves. Sessions sketched a scanty piano version with several references directing himself to the orchestral sketch. "I already imagined a lot of things for full orchestra in the beginning.''[21] The piano sketch for the Dance movement, at the Library of Congress, is of interest not only because we can observe the composer's crossed-out alternative musical ideas, but also because the abundance of the play's cues found in the sketch reveals how closely he followed four pages of script—found in the middle of scene 1—in his music. Sessions spent more time composing this movement than the following ones; they were written in relative haste.

Next, Sessions fashioned the first orchestral score. The instrumentation was limited to what he calls "a scratch orchestra": flute, oboe, B-flat and E-flat clarinets, bassoon, horn, two trumpets, trombone, tympani, percussion, piano, and strings. A note in an early orchestral score indicates Sessions was already thinking of the music as an independent piece: "In case of performance in concert form, a special concert ending will be provided. The present score leads simply to the music improvised during Scene IV by an organist behind the scenes.'' That organist was Sessions.

The orchestral holograph kept at the Americana Collection of the New York Public Library is a copy in Sessions's hand of the Incidental Music made in the second half of 1923. He began revising the work soon after the play was produced in June 1923, for at the end of the score one finds "Cleveland—Hadley Feb. 11–June 9, 1923. Revision completed Dec. 31, 1923.'' The dedication, "To Ernest Bloch,'' appears here for the first time. Numerous cuts and additions indicate that Sessions worked from this manuscript to forge the Orchestral Suite. Several movements were simply cut. Internal cuts consisted mostly of the elimination of brief repetitions, thereby tightening the structure. Here he adds piccolo, English horn, and contrabassoon to the instrumentation. Sessions again expanded the instrumentation for the published score.

Andreyeff's rubrics concerning music are clear. Four times he indicated specific instruments in his play. These Sessions faithfully incorporates: (1) castanets for the Old Woman, no. 6 ff;[22] (2) an organ for the funeral in scene 4, no. 79 ff; (3) trumpets in scene 3, two bars after no. 68 (where "the Black Maskers mount the musicians' balcony, seize the horns, and trumpet wildly") and echoed in the Dirge at nos. 75 and 79; and (4) the trumpets announcing the death of Lorenzo at no. 81.

Sessions wrote: "The music was conceived throughout as an expression of certain moods felt behind the incidents of the play, rather than as their descriptive counterpart."[23] However, examination of the music accompanying Andreyeff's rubrics, which Sessions wrote into sketches of the Incidental Music, reveals that the composer closely described the scenes in music. Paul Rosenfeld, who did much to generate enthusiasm for this relatively unknown composer, also observed this when he wrote:

> The nine numbers supplied by the composer brought perfectly to Andreyev's drama the extension through music required by him. They are a re-creation, in a sister medium, of the play itself; flowing from a vision of it so profound and exact that it seems the composer must have stood while composing close to the point at which the dramatist stood when he made the dialogue.[24]

If we trace the music associated with Andreyeff's rubrics from the early versions to the published edition of the Orchestral Suite, we shall be able to see how closely the music fits Andreyeff's play. In the following sections measure and rehearsal numbers refer to the published score of the Suite. Italicized lines are those found both in the play and in Sessions's manuscripts.

I. Dance

The music of the Dance is tied to the action of the play like an opera is to its libretto. The entire four-minute dance is allied to only four pages of script. Referring to the need to synchronize the music with the play, Sessions says: "You've got to time it in your imagination."[25] Some examples of this close adherence follow.

I. Dance. The musicians begin a wild melody in which are heard malicious laughter, cries of agony and despair, and someone's low, sad plaining. The opening of the Dance.

No. 6. *The Old Woman* [running up with castanets] *The bridegroom is coming, &c.* Castanets appear in the music.

No. 8.   Lorenzo: *"Ah, I see. The tones are masked . . .* I was not aware that tones could put on such repulsive masks." Here the texture suddenly lightens while two flutes play a languid, but highly chromatic, passage supported by insistent piano eighth-note Es (see ex. 2.1). The sharps and double sharps allegorically "mask" the tones.

Example 2.1.   *The Black Maskers* Orchestral Suite, I, Dance, one measure after no. 8, two flutes.
© 1960 Edward B. Marks Music Company. Used by permission.

Five measures before no. 17.   Ecco [weeping]: *"I am afraid of your guests, Lorenzo."* Ecco's fearful weeping is portrayed in the flute, clarinet, and muted trumpet lines.

No. 26.   Lorenzo [addressing a newly arrived and very beautiful masker]: *"Greetings, Signora.* You are as entrancing as a vision. You are as delicate as a silvery moonbeam." A triangle softly strikes every second and third beat. Not recognizing her, he asks, "Who are you, Signora?"

One measure before no. 30.   A Grand Pause. She answers, "I am your falsehoods, Lorenzo."

No. 30.   A return to the opening dance material.

No. 34.   A shapeless Thing appears. ["It speaks with many voices."] *"We are your thoughts, Lorenzo."* The woodwinds and brass play fast eighth notes, aided by sharp snaps in the percussion. The active counterpoint indicates "many voices."

Two measures before no. 36.   [Lorenzo, clasping his head]: "Oh, this horrible music! It is enough to drive one mad. *Luigi, or somebody there . . .* Unmask the tones." The tones eventually relent: Twelve measures later the Dance ends, the climax followed by two trombones petering out in eighth notes.

Not included in the Orchestral Suite is a Wedding March, which lasts only nineteen measures and bears Andreyeff's rubric *"The musicians play wild strains faintly resembling wedding music, but the music is that played in hell at the masquerade wedding of Satan"* (see ex. 2.2). Both the melodic stress on the weak beat and the insistent downbowed string ostinato underlying that melody betray Sessions's familiarity with the orchestral score of *Le Sacre du Printemps,* published the previous year. Compare the accompaniment with no. 13 of the *Sacre,* the Dance of the Adolescents.

Example 2.2. *The Black Maskers* Incidental Music, Wedding Music. New York Public Library.

Ia. Romualdo's Song

Andreyeff describes Romualdo's Song:

> The accompaniment begins with a beautiful soft, and tender harmony, pure and clear as a cloudless sky or as the eyes of a child; but with each successive measure which the masked artist sings the music becomes more fragmentary and more restless and soon passes over into wild cries and laughter, expressive of tragical but incoherent emotion. It closes with a solemn and melancholy hymn.

Never revised, Romualdo's Song appears exactly as written in 1923; therefore, it represents Sessions's earliest published work. Writing in uncharacteristic haste, Sessions finished Romualdo's Song in one night in Hadley, Massachusetts. He changed a few of the words. The inspired change was the omission of the word "black" three times prior to the last section of the song, thus saving it for "black depths of my heart" and "black depths of my thought" and rendering those words far more dramatic.

II. Scene

At no. 37ff *"Lorenzo enters."* The situation certainly warrants the dramatic music, because Lorenzo appears with a blood spot on his heart. However, this music probably represents Sessions's vision of the Black Maskers themselves. We can infer this because it reappears at no. 42, there marked *"The number of the Black Maskers increases"* and, one measure later, *"one of them mounts the stairs."*

Characterized in act 1, scene 1 as "a strange, deformed creature like a living fragment of darkness," the Black Maskers are further described by Andreyeff as "hairy and black from foot to crown, some resembling orangoutangs and others those uncouth hairy insects which in the night-time fly toward the light," which

Figure 2.2. The Original Production of *The Black Maskers* at Smith College, 1923. The characters include, from left to right: the Spider (hunched over), Donna Francesca, Lorenzo, Ecco (a dwarf), a masker, and the Heart (with a serpent).

they extinguish. Although the music seems to evoke the ominous power of the Black Maskers themselves, actually it was composed long before the commission of the work. Sessions had already sketched this music as the possible first movement of a symphony, discarded it, then reclaimed it for this scene.

The music at no. 54 in the Suite parallels the play where *"he* [a Black Masker] *tries to embrace the Spider."* This leads directly into Lorenzo's Song, no. 56, described by Andreyeff as ''a simply touching air, such as mothers sing when they lull their children, and strangely, with low and tender harmonies, the strains of the orchestra answer to the song.'' This hummed song was given to the alto flute in the Suite.

Between no. 60 and two measures after no. 68 the murder of another Lorenzo is discovered in the tower, Lorenzo insanely tries to rip off his own skin (attempting to prove he does not wear a mask), and the Black Maskers burst in through the windows. At that instant Lorenzo utters his ''wild cry'' and falls while window frames crash (two measures after no. 68, on the third eighth note.) This ushers in *"the Black Maskers* [who] *seize the trumpets of the musicians and trumpet wildly."*

III. Dirge

Act 2, scene 4 takes place in a chapel in the castle in which Lorenzo lies in state and a second black-clothed Lorenzo speaks to the dead one. Twice trumpets remind us of the triumphal triplet music of the last scene. Andreyeff's rubrics read: ''Now and then a prolonged and mournful blare of trumpets carries abroad the sad news of the death of the Duke of Spadaro.'' In the orchestral holograph Sessions crossed out his previous title, ''Prelude to Scene 4,'' and printed ''Dirge,'' suggested perhaps by Andreyeff's rubric at the end of scene 4: ''The last mournful strains of a funeral dirge are heard.''

''In the intervals of silence the solemn notes of an organ and the voice of a priest can be heard,'' Andreyeff writes. The organ music in the Suite lasts only nine measures and ends the Dirge. Sessions remembers: ''In the performance I improvised on a little reed organ behind the scenes. Rather amusing occasion because I sat improvising these sort of pseudo-Medieval quasi-Gregorian things on the organ. Well, now in the Suite, I put just the beginning of that.''[26]

IV. Finale

Lorenzo's guests, seeing a fire, cry out. The fire is portrayed by a slow-moving clarinet line surrounded by constant chromatic sixteenth-note quintuplets in the flutes and violas. *"The fire breaks through everywhere"* at no. 90. At no. 92 *"outside . . . appear the Black Maskers,"* who struggle to gain entrance through the broken windows but are repelled by the fire. The music representing the Black Maskers appears again in the low strings at no. 92. Engulfment by fire is vividly portrayed. At no. 96 Lorenzo's last speech begins: *"Up, up, Ecco, the Lord is coming.''* The Black Maskers quickly disappear; two measures after no. 96 we hear the last of them in the English horn and bass clarinet. At no. 97 Lorenzo solemnly proclaims: *"I greet thee, O Lord."*

Although Stravinsky's influence can be found in Sessions's woodwind and rhythmic patterns in the earlier movements, here the influence of Debussy is felt. The last nine measures end quietly in contrast to the flaming destruction taking place on stage. About this the director of the play, Sam Eliot, Jr., and the composer disagreed; Eliot proposed a grandiose ending and Sessions defended a pianissimo close. In the Incidental Music Sessions adhered to Eliot's wishes (see ex. 2.3). In his Suite, however, he reverted to his original ppp close (see ex. 2.4).

Example 2.3. *The Black Maskers* Incidental Music, Finale, last seven measures.

Example 2.4. *The Black Maskers* Orchestral Suite, IV, Finale, last five measures.
         © 1960 Edward B. Marks Music Company. Used by permission.

The last five measures of the Suite employ a combination of instruments Sessions first hit upon in fourteen measures of his two-movement Symphony in D Major; there he scored three trumpets supported by bass clarinet. In the Suite, four trumpets appear—in D (an instrument not now frequently found that Sessions needed for its high C♯), in C, and two trumpets in A, which replace the two B-flat and one F trumpets of the Incidental Music. All are accompanied by a bass clarinet, one of Sessions's favorite instruments.

Sessions comments on the last movement of the Incidental Music: "The last movement in the first version is much simpler, because the kind of thing I'd like to have done wasn't possible with that bunch, the change of meters, and so forth."[27] When he rewrote the movement in Northampton in 1928 he basically "tightened it up and put in a big orchestra. A lot of detail is here that isn't in the original score at all."[28]

The Finale was the most thoroughly revised movement in *The Black Maskers* Suite. Sessions's original rearrangement had been lost in the mail between Europe and Cincinnati. He then rewrote the Finale, "a still better rearrangement,"[29] in time for the premiere conducted by Fritz Reiner in Cincinnati in 1930. "So, there are theoretically three versions of the last movement."[30]

At the original performance in 1923 Sessions conducted behind the stage. Eliot balked at the idea of a pit orchestra, declaring it ruinous to his production because the lights of the music stands would glare during those times when the Black Maskers are supposed to devour all light. To conduct the actresses from behind the stage (women students played all roles) Sessions listened through the set (see fig. 2.2). "The girl who sang on the stage didn't always get it. She heard it and came in and it was God-awful, that's all I can say. There was this scene where she had to hum. I mean she couldn't sing my music at all."[31] Instrumentalists were imported from as far away as Boston and New Haven. Sessions's friend Quincy Porter played violin in the orchestra.

The music profoundly stirred its audience. In a prophetic article Paul Rosenfeld was one of the first to bring Roger Sessions's music into public awareness and uncannily predicted Sessions's future success. He praised the director as "the immediate producing cause of one of the most important events in the life of music in America."[32] He compared the joy of listening to *The Black Maskers* to that of hearing *Pelléas et Mélisande,* Bloch's *Psalms,* and Wolf's Möricke songs.

The director, Samuel Eliot, Jr., remembers the audience's reaction:

> The older alumnae *hated* it! President Neilson sat between two of them and told me that they so continuously protested to him he couldn't hear the play. He advised me to do no more Senior plays, so I didn't in '24, '25 and '26. The Alum. Quarterly of Aug. '23 had many attacks on *BM,* but that of November had 2 letters defending it.[33]

Sessions's former teacher, Ernest Bloch, to whom the work was eventually dedicated, came from Cleveland to hear the performance. His daughter Suzanne, remembers his amused reactions. "His description of Roger Sessions when he came back—I can see that. He said, 'Do you know, at the rehearsals there was Roger Sessions with his beautiful work conducting with a lollipop in his mouth!' He was moved to the thing."[34] Undoubtedly, Bloch's enthusiasm for this work benefited Sessions's career more than Rosenfeld's literary flurries. When Sessions showed him the work in progress, Bloch stressed that it be performed independently. He made a scene in the audience: "Show me the ass who produced this work!" he ranted in reference to hiding the musicians behind the stage. It was Bloch who raved about the orchestration. Thinking he had heard two contrabassoons where none were scored, he was the expert Rosenfeld referred to. He also pressed conductors to perform the work.

The first New York performance of the Incidental Music, and its only other public performance, was presented in a Copland-Sessions concert on 15 March 1931 with Aaron Copland's *Music for Theater,* conducted by the composer; Hugh Ross conducted the Sessions piece. Fritz Reiner conducted the first performance of the Orchestral Suite in 1930 in Cincinnati. Leopold Stokowski presented the Philadelphia premiere of the Suite on 4 November 1933, here called "Music for the Drama of Andreieff, The Black Maskers." At this early date the press had already begun reacting to Sessions's music in a manner typical of later criticism: "In influence, *The Black Maskers* seems Stravinskian, and in essential identification cerebral rather than emotional, as is the play."[35] The work has since been played by many American orchestras, including Otto Klemperer's performance with the Los Angeles Philharmonic and Pierre Monteux's with the Boston Symphony Orchestra. On 15 October 1958 the Suite (minus its first movement) was performed in Moscow, a homecoming for the Russian work.

Sessions continued his fascination with Poe's symbolism. He began an opera in the mid-1920s on *The Fall of the House of Usher,* a subject to which Debussy had twice given his attention, in 1908 and 1918. The director of *The Black Maskers,* Sam Eliot, Jr., produced a libretto, and Sessions had sketched out quite a bit of the story before discovering he really "wasn't interested in doing it."

Sessions's music continued to remain close to drama, whether he overtly obeyed a playwright's or librettist's instructions or whether, on a more abstract level, he followed a hidden play, one whose characters he developed thematically and whose dramatic conflicts he portrayed with musical contrasts. With *The Black Maskers* Sessions learned firsthand the relation of music to theater, and over the next 60 years he never forgot this lesson.

Notes

1. Ronald Duane Henderson, *Tonality in the Pre-Serial Instrumental Music of Roger Sessions* (Ph.D. diss.: Eastman School of Music, 1974), unpublished.

2. Elliott Carter, "Current Chronicle," *The Musical Quarterly* 45 (July 1959): 375–81.

3. Henderson, *Tonality,* p. 435.

4. Ibid., p. 170.

5. Ibid., p. 435.

6. Ibid., p. 315.

7. Ibid., p. 442.

8. Carter, "Current Chronicle," p. 376.

9. Ibid.

10. Ibid.

11. Ibid.

12. Taped interview 16 October 1974. *See* Leonid Andreyeff, *Plays*, trans. by Clarence L. and Fred Newton Scott with an introduction by V.V. Brusyanin (New York: Charles Scribner's Sons, 1915).

13. All Gorki quotations from Maksim Gorki, *Reminiscenses of Tolstoy, Chekhov and Andreev* (1931), trans. by Katherine Mansfield, S.S. Koteliansky, and Leonard Woolf (London: The Hogarth Press, 1968).

14. Elliott Carter, "Expressionism and American Music," *Perspectives on American Composers*, ed. by Benjamin Boretz and Edward T. Cone (New York: W.W. Norton & Co., 1971), p. 224.

15. This description fits Sessions's later music as well. Only twice, in the Second String Quartet and the Violin Sonata, does Sessions recapitulate material exactly; far more frequently, opening material recurs in a varied recapitulation.

16. Columbia University Oral History Collection, pp. 228–29.

17. Edward T. Cone, "Conversations with Roger Sessions," *Perspectives on American Composers*, ed. by Benjamin Boretz and Edward T. Cone (New York: W.W. Norton & Co., 1971), p. 96.

18. Taped interview 16 October 1974.

19. Paul Rosenfeld, *Port of New York* (New York: Harcourt & Brace, 1924), p. 149.

20. Taped interview 16 October 1974.

21. Taped interview 2 November 1978.

22. Sessions initially scored crotales for castanets, thinking them identical. Pierre Monteux corrected him.

23. Roger Sessions, "The Black Maskers," *Desto* 404 liner notes.

24. Rosenfeld, *Port of New York*, pp. 146–47. It should be remembered that Paul Rosenfeld did not actually attend the Smith performances, despite the "I was there" tone of his article. Sessions played the piano version for Rosenfeld in New York City.

25. Taped interview 15 November 1978.

26. Taped interview 16 October 1974.

27. Ibid.

28. Conversation 15 November 1978.

29. Taped interview 16 October 1974.

30. Ibid. The Finale was transcribed for band by B. Richard Bancroft (Marks Music, 1963).

31. Taped interview 16 October 1974. Marion Watts played Lorenzo, Martha Morse Ecco.

32. Rosenfeld, *Port of New York,* p. 146. Rosenfeld's enthusiasm for Sessions's music wavered. He disliked Sessions's First Symphony; however, he liked the First String Quartet.

33. Eliot letter to the author 17 November 1978.

34. Taped interview with Suzanne Bloch 17 March 1977.

35. "Black Maskers by Roger Sessions Is Introduced to Philadelphians," *Musical America* (10 November 1933).

3

The Music Written in Europe: 1924–1935

The European Years

Sessions first visited Europe in the summer of 1924. Introduced by a letter from Ernest Bloch and in person by Theodore Chanler, he met Nadia Boulanger in Paris. Sessions traveled to London and to Lake Geneva, where he visited Jean Binet, who, with Bloch, had been a pupil of Jaques-Dalcroze in Geneva. Sessions also visited Florence, Italy, the city that became his world favorite.

At the end of the academic year 1924–1925 Bloch and Sessions left the Cleveland Institute. In the summer of 1925 Sessions traveled in Europe for ten weeks, visiting Florence, Paris, London, and Switzerland. At the beginning of that summer Sessions had applied for a Guggenheim Fellowship, but the application was received too late. Asked by his father what he would like to do, Sessions replied that he wanted to live in Europe. Archibald Sessions generously offered to support him in Europe for the next year. In the two following years Sessions did receive Guggenheim Fellowships.

The first year (1925–1926) Sessions and his wife lived at 25 Via dei Bardi in Florence. Bernard Berenson's sisters, whom Sessions had known at Smith, introduced Sessions and his wife to the art critic. From 1926 through the spring of 1927 they stayed in the guest house of Berenson's villa, I Tatti, in Settignano, where Sessions worked on his Symphony No. 1. The environment in which Sessions lived and worked is described in Ernest Samuels's biography of Berenson:

> In the austerely elegant precincts of I Tatti, surrounded by his great library and treasures of Renaissance paintings, [Berenson] held a kind of court for art historians and artists, poets and novelists, statesmen and tycoons, and dignitaries from every walk of life. Here too came in increasing numbers the merely curious, who were drawn by anecdotes of the ritual of the semimonastic household.[1]

At Berenson's house the Sessionses met and dined with Carlo Placci, Kenneth Clark, Alberto Moravia, Robert C. Trevelyan, Walter Lippman, and Berenson's secretary, Nicky Mariano.

During the summer of 1926 the Sessionses spent a month in Paris, where they met Aaron Copland. Barbara Sessions studied the art of Paolo Uccello and took classes at the Sorbonne. They lived in Juziers, fifteen miles outside of Paris. Sessions never formally studied with Boulanger (unlike many of his American contemporaries), but he did show her his music. Nadia Boulanger "was the first European and musician of distinction to take American composers seriously. Then she tended more and more to really take over."[2] Other factors eventually contributed to a breach with Boulanger: "I think the root of the whole business is that she never forgave me for going to live in Berlin instead of coming to live in Paris."[3] Later Boulanger and Sessions parted ways over Sessions's divorce, which she opposed.

During the summer of 1927 the Sessionses lived for six weeks in a twelfth-century house on a hill on the Via delle Campora owned by two "haughty and arrogant old Scottish ladies." In the spring of 1928 Sessions returned to the United States, taught a course at Smith, and began his Sonata for Piano No. 1. In Northampton he heard a concert that included pieces by both Stravinsky and Schoenberg. Sessions remarked to himself: "Well, after all, Schoenberg and all that he represents, that's one of the facts of musical life today, too, and I'd better really come to terms with it."[4] Sessions elaborated on his comment: "I felt I was more in the Stravinsky camp than the Schoenberg camp, which were looked upon as half mutually exclusive. These two pieces stood out from the rest of the concert."[5]

In 1928 Sessions applied for the three-year fellowship at the American Academy in Rome. Walter Damrosch, a trustee of the Academy, was also the chairman of the music jury, which included Richard Aldrich, John Carpenter, Edward B. Hill, and Leo Sowerby. The prize in composition had been established a few years earlier, and the previous winners were Howard Hanson, Randall Thompson, Leo Sowerby, George Elwell, and Walter Helfer. The award consisted of a stipend of $1,500 a year and $500 a year for travel, plus a studio, meals, and living quarters. Funds were established by Frederic A. Juilliard, Walter Damrosch, and Horatio Parker; these prizes were held in 1928 by Alexander L. Steinert, Sessions, and Robert Sanders, respectively.

In two senses the awarding of the Rome Prize to Sessions was unusual. First, Sessions's oeuvre was small. The only works he considered presentable were *The Black Maskers*, the Choral Preludes for Organ, and the First Symphony, and none of his works were published. Second, the Academy had distinct eligibility requirements. A candidate could not be married and had to be under the age of 30. Sessions had been married for 8 years and was 31 at the beginning of his 3-year sojourn. Obviously, Damrosch was sufficiently impressed by Sessions's music—and perhaps by the success of *The Black Maskers* and the Boston Symphony performance of the First Symphony—to override the rules.

Since women were not allowed to live at the Academy, the Sessionses lived at the Villa Sforza, a "spectacular hilltop house" owned by three White Russian families. Here Sessions learned Russian and began reading *War and Peace*; he memorized the first ten pages.

Sessions's interest in literature is understandable considering the people with whom he came into contact in Rome: Mario Labroca, a newspaper critic for *Fascist Labor* and a composer; Emilio Cecchi, at whose party Sessions met Pirandello; Umberto Morra; Guglielmo Alberti; and Cesar Searchinger, a journalist in charge of the London CBS radio and through whom Sessions met Pierre Monteux and Otto Klemperer when they were guest conductors at the Augusteo. He knew composers Alfredo Casella, who kept young Italian composers united, Petrassi, and Molinari, the permanent conductor of the Augusteo. Sessions attended rehearsals of the Augusteo. In the months of July, August, and September (1929) he went to Switzerland and afterwards visited Paris.

According to the annual reports of Felix Lamond, Professor in charge of the Department of Music at the Academy, in 1928–1929 Sessions "worked diligently on sketches for a new symphony,"[6] and on 27 March 1928 he gave a short address on "Some Aspects of Contemporary Music" before the Fellows of the various national institutions in Rome. In 1929–1930 "Sessions' work comprised a revision of his piano sonata and a ballata, illustrative of scenes in Boccaccio's 'Decameron.' He also prepared sketches for a violin concerto." In 1930–1931, when Sessions shared the Fellowship with Normand Lockwood and Werner Janssen, he "made considerable progress on an orchestral work entitled 'Strophes.' "[7] Lamond announced prematurely the premiere performance of the Violin Concerto for the 1931–1932 season with Max Strub and Otto Klemperer. It was also to have been played in Rome. Sessions was, however, receiving performances of his First Symphony (6 April 1929 in Geneva) and his First Piano Sonata (3 March 1930 in London and in July at the International Society for Contemporary Music Festival), as well as publications of his First Piano Sonata (Schott) and *On the Beach at Fontana* (Oxford University Press). (See the cover for a painted likeness of Sessions during this period.)

In 1929–1930 Sessions spent his travel period in the United States. In 1930–1931 he traveled for two months in Germany, spent time in Oxford and London, and stayed two months in Berlin in the spring.

At the ISCM meeting in 1931 in Amsterdam, Malipiero and Sessions together favored a composition by Luigi Dallapiccola, whom Sessions had not yet met, but who later would become a close friend. Works in the Festival were Copland's Variations for Piano, Mark Brunswick's Viola Solo, and a piece for oboe by Ruth Crawford.

In Rome in 1930–1931 Richard Strauss conducted his Alpine Symphony and *Don Juan* at the Augusteo. Sessions felt that Strauss was "a good conductor, conducted his own works better than anyone else."

Aaron Copland first approached Sessions with the idea for a series of concerts during the semester Sessions taught at Smith, spring 1928. Immediately after their discussions, Sessions won the Rome Prize and lived mainly in Europe, so he did not participate fully in Copland's plan. The purpose of the Copland-Sessions Concerts was to "satisfy the need of [the younger generation of American composers] to hear and test their work in public performance" and "to stimulate composers to more prolific activity and to develop a stronger sense of solidarity among the creators of a growing American music."[8]

Copland and Vivian Perlis explain Sessions's involvement in the concert series in *Copland/1900–1942.* Sessions was responsible for the inclusion of music by Nino Rota, Jerzy Fitelberg, and Jean Binet. Sessions's letters to Copland were frequent and "long, affectionate, worrisome, apologetic, and occasionally contradictory." Characteristically, Sessions worried about his silent role (22 March 1929):

> The point is simply that I have no means of knowing the situation in any real sense when I am absolutely ignorant of some of the music that is being played. I have as much confidence in you as I would have in anyone; and yet—in spite of the fact that I myself am wholly responsible for this situation—I am beginning to realize the very great inconveniences as well as the risks involved in my being a completely irresponsible partner. I have to all intents and purposes signed a blank page, and sponsored, as a musician and a composer, something for which I have no responsibility at all; and I have no sure means of knowing, as things are now, whether I would be willing to take that responsibility for the works that are played at the concerts.[9]

The concerts took place between 22 April 1928 and 16 December 1931 in New York (the Broadhurst Theatre, the President Theater, Steinway Hall, the Little Theater, and the Edyth Totten Theater) and spilled over into Europe—to Paris on 17 June 1931 in the Salle Chopin and to London on 16 December 1931 in the Aeolian Hall. Only two of Sessions's works were played. John Duke performed the unfinished First Piano Sonata on 6 May 1928; the completed work was played by Irene Jacobi in the London concert. *The Black Maskers* Incidental Music was performed on 15 March 1931.

In 1931 Sessions was awarded a Carnegie Corporation grant. Encouraged by Klemperer, he moved to Berlin, the European city that most attracted him musically. Berlin had not only three orchestras but three opera houses as well: the Staatoper on Unter den Linden Strasse, conducted by Wilhelm Furtwängler, Bruno Walter, and Erich Kleiber; the more interesting and daring Kroll Opera, conducted by Klemperer; and the Städtische Oper, conducted by Fritz Stiedry.

Klemperer found Sessions a place to stay with Max Strub, the concertmaster of the Berlin Philharmonic with whom Sessions worked on the Violin Concerto. Klemperer spoke English and Sessions learned German. Barbara Sessions earned some income translating French.[10]

Among the people Sessions knew in Berlin were Ernst Toch, Paul Hindemith, Paul Dessau, Stiedry and his wife, Erica Wagner, one of the first singers to perform Schoenberg's *Pierrot lunaire,* and Artur Schnabel. After concerts, these people frequently got together in a "friendly atmosphere, everyone knew everybody. There was no social nonsense involved."[11]

Figure 3.1.   Roger Sessions, Gian Francesco Malipiero, Alban Berg, and Egon Wellesz in Florence, Italy. May 1933.

The most exciting aspect of Berlin was, of course, concertgoing; here Sessions heard *Falstaff* and *Elektra* for the first time, and *Così fan tutte* and *Oberon*. The fiftieth anniversary of Wagner's death was observed in 1933, and Sessions attended performances of *Parsifal, Tannhäuser, Das Liebesverbot, Rienzi, Die Meistersinger,* and *Der fliegende Holländer.*

In addition to this dose of opera, Sessions heard Klemperer's uncut performance of the *St. Matthew Passion,* Schoenberg's *Serenade,* and Stravinsky's Violin Concerto played by its dedicatee, Samuel Dushkin. Although he did not frequent the Berlin Philharmonic, he did hear such performers as Serkin, Feuermann, Busch, and Hubermann at the Singakademie and at concerts given in the Städtische Oper. Sessions and British foreign newspaper correspondents frequently drank beer together and talked at the Stammtisch. Through these conversations and his own observations, Sessions drew to fear the consequences of the political trend in Germany, and these events hastened his departure.

In 1933 Sessions was invited to Florence, along with Berg, Milhaud, Křenek, and Malipiero. It was there that the photograph in figure 3.1 was taken. At the ISCM Festival he gave a talk on American opera. In preparation he studied scores in the Berlin library and came to the conclusion that the two best American scores were *Mona* by Horatio Parker and *Natoma* by Victor Herbert. At the festival he met Darius Milhaud, who became a loyal friend. Sessions first met Schoenberg in Berlin.

The list of Sessions's music produced in the European years begins with the Three Chorale Preludes for Organ and ends with the Violin Concerto, the culmination of Sessions's second creative period.

Three Chorale Preludes for Organ   1924 and 1926

Dedicated to Douglas and Emily Moore (I), Theodore Chanler (II), and Dore Landau (III).
Published by Cos Cob Press, 1934. Manuscripts at the Library of Congress.
Premiere: December 1927, New York City, Joseph Yasser, Organ.
I. Adagio (Florence, August 1924)
II. Largo (Paris, May 1926)
III. Ben ritmato (Paris, May 1926)

Sessions's inscription to Theodore Chanler refers ironically to their recent past at the Cleveland Institute. It reads: "For Teddy Chanler. In memory of the 'heroic age' of the late 'Cleveland Institute of Music' (or should I call it the Romantic Age?) Roger H. S. (October 15, 1925)."

Sessions's only self-conscious change of style took place after writing *The Black Maskers.* He explains:

> One thing that bothered me about it was the play. It was an expressionistic play; it was a play about complicated psychology. I didn't want to get into the way of writing music in which this contributed a very important part of the interest. I wanted to write music that was essentially simple and very direct in its musical impact. So I wanted to get away from picturesque states of mind.[12]

The influence of Stravinsky on the music of *The Black Maskers* is acknowledged; it was hearing Stravinsky's music that gave Sessions the courage to write in a bold harmonic manner. However, "I wanted to *not* write works like the Stravinsky works, where the harmonies were in blocks. They don't flow exactly, but they shift."[13] One day in Florence Sessions found himself writing the first of the Preludes and realized the direction in which he wanted to proceed. "What I really did was to go into more of an emphasis on line, and less on color."[14]

Henderson's dissertation provides a concise description of these pieces: "The Three Chorale Preludes are short, monothematic, three-voice organ preludes in basically non-imitative tonal counterpoint, with a self-composed, ornamented chorale melody in the upper voice. Each prelude has a main point of division near the middle and a repeat of the first section."[15]

The first Prelude, based on Bach's motet, *Jesu, meine Freude,* is in E minor and goes to B minor. The second Prelude is less amenable to fitting tonal categories—despite the key signature, it is not in B major. It is perhaps G-sharp minor, or modal. It progresses from B minor to G-sharp minor and an A sharp major triad, with its final chord, D sharp major (G-sharp minor: V/V to V) is enharmonic with the tonic of the third Prelude in E-flat major. The third Prelude ends on the dominant of G-sharp minor. Sessions favors dominant endings in his tonal works. Seventh and ninth chords, as well as root movement by second, play a larger role in the second Prelude than in the first.

Varying degrees of tonal ambiguity are illustrated within this one work. "The borderline between tonality and atonality is a very, very wide one. You don't step over the threshold from one to another. You have to go down a long, long, long corridor."[16] The Organ Preludes are the beginnings of that journey.

Symphony No. 1 in E Minor   1926–1927
(Score Marked Settignano-Firenze, 31 January 1927)

Dedication: "To my Father"
Published by Cos Cob Press (Large Score), 1929, and Arrow Music Press (Small Score), 1929.
   Manuscript at Houghton Library, Harvard University.
Premieres: 22 April 1927, Boston, Massachusetts, Boston Symphony Orchestra, Serge Koussevitsky
   Conducting; First New York Performance, 1949.
I. Giusto
II. Largo
III. Allegro vivace

When asked what inspired him to write a symphony, Sessions replied:

Actually, I wanted to write a piano quintet; I wasn't always satisfied with the first idea. Then
I realized that I was thinking of an orchestral piece instead. I sketched a hundred different versions of the first idea, just systematically. And then I realized that one of them was much better
than the others, and curiously enough, that was the simplest one. I was surprised, because it
seemed extremely simple, but yet it was the best one[17] [see ex. 3.1].

Example 3.1.   Symphony No. 1, I, trumpet line and accompaniment, mm. 1–12.
© 1929 by Edward B. Marks Music Company.
Copyright renewed. Used by permission.

Sessions discarded his sketches for this symphony. However, he forgot that he gave Nadia Boulanger a manuscript copy, now at the Harvard Library. It took Sessions the winter of 1926–1927 to write the first movement. This was to become a pattern—writing the first movement slowly and the remaining movements more quickly. He had sketched large portions of the work in $\frac{2}{4}$ time and, following the principle that a downbeat is not the same as an accent, later changed the barlines and shortened measures by eliminating eighth notes. An example is the chord on the first beat of no. 10; originally it came on the second beat. The $\frac{8}{8}$ measure three bars before no. 14 is in reality three smaller units (3+2+3) combined in one measure.

In Paris he played the First Symphony for Mlle. Boulanger. She felt that the recapitulation was too long, but Sessions did not agree. She told him that he would hear it himself in a performance. Boulanger was not the only one with ideas about the work. Serge Koussevitsky felt that the trumpet's opening line (see ex. 3.1) ought to be played as a kind of recitative. To the reknowned conductor's amused surprise, Sessions argued with him.

The piece was performed by Koussevitsky on 22 April 1927 in Boston. Sessions did finally realize that there were problems with the first movement. In performance the tempo sagged and seemed uncertain two bars before no. 10. Koussevitsky suggested that the music at no. 28 did not belong. Hearing the piece, Sessions understood the difficulty: From no. 17 to no. 28 the music was "underdeveloped and needed building up to a bigger climax." Sessions returned to Italy, took the work apart, and sewed it back together again. Between two bars before no. 23 and no. 26 he added a new idea and made other changes. By doing this he had changed the proportions of the whole and solved the problems pointed out by both Boulanger and Koussevitsky, the recapitulation and the sagging tempo, respectively.[18]

The second movement was written quite rapidly. Sessions had received a telegram stating that his father was seriously ill. He wrote quickly through the night, obsessed by the irrational feeling that when he finished the movement, he would receive another telegram saying that his father was better. The next telegram, however, contained the news that Archibald Sessions had died on 6 January 1927. The slow movement is dedicated to his father, who made the composer's European stay possible.

More information about the second movement comes from the Columbia University Oral History Collection: "The second movement was perhaps consciously modelled on Bach, a little. The last movement was somewhat consciously modelled on Mozart. This seems ridiculous to me now, because Bach and Mozart are quite impossible to imitate."[19] Nevertheless, the work came to be known as an example of neoclassicism in Sessions's output.

Sessions realized who influenced the writing of this symphony. He wrote about the work in his program notes for the 1927 Boston Symphony Orchestra performance:

I am aware of the strong influence in my work of two, above all, among modern composers—Bloch and Stravinsky. These influences I have tried to absorb rather than to escape, since I have no sympathy with consciously sought originality. My interest is in form; and by this I mean that I accept my musical ideas, try to give them living shape, without theorizing as to their source or their other than musical meaning.[20]

Andrew Imbrie writes about the First Symphony and neoclassicism.

The First stands a little apart from the others in that it exhibits certain stylistic mannerisms that were beginning to be fashionable at the time it was written: a diatonic jazziness, an obsessive reiteration (in fast tempi) of short motives, syncopated and aggressively accentuated. The orchestration is hard-edged: the violins play only pizzicato in the first movement, and the lyricism of the second is dominated at first by the astringent sound of divided violas, later by woodwinds. But beneath this austere surface the listener can already discover much that is characteristic of the mature Sessions, including particularly his overriding concern for line.[21]

The first and third movements are clearly in sonata-allegro form, while the second is a three-part form with a trio in the middle. Characteristics of the symphony include the use of an ostinato, the retaining of the identity upon recapitulation of the subordinate and closing themes of the first movement (a rare use of literal repetition for Sessions), pandiatonicism, the "long line" (especially in the second movement), thirteenth chords, and rootless diatonic sonorities in the third movement. Sessions feels the third movement is the most obviously Italian.

By 1929 Sessions had remodeled the symphony, and on 6 April it was performed at Victoria Hall in Geneva at the ISCM Festival. Ansermet conducted. The English critic Edwin Evans wrote in the *Musical Courier* (4 May):

> Sessions' Symphony in E minor opened the Festival and aroused more interest than any American work hitherto performed on these occasions. It was felt to be at once a contribution to the main stream of present-day musical thought and representative of something apart from that stream; and that something was assumed to be the American outlook . . . . It was warmly welcomed and appreciated.[22]

Aaron Copland arranged a Berlin performance, 9 December 1931, also sponsored by the ISCM and conducted by Ansermet.

The work was not warmly welcomed in 1935 in Philadelphia. The *New York Times* reports of the Philadelphia Orchestra performance: "Alexander Smallens . . . was the guest conductor today, but that did not prevent hisses and boos from the audience during the playing of Symphony No. 1 by Roger Sessions, modern American composer. The work, never before heard in Philadelphia, aroused hisses and caused several to walk out."[23]

Even in 1960, when the recording was released, the work was still not familiar. Eric Salzman, a student of Sessions, writes: "His First Symphony is not only a fine piece, but it also is one of his most direct and accessible works. Yet it is virtually unknown, even to specialists."[24] At least one specialist, Elliott Carter, knew the work well, having copied it out for analysis. In writing his own First Symphony in 1942 Carter "borrowed Sessions's cross-accented rhythms and continuous development, but not his motoric, neo-baroque style."[25]

Salzman also writes: "All three movements have brilliant endings; this is characteristic of Sessions. They are unexpected yet utterly logical and right in that they lock the movements tightly shut with the firmest and most inevitable finality."[26] The E minor first movement ends in E major. The presence of an emphatic picardy third cadence at the conclusion of a movement became a trademark of American neoclassic composers who were influenced by Hindemith.

Although Sessions was often to attempt symphonic writing in the next two decades, Symphony No. 1 remained his only completed symphony until 1946. Perhaps the memory of his problems writing this work plagued future efforts. By 1946 (Symphony No. 2) his style had evolved and changed. The stylistic difference is greater between the First and the remaining symphonies than between any of the other symphonies.

On the Beach at Fontana   **1930**

Text by James Joyce
Published in *The Joyce Book,* Oxford University Press, 1933, pp. 36-41; *New Vistas in Song* by
     Edward B. Marks, 1964, pp. 50-52. Manuscript Lost.
Premiere: Winter 1930, London.

This work was written for a volume of songs, *The Joyce Book,* based on poems
by James Joyce and given to him on his fiftieth birthday.

> And there's a very funny story about that. It's a poem about—I interpret it as an older woman
> who loved a younger man, and they're walking on the beach in Italy, and there's a storm com-
> ing up. And she feels very protective. Okay. So I set it for soprano and piano. Well, the man
> who played my First Piano Sonata came to Rome, and I showed him this piece. He said, "But
> you set it for soprano. That's a homosexual song." And I said, "Well, I felt there was something
> not quite right, but that's the only way I could interpret it." So I left it for soprano. Okay.
> So the song was published and sung. Then, several years later, when I was back in New York
> in the mid-thirties, I was invited by a lady to come and have tea—one had tea in those days—
> and there was a singer named Radiana Pazmor who was there. She [the lady] said, "Please
> bring your song, because the son and daughter-in-law of Joyce will be there, and Mrs. Pazmor
> would like to sing it." And I said, "Well, I don't think it can be read at sight." She said, "Well,
> *she* can." (I'd never heard of a singer who could read at sight at that time. They're much better
> trained musically now.) I took it over, and she *did* sing it at sight. She looked it over first,
> and then we just played it. And then I went and sat next to Mrs. Joyce, and she said, "I'm
> awfully happy to meet you, and I'm awfully happy that you set that song, because this is my
> favorite poem of my father-in-law's. You know it was written for my husband." Never having
> had children myself, I couldn't imagine that it was about a father and his son.[27]

In an acoustical discussion of the treatment of timbre in this song, Robert Cogan
demonstrates that details of timbre and melodic line almost completely correspond.[28]

Sonata for Piano No. 1   **1927-1930**

Dedicated to Rosamond Foster (on Holograph Only)
Published by B. Schotts Söhne, 1931. Sketches at the Princeton University Library. Manuscript in
     John Duke's possession.
Premieres: 6 May 1928, Copland-Sessions Concert (Work Incomplete), New York City, John Duke,
     Piano; 3 March 1930, Bad Homburg, Germany, Frank Mannheimer, Piano.
Andante
Allegro
Andante
Poco meno mosso
Tempo I°
Molto vivace
(Played without Pause)

Aaron Copland wrote about Sessions's First Piano Sonata: "To know the work
well is to have the firm conviction that Sessions has presented us with a cornerstone
upon which to base an American music."[29]

Sessions rarely discusses his own music in his published prose. An exception is a description of the genesis of this work in *The Musical Experience of Composer, Performer, Listener.*

> The first idea that came to me for my first Piano Sonata, begun in 1927, was in the form of a complex chord preceded by a sharp but heavy up beat [see ex. 3.2]. This chord rang through my ear almost obsessively one day as I was walking in Pisa, Italy. The next day, or, in other words, when I sat down to work on the piece, I wrote the first phrase of the Allegro [mm. 27–32]; . . . the chord had become simpler—a C minor triad, in fact, and its complex sonority had given way to a motif of very syncopated rhythmic character[30] [see ex. 3.3].

Example 3.2.   Piano Sonata No. 1, first idea: chord with upbeat.

Example 3.3.   Piano Sonata No. 1, Allegro, mm. 27–32.

In a letter to pianist Beveridge Webster Sessions elaborated:

> When I discovered, however—after a surprising length of time—that the vague but all too strong dissatisfaction I felt with this beginning was due to the syncopated rhythm before any regular beat was established, I immediately thought of the music of the andante Introduction in B minor, and realized that I wanted to bring it back later as the real slow movement of the piece. It was one day somewhat later that, following a semi-conscious train of thought from the chord of measure 234, I found myself back, exactly as in the final text of the Sonata, at the B minor of the Introduction, and realized that this key relationship had been subconsciously in my ear all the time.
>
> When I composed the section beginning measure 252 I felt that it was something quite new and possibly the beginning of a quite new phase in my music, and in a way which I would find it very difficult to define I still feel that it is very close to my later music, perhaps closer than anything else in the Sonata except perhaps certain passages in the Finale.

The last movement gave me a lot of trouble particularly in the choice of a key. I originally had planned to write it one tone lower, i.e., in what I thought of as the key of B major, starting on C sharp instead of D sharp. This however seemed to me to fall flat. I realized that my ear was pulling me towards the D sharp, and then only much later, when I was well along in the actual work on the movement I realized that the D sharp was the real tonic of the piece, and the note on which it had to end.[31]

The structure of the sonata is three movements. The Andante introduction is actually the beginning of the slow middle movement. The Andante is interrupted by the fast movement, then continued. The first and third movements are in sonata-allegro form and in C minor; the opening and recurring slow sections are in B minor. In each movement the principal theme returns as a recapitulation in the tonic key of that movement. The length, key, and uninterrupted flow of the sonata suggest Liszt's B-minor Sonata as a possible formal inspiration.

Other composers might have influenced Sessions. The C-minor section is reminiscent of Beethoven's *Hammerklavier* Sonata, Op. 106. The large-scale structural dissonance of a half tone in the Beethoven sonata (B-flat major and B minor) is similar to that in the Sessions sonata (B minor and C minor). The B-minor sections frequently remind listeners of Chopin, possibly because of the Chopinesque harmonic rhythm, pedal changes, and wide spacing in the accompaniment's chords.

I might say also that while the introductory melody has often been likened to Chopin, I conceive it as something rather different—the nearest thing in the music of the past would be a Bach "aria" (Italian Concerto) or perhaps still better, such a Mozart slow movement as that of the little C major Sonata—in other words the long phrases and not the detail are the real key to the expression.[32]

About performing the work Sessions writes:

I believe also, at this late date [1952] the First Sonata is not likely to be played in the completely frigid manner in which many of its earliest performers tried to play it. The relative paucity of expression marks in the text was due, believe me, not to any dogma regarding "objectivity" but to an all too naive belief that the character of the music would naturally suggest its own mode of performance—a "singing" tone, a long breath requiring a real dynamic curve, and a ringing tone quality. The greatest mistake from this point of view lay in the fact that (I am afraid out of sheer helplessness) I indicated only a very few pedalings. Actually I assumed that the pedal would be used rather freely throughout, as it certainly should be.[33]

Originally intended for the first Copland-Sessions Concert, the work was not completed in time; the first two movements were performed at the second concert. "I was being so hypercritical that until it moved naturally, it was torture. But it does move naturally. It was just the experience of writing this whole thing was much the toughest time I've ever had as a composer."[34] Sessions's former teacher, Edward Burlingame Hill, wrote of this first performance of the sonata:

Mr. Sessions' *Sonata*, (was it wise to play it incomplete?) also redolent of Stravinsky's procedures, was on the whole better music than Stravinsky has written of late. It had in the *Allegro* movement assertiveness, strength and interesting development of themes that were never wholly original. The *Andante* following, worked out with a sensitive feeling for line and climax, ideas suggestive again of Stravinsky, but a Stravinsky who, in striving to get "back to Handel," stalled on reaching César Franck.[35]

In Michael Campbell's dissertation on all three of the sonatas, the author describes the First Sonata:

The First Sonata displays a conservative use of the musical elements: clear pulse, restricted contrast in surface rhythm, often conjunct melody, moderate range, and predominately melody plus accompaniment texture. These features, coupled with a well-demarcated formal outline, suggest superficially Sessions's affinity for the neoclassical trend of the period. Yet the quality of movement, the relentless energy of the fast movements and the unbroken flow of the slow movements, the consistent intensification within gestures and the strong linear connections through punctuations, clearly identify the First Sonata as a composition by Sessions.[36]

The first performer was John Duke, Sessions's colleague at Smith College. He recalled that the music was brought to him almost page by page:

But as time went on, and it wasn't finished, Roger was in a terrible state about it and finally decided to just have me play the first two movements with an improvised ending to the second movement. I'll never forget the struggle he had. He used to stay up drinking black coffee, and by the time we went to New York, Roger was about all in. We had to change trains in Springfield, and he had to lie down on the station seat there. But we made it to New York and I actually played the Sonata at the concert.[37]

The work was completed in Rome, performed in Europe, and published shortly afterward by B. Schotts Söhne. Felix Lamond describes the reception of the 24 July 1930 performance at the ISCM Festival as "excellent . . . we were proud of the numerous recalls that the composer received." *The London Times* said of this work: "It began well with a delicately poised and thoroughly pianistic theme. What followed did not completely fulfill the expectation raised by the opening, but the finale is a remarkably brilliant piece of writing." It also received favorable comments from the music critics of the continental press. *L'Indépendance Belge*, Brussels, wrote: "The Sonata of Sessions is one of the rare works of the festival which left in us the impression that it is a masterly work, of profound sentiment (the first theme is of exceptional serenity) most adequately expressed."[38]

Four Pieces for Children   1935–1939

Scherzino 1935

Published by Carl Fischer, 1936.
Manuscript at Princeton University Library.

March 1935

Published by Carl Fischer, 1936.
Manuscript at Princeton University
Library.

Waltz for Brenda 1936

Published by Edward B. Marks in
American Composers of Today,
1965.

Little Piece (for John, Age 1) 1939

Published by Edward B. Marks in
American Composers of Today,
1965.

The Scherzino and March were published by Fischer in a collection of children's piano works. The one-page Scherzino, in F major, is reminiscent of Bartók's *Mikrokosmos,* using a similar ostinato and modal scales. The March is constructed in ABB form and is in B-flat major. Sessions wrote the Waltz for the daughter of a California neighbor. This D-minor ABA Waltz is reminiscent of Chopin's Grande Valse Brillante, Op. 34, No. 2. Of the Little Piece, Sessions says: "The Piece for John I used to sing to my son when he was a baby. I used to sing him this little tune I made up. So I harmonized it in my own inimitable way."[39] Like his other occasional pieces, these works are not especially representative of Sessions's music.

Concerto for Violin and Orchestra 1930–1935
(Score Marked San Francisco, Calif. August 1935)

Dedication: "To Barbara Sessions"
Published by Affiliated Music Corporation, 1937; Edward B. Marks, 1937. Manuscripts at the Princeton University Library and the Library of Congress.
Premieres: 8 January 1940, Chicago, Illinois, Robert Gross, Violin, Illinois Symphony, Izler Solomon Conducting; 15 February 1959, New York City, Tossy Spivakovsky, The New York Philharmonic, Leonard Bernstein Conducting.
I. Largo e tranquillo
II. Scherzo—Allegro
III. Romanza (Played without Pause)
IV. Molto vivace e sempre con fuoco

The Violin Concerto is a transitional work in two senses of the word, locational and stylistic. The first movement was begun in Rome in 1930. In the summer of 1931 Sessions continued the work at Lutjenburg, a resort on the Baltic Sea. Most of the movement, however, was written in Berlin and in Hamburg. The second movement was composed in Berlin, as was the third, which was completely sketched in Berlin and finished in Massachusetts. While he was writing the Concerto, he bridged the difficult transition between living happily with his wife in Europe and returning in 1933 to the United States, where he had little money and no regular job. Here he separated from his wife. The last movement was almost entirely written in California in the summer of 1935 and, although the score is dated "San Francisco, Calif., August 1935," the orchestration was completed that fall in New York.

The Concerto was still not performed when he remarried. "So it covers space and time and history, so to speak." [40]

Elliott Carter comments on the significance of the piece:

> It was finished just before the Violin Concerto of Alban Berg, but under cultural conditions so vastly different that the achievement of such an outstanding work represents an even more remarkable artistic triumph—a triumph over the apathy, cultural confusion, and uncertainty that caused its subsequent neglect. [41]

The performance history of the Violin Concerto is the most tortured of any of Sessions's works. To a composer approaching 40 the largest and most recent work acquires added significance, especially since this composer did not have a large catalogue. That the Concerto be played and accepted was vital to Sessions's career and reputation. However, circumstances did not allow this.

Albert Spalding canceled his 1937 performance, which was to have been with the Boston Symphony Orchestra with Koussevitsky conducting. For reasons unrelated to the Concerto, Koussevitsky subsequently refused to conduct any of Sessions's music—a devastating blow to Sessions's career. In addition, rumors that the composer had not completed the Concerto further damaged his reputation.

The violinist Louis Krasner traveled to Boston to hear the performance. He was dismayed to find "Canceled" plastered over the Boston Symphony Orchestra's poster. By coincidence he encountered Sessions on the train returning to New York. Sessions told Krasner that Spalding had changed some of the notes in the last movement and he could not allow a performance that differed from his original version. A few days later Krasner received a letter from Sessions detailing what had transpired with Spalding:

> . . . I did not have the opportunity of going over the Concerto with him until the fall of 1936; I waited until his return from a European tour, early November. At that time [the month of Sessions's marriage] I spoke to him over the 'phone; he told me that he had gone to Europe confident of knowing the Concerto perfectly; but that on his return he had found that he did not remember it well, and that at the performance, set for one month later, he might have to use the notes. Since I had absolutely no objections to this, I was, of course, not disturbed.
>
> Ten days later I went to an appointment which we had made—the performance was scheduled for two and a half weeks later. At that time Spalding told me that he had asked Koussevitsky to postpone the performance, simply because he did not know it sufficiently to play it. At the time, he was not sure whether the performance could take place in the following March or would have to be delayed until *this* season. . . . He also told me he felt the last movement was "unrelieved" and asked me if I would be willing to make changes. I told him that a large part of the character, which I had in mind, lay in the very intensity of the movement, especially toward the end, but that I felt that this also was relieved most especially by the episodes, lighter in character, beginning at No. 112 and at No. 129. . . . About a month later . . . he reiterated his feelings that the finale was "unrelieved" and spoke this time of a "relentless staccato."
>
> I considered the matter very carefully and went over my score,—as I felt quite able to do—in the most objective manner possible; for I wanted to give Mr. Spalding's criticism every benefit of the doubt. [Spalding had himself composed several violin concertos.] My only possible conclusion was the one I might have anticipated—I had written exactly what I had intended to write,

and it would have been quite out of the question to make the kinds of radical changes which Mr. Spalding demanded. I wrote him to this effect, saying that I felt the movement was fundamentally unsympathetic to him and that, therefore, I did not wish to hold him to any obligation to play it. He wrote me that he could not feel the conviction in regard to it that was necessary in order to do the work justice.

If there is a chance of your caring to undertake the premiere of the work—this season if possible, and early next season at the latest—I should appreciate your letting me know as soon as you can do so. Since the work is over two years old I am anxious to "launch" it as soon as possible; but I am also anxious to have you play it, and, should there be a chance of your doing so, would be willing to wait a little longer, if necessary.[42]

Ultimately, Krasner did not give the premiere of the Sessions Concerto as he had done the Berg, although he did perform the Concerto later in Minneapolis. Sessions was destined to wait three more years.

The Concerto was not performed with orchestra until 1940 when the Illinois Symphony played it with Robert Gross. In 1949 Sessions showed the piano reduction of the Violin Concerto to Tossy Spivakovsky. Around 1950 Spivakovsky approached Dimitri Mitropoulos with the idea of their performing it together. Mitropoulos had already studied the work, as indicated in the following letter:

The three important works that I am going to study this summer are: a symphony that Ernst Krenek just finished for me, . . . the Alpine Symphony of Richard Strauss and the Roger Sessions Violin Concerto—one of the greatest American achievements in musical composition. You might not have heard of that composer, but I think he is the only one who could compete with the rest of the great.[43]

Mitropoulos intended to proceed with the performance; however, the manager of the New York Philharmonic (as well as of the Philadelphia Orchestra), Arthur Judson, forbade the work on the grounds of length. Spivakovsky waited ten years to play the work with orchestra.

Twenty-four years after the completion of the work the Violin Concerto was heard finally in New York when, in 1959, Tossy Spivakovsky and Leonard Bernstein gave the New York premiere performance (see fig. 3.2). By the time of the New York premiere, audiences and critics were more accustomed to the dissonant sound of Sessions's music from this period. The piece received good reviews from the *New York Times*[44] and from the *New York Herald Tribune*.[45]

Spivakovsky compared the difficulty Sessions experienced getting the Violin Concerto performed, not to mention accepted into the standard repertoire, to Beethoven's Violin Concerto, which took nearly 40 years to become popular.[46] Spivakovsky's enthusiasm for Sessions's music has not wavered—he has performed the Duo for Violin and Piano and he has learned the solo violin part to the Double Concerto in the hope of performing it. He wrote of the Violin Concerto:

Sessions's Violin Concerto has grandeur, depth and intensity of feeling. Its masterful construction, nobility of idiom (which never permits effects for effect's sake)—although the finest

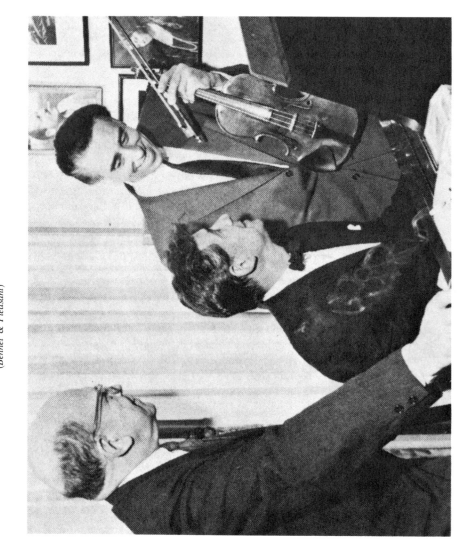

Figure 3.2. Roger Sessions, Leonard Bernstein, and Tossy Spivakovsky preparing for the 1959 performance of the Violin Concerto. *(Bennet & Pleasant)*

possibilities of expression of the violin are made use of—mark it as one of the most important works of the music literature of our time. . . . Roger Sessions possesses, as only the very greatest do, that power of the imagination by which ideas can be expressed in the most complicated combinations without thereby losing in freedom or depth of feeling.[47]

A postscript to the performance history of the Concerto regards the "return" of the work to Boston. It has still not been performed by the Boston Symphony Orchestra; however, on 15 April 1981 Eric Rosenblith gave the Boston premiere with the New England Conservatory Orchestra conducted by Eiji Oue. The Boston reception of the Concerto was more enthusiastic than the response it had received in New York 22 years earlier. Calling the Concerto "a major masterpiece of 20th-century music," *The Boston Globe* continued, "it is also necessary to say that it remains difficult in its very nature, that, like some of the greatest music of Bach and Beethoven and other masters, it will *always* be difficult, the way some of the enduring aspects of our universe are."[48] Happy at this, the composer nevertheless continues to adhere to what he wrote shortly before the completion of this work: "I am convinced that every mature or really talented composer, however much he may be momentarily pleased by a 'good' criticism or irritated by a 'bad' one, will and must remain—through the strength of his creative impulse and for the good of his art—fundamentally indifferent to it."[49]

About neoclassicism and this work the composer has said:

> I suppose that people who talk about my neo-classic period might consider this [first movement] 'neo-classic.' I would say other movements, not at all. It's almost an instrumental conception that is neo-classic if anything. It's a very, very long line for the violin, insofar that if I was thinking of anybody from the past at that time, I was thinking of a composer like Corelli, with a big singing line, you see.[50]

Elliott Carter describes the Concerto: "More and more the notion of extended, continuously flowing sections during which ideas come to the surface, gain clarity and definition, and then sink back into the general flow has characterized Sessions' unique style, and he seems to have striven for this first here."[51]

The Concerto begins and ends clearly in B minor, seemingly a favorite key for Sessions, as is E minor, the key of its subdominant. (The First Piano Sonata is also in B minor and the First Symphony and First String Quartet are both in E minor.) In a detailed analysis of the opening of the first movement, Andrew Imbrie views the opposition of tonic to supertonic as one of its most important form-engendering principles.[52] Unity among the movements is achieved by references to motives stated at the beginning of each movement. The motives are themselves related to each other, as Elliott Carter has pointed out.[53]

The first movement is constructed in a large ABA form, each section introduced by the same musical idea (given in ex. 3.4). This opening orchestral idea returns at no. 12 and at no. 20, but after nine bars dissolves into a quasi-cadenza, "an organic part of the movement." At no. 22 the upper line of the violin double stops contains the main idea; the lower line is its accompaniment, an adaptation of the original accompanying idea at no. 3. The bassoon continues the pattern while the horn takes the melody. Each of the three sections supports a seventeen- to nineteen-measure-long phrase in the violin, examples of Sessions's famous *grande ligne*.

Example 3.4.   Violin Concerto, I, Largo e tranquillo, mm. 1–2.
© 1937 by Edward B. Marks Music Company.
Copyright renewed. Used by permission.

The type of ending Sessions employs at the close of the first movement was to become a kind of trademark in his later music. The instruments of the orchestra drop out in descending note patterns, leaving a single, slow, bass pitch remaining, which dies out softly. Later works that also incorporate this "Sessions ending" are the Quintet (second movement), the Seventh Symphony (last movement), *Montezuma*, the Eighth Symphony, and *When Lilacs Last in the Dooryard Bloom'd*.

The Scherzo is in $\frac{2}{4}$, although it is not common for the composer to remain in one meter for an entire movement. Its structure is ABA-coda. The B begins at no. 44, A returns at no. 59, and the coda begins at no. 75. Characteristic of Sessions's scherzolike movements, it is the most chromatic movement of the piece.

The Romanza, constructed in a small ABACA form, is the only movement with no key signature. Its implied keys are A minor, C major, and E Phrygian. Sessions describes the form of this short movement as "just a song in three verses."

The fourth movement begins a perpetuum mobile and never unwinds. Sessions's original idea was that the movement be a tarantella, "a wild, mad dance," where the legendary tarantula-bitten victim dies dancing. When the orchestra enters at no. 88, the violin sounds like a fast-motion parody of the previous movement. The movement is a sonata. Dancelike sections at nos. 112 and 114, which return at no. 129, sound like "demonic waltzes" reminiscent of the grotesque dance in *The Black Maskers*. In the movement strict inversion is employed. The violin's opening fifteen bars return in exact inversion at no. 152.

Often during the movement Sessions metrically modulates from duple to triple divisions, as for example the $\frac{6}{8}$ two bars before no. 112 L'istesso tempo. Duplets prepare the way for the $\frac{3}{4}$ (see ex. 3.5). Elsewhere he simply alternates between duple divisions and triplets, as at no. 115ff. After no. 118 the A clarinet plays triplets against the solo violin's duple divisions of the beat. At no. 119 the E-flat clarinet persists in the triplet subdivision and eventually (five measures after no. 120) the violin succumbs, taking over in triplets.

Example 3.5.   Violin Concerto, IV, four measures before no. 112ff, solo violin line.
© 1937 Edward B. Marks Music Company.
Copyright renewed. Used by permission.

Time, expressed in meter, helps to articulate form. The first theme originally appears in $\frac{6}{8}$, when it returns in the recapitulation, beginning at no. 132, it is in $\frac{9}{8}$. Conversely, the second theme appears first in $\frac{9}{8}$ and returns in $\frac{6}{8}$ at no. 139. The entire movement contracts like a stretto: One measure of $\frac{9}{8}$ corresponds to two measures of $\frac{6}{8}$. Sessions says, "everything is foreshortened. That's sort of in the spirit of the piece. The proper performance of the last movement is one in which the violinist drops dead."[54]

Another type of contraction starts at no. 153. In the $\frac{3}{4}$ meter six eighth notes occupy each bar, but the phrasing and accentuation produce patterns of five notes, four notes, three notes, and finally, by means of alternating pitches, patterns of two notes. This is reminiscent of the Brahms Violin Concerto in which an accelerating rhythm pulls against a steady pulse and ultimately produces a contraction. In both concertos this rhythmic foreshortening helps to produce a sense of musical vertigo as well as to propel the piece to its conclusion (see ex. 3.6). From no. 153 to the end is an extension and elaboration of the final cadence, moving from A minor to B minor.

Orchestration has always been one of Sessions's fortes. The most dramatic stroke in the Concerto is the absence of first and second violins, so as not to compete with the sound of the solo instrument and to highlight the woodwinds and brass. Possibly Sessions got the idea of eliminating the violin section from Stravinsky's *Symphony of Psalms,* written in 1930. To separate further the soloist from the accompanying instruments, Sessions keeps the violin in the high register. The part is played almost exclusively on the E string, infrequently on the A, and only occasionally on the D or G strings.

Example 3.6.   Violin Concerto, IV, no. 153ff, phrasing and accentuation in the solo violin line.

In the introduction to the third movement, Sessions pairs the solo instrument with the basset horn (whose part can be played by an alto clarinet in F). The idea to use this unusual instrument came from Strauss's *Elektra*, but Sessions abandoned the basset horn after this work because orchestras had trouble finding a player.

It was stated above that the Violin Concerto is a transitional work in two senses. The first was physical: the changes of locales and circumstances under which it was written. The second is its summation of his second-period style and the launching of the third. Referring to the late 1920s, Sessions writes:

> This was the period in which Stravinsky was entering on his "neo-classic" phase; and that seemed to me to offer a direction from which I could gain the resources which I needed. Looking backward I can realize that my approach was a quite different one from Stravinsky's and that a part of the experience consisted in fighting stubbornly against the reservations which I always felt regarding the final validity of such an approach as his. Naturally every work has its own value and I do not mean to deny in any degree whatever the validity of these works themselves, when I say that my First Symphony, my First Sonata, and even to some extent my Violin Concerto were all stages in the process of finding my way back to the music of which I was dreaming when I wrote *The Black Maskers* in 1923. It was not, of course, really a "way back," but an extremely important phase of my development.[55]

Notes

1. Ernest Samuels, *Bernard Berenson: The Making of a Connoisseur* (Cambridge: Harvard University Press, 1979), p. xiii.

2. Untaped interview 27 November 1979 (shortly after Boulanger died, 22 October 1979). For an elaboration of Sessions's view about Boulanger, *see* Aaron Copland and Vivian Perlis, *Copland/1900–1942* (New York: St. Martin's Press, 1984), pp. 149–50.

3. Ibid.

4. Columbia University Oral History Collection, p. 166.

5. Untaped interview 27 November 1979.

6. Felix Lamond, "Report of the Professor in Charge of the Department of Music," *American Academy in Rome—Annual Reports 1928–29* (New York: Offices of the Academy, 1929), p. 43.

7. Felix Lamond, "Report of the Professor in Charge of the Department of Music," *American Academy in Rome—Annual Reports 1930–31* (New York: Offices of the Academy, 1931), p. 39.

8. "The Copland-Sessions Concerts of Contemporary Music," 22 April 1928, Program at the Music Division, New York Public Library. *See* Carol J. Oja, "The Copland-Sessions Concerts and Their Reception in the Contemporary Press," *The Musical Quarterly* 65 (April 1979): 212–29.

9. Copland and Perlis, *Copland/1900–1942*, pp. 144, 159.

10. In 1953 she translated Jean Seznec's *The Survival of the Pagan Gods.*

11. Untaped interview 11 April 1978.

12. Columbia University Oral History Collection, p. 236.

13. Taped interview 23 October 1974.

14. Ibid.

15. Ronald Duane Henderson, *Tonality in the Pre-Serial Instrumental Music of Roger Sessions* (Ph.D. diss.: Eastman School of Music, 1974), unpublished, p. 19.

16. Taped interview 23 October 1974.

17. Taped interview 5 November 1974.

18. In the only recording of the First Symphony (*see* appendix 3) the tempo of the first movement is radically wrong. The written metronome marking is quarter note equals 116, not 152.

19. Columbia University Oral History Collection, p. 232.

20. Roger Sessions, "Symphony No. 1," Boston Symphony Programs, 1926–1927, pp. 1874–78.

21. Andrew Imbrie, "The Symphonies of Roger Sessions," *Tempo* 103 (1972): 24.

22. Quoted in Lamond, *Annual Reports 1928–1929,* p. 43.

23. "Philadelphia Boos Music," *New York Times,* 21 December 1935.

24. Eric Salzman, *New York Times,* 19 June 1960.

25. David Schiff, *The Music of Elliott Carter* (London: Eulenburg Books, 1983), p. 115.

26. Eric Salzman, *New York Times,* 19 June 1960.

27. Taped interview 13 November 1974.

28. Robert Cogan, "Toward a Theory of Timbre: Verbal Timbre and Musical Line in Purcell, Sessions, and Stravinsky," *Perspectives of New Music* 8 (Fall 1969): 75-81.

29. Aaron Copland, "Contemporaries at Oxford, 1931" *Modern Music* 9 (November 1931): 23.

30. Roger Sessions, *The Musical Experience of Composer, Performer, Listener* (Princeton: Princeton University Press, 1950), 52ff.

31. Roger Sessions, letter to Beveridge Webster 28 November 1952.

32. Ibid.

33. Ibid.

34. Taped interview 20 November 1974.

35. Edward Burlingame Hill, "The Young Composers' Movement," *Modern Music* 5 (May–June 1928): 32–34.

36. Michael Ian Campbell, *The Piano Sonatas of Roger Sessions: Sequel to a Tradition* (DMA diss.: Peabody Institute, 1982), p. 111.

37. Quoted in Copland and Perlis, *Copland/1900–1942*, p. 149.

38. Quoted in Lamond, *Annual Reports 1930–1931*, p. 40.

39. Taped interview 18 December 1974.

40. Columbia University Oral History Collection, p. 234.

41. Elliott Carter, "Current Chronicle—New York," *The Musical Quarterly* 45 (July 1959): 380–81.

42. Roger Sessions, letter to Louis Krasner 26 October 1937. Letter at the Houghton Library, Harvard University.

43. Dimitri Mitropoulos, *Dimitri Mitropoulos-Katz Katsonyanis; A Correspondence, 1930–1960* (New York: Martin Dale Books, 1973), p. 61.

44. Howard Taubman, "Music: Sessions Violin Concerto," *New York Times* (21 February 1959), p. 24.

45. Louis Biancolli, "Sessions Concerto Has N.Y. Debut," *New York Herald Tribune*, 16 February 1959.

46. Interview with Tossy Spivakovsky, 2 December 1980.

47. Spivakovsky's Program notes, in his personal collection.

48. Richard Dyer, "Sessions Work Handled Well," *The Boston Globe* (20 April 1981), p. 43.

49. Roger Sessions, "Composition and Review," *New York Times,* 11 March 1934.

50. Columbia University Oral History Collection, p. 233.

51. Elliott Carter, "Current Chronicle," p. 380.

52. Andrew Imbrie, "Roger Sessions: In Honor of His Sixty-fifth Birthday," *Perspectives of New Music* 1 (Fall 1962): 127ff.

53. Elliott Carter, "Current Chronicle," pp. 375–81.

54. Taped interview 26 February 1980.

55. Roger Sessions, letter to Beveridge Webster, 28 November 1952.

4

"The Wars of the Present also Endure":
The Music from 1936–1947

University Life

Sessions's return from Germany to the United States in 1933 signaled the end of his marriage as well as his most difficult career crisis. By the fall of 1934 he and his wife had separated, and for the rest of the decade Sessions's career suffered due to the delays of the premiere of the Violin Concerto. Depression-ridden America could not compete with the glamour and excitement of Europe. More upsetting was the unwillingness of many of Sessions's friends to believe the worst about the course of the political events in Germany.

Considered an expatriot, Sessions also felt culture shock in the musical world. Milton Babbitt explains: "Europeans regarded Sessions as an American composer and Americans thought of him as European. He was caught in the middle."[1] Sessions recalls: "This was the worst period of my life. I felt totally alone, because I was entirely opposite the current that was going around here."[2] He maintained a sensible attitude, as Edward T. Cone recalls: "Sessions had always rightly insisted that the American past is the European past and that the foundation provided by the great line [in music] is basic to the development of music in the United States as well as in Europe."[3]

As if the saga of his parents' marriage were repeating itself, Sessions began to spend more time in New York and Boston, while his wife remained in Hadley. (Recall that Sessions's father had lived in New York, while Ruth Sessions lived at Smith College near Hadley.) During 1933–1934 Sessions commuted to New York to give talks on contemporary music and teach the fall term at the New School for Social Research. Sessions also commuted to Boston to teach at the Malkin Conservatory and Boston University. (Arnold Schoenberg also taught at the Malkin Conservatory, but the two never met there.)

In the second term of 1934 Sessions taught at the Dalcroze School headed by Paul Boepple. Among his pupils were Hugo Weisgall, David Diamond, Vivian Fine, Miriam Gideon, and Irwin Heilner. Boepple and Sessions combined forces the next year to found and teach at the New Music School. Because Sessions drifted away from the Dalcroze method by bringing in non-Dalcroze people, Boepple resigned. In the fall of 1934 Sessions began teaching at Princeton University. At this time Sessions and his wife formally separated.

Sessions drove a Plymouth named Annabelle about 500 miles a week. He commuted from Rosedale, New Jersey, to New York one day a week, teaching in Miriam Gideon's apartment and renting a studio on Third Street and Sixth Avenue and a $10-a-month piano. (He continued to commute to New York until 1945.) He also commuted two days a week to the New Jersey College for Women, now Douglass College, in New Brunswick, from 1935 to 1938.

Sessions had resumed his career writing prose in 1926, and between 1933 and 1938 he published fifteen articles, mostly in *Modern Music*. The mid-1930s were, for Sessions, a period of evaluation, change, and adjustment. His reviews of Schenker, Křenek, and Hindemith's theoretical work and his own political writing reveal both his critical insight and emotional ferocity.

Milton Babbitt thinks Sessions wrote these reviews because he was reevaluating his views toward composition. One of the first to publish Heinrich Schenker's theories in English, Sessions contributed the English translation of Schenker's *Tonikalisierung* as "tonicization," much more manageable than the literal "tonicalization." In "Heinrich Schenker's Contribution" (1935) Sessions writes that he finds Schenker's "doctrines . . . forced, untenable, and essentially sterile in tendency." Sessions argues that Schenker's true contribution to musical theory consists of delineating a relationship between form and harmony. Sessions objects to Schenker's principal concepts of *Urlinie* and *Ursatz*. First, it is "far too primitive a description of actual musical events"; and second, "it is in essence the Alexandrian or ex post facto conception which envisages creation as the painstaking and meticulous embodiment of principles that were once vital and in process of development, but whose very definiteness and, so to speak, formulability proclaim either their insufficiency or their exhaustion."

Sessions writes in "Escape by Theory" (1938) that *Der Freie Satz* is "repulsive, sterile and repellent reading." Here, only three years after his first article on Schenker, which was generally laudatory and milder in its criticism, Sessions attacks the concept of the *Ursatz* as "attenuated, inflexible, and devoid of any dynamic quality." Undoubtedly, the 29-page, self-serving introduction to *Der Freie Satz*, accentuated by Sessions's awareness of current history, only annoyed him further against Germanism. Schenker's chapters on "Diminution," "Articulation," and "Metre and Rhythm" Sessions finds "genuinely profound, illuminating, . . . and important." However, he voices a "fundamental divergence" from Schenker's viewpoint, one that Sessions regards as "categorically false." The "escape" that appears in the title of the review refers to Schenker's escape from the present into the more comfortable past.

The differences in point of view between these two articles, spanning only three years, reveal the intensity with which Sessions first examined and embraced

Schenker's theories, only to discard soon afterward what gave them their impact. During these years—1935–1938—Milton Babbitt studied composition with Sessions and observed that his teacher then underwent a profound rethinking of his own views concerning theory, pedagogy, and composition.

In reviewing Ernst Křenek's *Über neue Musik,* in "Exposition by Křenek" (1938), Sessions was forced to examine "an extraordinarily clear, illuminating, and persuasive exposition of the technicalities and specific aesthetic problems of the twelve-tone system." Křenek's argument is "masterly, convincing, and completely evolved." However, "this writer has come to the conclusion that this is so; that what one hears in twelve-tone music is often plainly at variance with the conceptions that go into its construction." For Sessions "the system is suspect."

Reviewing Hindemith's "extraordinarily interesting and provocative book," *Unterweisung im Tonsatz (The Craft of Musical Composition),* Sessions finds Hindemith's observations "always illuminating and vital; they are also clear, shrewd, and, granting his premises, generally consistent." Having said this, the reviewer "finds himself in complete disagreement with much in the book." Sessions feels that Hindemith "assigns far too great an importance, in the construction of a musical theory, to the physics of sound" and that he emphasizes the acoustical at the expense of the psychological aspects of music.

Partly in his effort to raise the consciousness of musicians to recognize the implications of the political threat in Europe, Sessions wrote about the famous Furtwängler-Goebbels exchange of letters. He drills his points home with uncharacteristically direct prose:

> But the impulse to create has nothing whatever to do with the impulse to proselytize . . . . The conception of art as propaganda appeals either to the type of artist who is so childlike as to be incapable of self-analysis, or to minds so academic, sterile, and tortuous as to be incapable of any but purely interested reactions.

Elsewhere in the same article, he reveals the scope of his political insight when he notes that "the most vulnerable points for the United Nations have been precisely those at which they have felt themselves most complacently secure."

Sessions views fascism as so deeply rooted as to pervade every aspect of society:

> Fascism . . . is simply the uprush of the most ruthless and resentful elements into a void which has been created in modern society by the prevalence of nihilistic cynicism, by economic, intellectual, and moral disorder, and by a crassly competitive spirit in human relationships.

And: "It's ultimate horror is not the fact that it is cruel beyond all conception but the fact that from beginning to end it is *phoney.*" He shows the breeding ground of fascism in our own most cherished concepts: "Each one of us has to struggle to some extent against the desire to preserve at all cost his own pet corner of status quo."

Sessions had financial problems and borrowed money frequently. Although his title at Princeton was Associate Professor, his salary was that of a lecturer. Sessions advanced to Instructor from 1936 to 1937, to Assistant Professor from 1937 to 1940, and to Associate Professor in 1940. On Thanksgiving Day in 1936, Sessions married a summer-school student from Spokane, Washington, Sarah Elizabeth Franck, a librarian ten years younger than he. She was called Lisl and was related to César Franck. On 6 March 1938, when Sessions was 41, his son, John, was born eleven weeks premature. John is now a cellist and teaches at Smith College. Elizabeth, born 5 September 1940, holds a Ph.D. in linguistics from Princeton and a M.S. from New York University. Each of Sessions's children has one child (see appendix 1).

In the summer of 1944 Sessions joined Rudolf Kolisch, Eduard Steuermann, Frederick Cohen, and Mark Brunswick at a seminar at Black Mountain College in North Carolina. The following summer he taught at Kenyon College in Gambier, Ohio, connected to the Black Mountain Institute.

During his last year at Princeton, 1944–1945, Sessions and his colleague Oliver Strunk translated Alfred Einstein's *The Italian Madrigal* into English. But by 1945 Sessions had grown tired of Princeton. At the time he did not feel that Princeton took creative work seriously. Sessions described his need for a change: "I didn't like the Princeton climate too much and my wife hated it. But mainly I wanted adventure. I wanted to move to another part of the country. . . . The minute I got to Berkeley, I began producing [music]. It was also a period when I needed to take stock."[4]

String Quartet No. 1 in E Minor   1936

(Score Marked New York, Pyramid Lake,
Nevada, Princeton, 1936)

Dedication: Mrs. Elizabeth Sprague Coolidge
Published by Arrow Music Press (Edward B. Marks), 1938. Manuscript at the Library of Congress.
Premiere: April 1937, Washington, D.C., Coolidge String Quartet.
I. Tempo moderato
II. Adagio—Allegretto—Adagio
III. Finale

For Sessions this quartet evokes memories of tumbleweeds, Western garb, and horseback riding. In 1936 he stayed on a ranch in Reno, Nevada, in order to establish the short residency required to obtain a divorce. His other memories are not as pleasant: the divorce itself; a letter from Boulanger urging Sessions to reconsider; and asking his aunt Adeline for money to be able to drive back East.

The first movement of the quartet is a triple exposition, three "stanzas": m. 89 marks the beginning of the second stanza, and m. 168 the beginning of the third. This structure is similar to the first movement of Beethoven's Op. 132, the A-minor Quartet, a work Sessions taught for a semester in 1979. Sessions describes the movement: "All the way through you have a kind of stretto." Each time an exposition occurs its three themes are varied. Example 4.1 compares the first theme in each of the stanzas. Compare also the second theme in each stanza: m. 37 (second violin), m. 124 (viola), and m. 188 (second violin). The closing theme in each stanza appears at m. 63 (viola), m. 144 (second violin), and m. 210 (second violin).

Example 4.1.   String Quartet No. 1, I, comparison of the first theme in each of the three stanzas. © 1938 by Edward B. Marks Music Company. Copyright renewed. Used by permission.

A specific tempo grants each of the three themes in the first movement part of its identity. At theme A (mm. 1–8) the quarter note equals 116; in the third section the quarter note also equals 116; and in the codetta it equals 100. At theme B (mm. 37–41) the quarter note is given a metronomic marking of 100; in the third section it is 96. The quarter-note tempo of theme C (mm. 64–67) is initially 120; in the third section it returns at 126.

The second movement begins with an Adagio and is continued by a brief scherzando interlude that leads back to the Adagio. The movement, explicity in B minor, modulates to G-sharp minor at m. 305. A description of E minor for the scherzo, as well as the other movements, would be tenuous; each bar could be interpreted in a different key. E minor is merely a point of departure. One unifying feature of the movement is the first three-note motive, which recurs at mm. 263, 271, 281, and 437 (see ex. 4.2). The contrast between the firm key areas of the Adagios and the ambiguity of the scherzando is fully intended. Canons appear in a secondary viola figure at m. 408 and again in the second violin at m. 416. Canonic devices, a dense web of motives, and a sense of controlled chromaticism within an expanded tonal framework represent an increase in technical complexity over Sessions's earlier music. About writing the movement Sessions says: "It seemed to me that I was writing like Alban Berg already." [5]

Example 4.2.   String Quartet No. 1, II, violin 1, mm. 241–42.
© 1938 by Edward B. Marks Music Company.
Copyright renewed. Used by permission.

The third movement, a sonata-allegro form, is Sessions's strictest standard form to date. The introduction is followed by the first theme in the viola; the second theme appears in the cello at m. 55. The development begins m. 629 and the recapitulation m. 726. The Vivace molto tempo (quarter note equals 120–132) and the $\frac{2}{4}$ meter never fluctuate throughout the entire movement (except four measures of $\frac{3}{4}$).

Every composer commits embarrassing mistakes. Here Sessions wrote a double stop for viola at m. 457 "that's quite unplayable because both these notes are on the C string. I remember Alfred Einstein was with me once when we were going to hear this, and I told him I was ashamed of one thing. He said, 'Oh don't worry about that, Mozart did that once too.' "[6]

Chorale for Organ   1938

Commission: H. W. Gray Co.
Dedication: "To my Wife"
Published by H. W. Gray Co., Inc., 1941. Manuscript at Princeton University Library.
Premiere: April 1938, Princeton, New Jersey, Robert Hufstader, Organ.

William Strickland, Sessions's student at the time, persuaded the H. W. Gray Company to commission this work for their Contemporary Organ Series. The overall model for the piece was the chorale prelude as written by Bach. The texture alternates between free fantasialike figuration and slower chordal sections. The organ is not Sessions's favorite instrument: "The trouble with the organ is you never know what you're going to get. It depends on the instrument, and of course on the player himself, and on the registration."[7]

Pages from a Diary   1937–1940

Dedicated to Milton Babbit (I), Edward T. Cone (II), Carter Harman (III), and Vivian Fine (IV)
Published by Edward B. Marks, 1947. Manuscripts at Princeton University Library.
Premiere: November 1939, New York City, Roger Sessions, Piano.
I. Poco adagio (Score Marked Princeton, May 1937–November 1939)
II. Allegro con brio (Colorado Springs, August 1939; Princeton, March 1940)
III. Larghissimo e misterioso (Colorado Springs, August 1939)
IV. Allegro pesante (Princeton, November 1939)

Sessions dedicated each of these four short piano pieces to one of his students: Milton Babbitt, Edward T. Cone, Carter Harman, and Vivian Fine. One of the discarded pieces of the set later became the second movement of the Second Symphony. The erroneous title From My Diary is the publisher's miscomprehension of the original title, Albumblätte.

The first piece cannot be divided into distinct sections. The second idea is parenthetical and represents a continuation of the first line in the Baroque sense of *Fortspinnung*. "I would say that in all of my music, perhaps even in my First Symphony, for instance, but certainly as my music developed, the harmonies are more and more derived from the movement of the lines." C minor was the point of departure for this movement.

Sessions's interest in rhythm's ability to distinguish a phrase can be traced in his music back to the First Symphony. In the second piece of this work rhythm itself becomes a criterion for formal organization. The opening section of the ABA form is built on an ostinato continuum of eighth note equals 456, which can be grouped into twos or threes. This type of asymmetrical additive rhythm is common to much American music. The B section also has one underlying division, one third of a beat equals 216 that can be grouped similarly. The return of A is expectedly a varied repetition of the opening material. Unity and variety are each maintained on a rhythmic level. Here again time is manipulated to distinguish form. Imbrie writes of this work:

> The second movement of Pages from a Diary . . . is an excellent illustration of his style at a point midway between the first two symphonies. It has divested itself of all symptoms of eclecticism, and sounds like the music of no other composer. We become aware of the sustaining power of extended phrases, especially now that the accompanying rhythms have become so much more elastic—to the point, in fact, where they can now adequately set off the principal melodies. These are spun out with such inventive fantasy that the co-operation of a truly responsive accompaniment is needed: one which is rhythmically complementary rather than neutral or indifferent. The sense of key is still quite strong, although interesting ambiguities arise, as in the

third movement of the same suite, where one critic assumed that the two sharps meant D major, and published a learned exegesis on that basis.[8] In fact the piece is in B minor, although it allows for the real possibility of being heard in E-flat major.[9]

Sessions characterizes the fourth piece as "sort of parodistic. It's a dialogue between something rather weighty and something slightly mocking."[10] The "weighty" first idea consists of a figure constructed from quartal chords built on A and the single tonic tone D. Contrapuntal, angular, and varried in length, the "slightly mocking" second idea is set at a softer dynamic level. It recurs several times and appears at no. 39 in inversion, after which a three-voice stretto leads to an ending.

The climax of the piece is in mm. 21 and 22, exactly midpoint. The first idea appears in the left hand against right-hand octaves in the highest register of the work. An overlapping occurs at the "denouement," the last eighth of m. 30: C#, E, and B are heard in the texture of the second idea, but Bb, the expected next note, arrives in the weighty texture of the first idea—a ff diciso accented chord. Mm. 31–36 continue to expand the second idea while descending in the lower voice three octaves and a fourth to Eb. This foreground descent is structurally an ascent from a Schenkerian view. The relationship between the two ideas is twofold: both are pentatonic in nature, and perfect fourths are a characteristic of the vertical sonority of the first idea, as well as an important melodic element of the second.

Example 4.3.   Pages from a Diary, IV, mm. 1–4. The first idea is in mm. 1 and 2, the second in mm. 3 and 4.
© 1947 by Edward B. Marks Music Company.
Copyright renewed. Used by permission.

Duo for Violin and Piano   1942

Dedication: Irene and Frederick Jacobi
Published by New Music Edition, 1947; Edward B. Marks, 1966. Manuscript at Princeton University Library.
Premiere: January 1943, Princeton, New Jersey, J. Antal, Violin, Roger Sessions, Piano.
I. Andante moderato, tranquillo ed espressivo
II. Allegro impetuoso
III. Tranquillo, espressivo, come al principio
IV. Allegro vivace e con fuoco
(Played without Pause)

Named Duo simply because Sessions tired of labeling works sonatas, the piece essentially follows sonata form. Sessions provided notes explaining formal divisions, here paraphrased.[11] The slow movement that begins the Duo is interrupted by a fast movement. The slow movement resumes, leading to another fast movement that contrasts strongly with the first one. The scheme of interrupting a slow movement with a fast one is also found in the First Piano Sonata.

The Duo opens "moderately slow, quiet, expressive" with a long melody in the violin over a flowing accompaniment. It has no key signature. After a contrasting section of somewhat more restless character, the movement gradually becomes quieter. It returns to the tempo, the mood, and the character of the beginning and leads to a pause on a sort of "half-cadence." The first of the fast movements is "rhythmic and dramatic in character."[12] Its three sections parallel the traditional sonata form. The recapitulation is a free variation of the exposition. The middle section of the movement consists of a "very brilliant" passage for the violin developing through three successive entrances of a steadily pulsating D♯ in the piano, punctuated by heavy chords. The slow movement resumes. "The melodic line and the expression at this point are more subdued, the development less expansive, and the movement quieter."[13] Compare mm. 1–8 with mm. 284–92.

The last movement begins "fast, gay, with fire."

A gradual retard leads to a heavy climax which brings back the general mood and two easily recognizable themes from the first [fast] movement. The second of these reminiscences leads directly to a resumption of the fragments given out at the beginning of the last movement; the passage in question, however, is this time much abbreviated and the motifs appear in inverted form. The recapitulation also brings back the main themes in order, but in a form which is much shorter and more concentrated in texture.[14]

Turn, O Libertad   **1944**

Mixed Chorus and Piano Four-Hands
Text by Walt Whitman
Published by Edward B. Marks, 1952. Manuscript at Princeton University Library.
Premiere: April 1944, New York City, Temple Emanu-El Choir, Roger Sessions Conducting.

During the Second World War the Temple Emanu-El commissioned works to salute each of the Allies. Sessions drew Russia and chose the Whitman poem with "some malice aforethought, addressed to Russia."[15] An orchestral version, requested by his publisher, has never been performed or published.

The piece, essentially in D major, is not difficult because excellent singers were not at the composer's disposal. *Turn, O Libertad* is therefore not especially representative. The reversion to tonality can be attributed to this circumstance.

Discussing the subject of creativity in conjunction with *Turn, O Libertad*, Sessions refers to the sensation of seeing the whole work before him, rather than its parts, as common in the experience of the creator. This concept is referred to as "preunderstanding," which is "a circular process."[16] Thus a "hermeneutic circle" results because we cannot know the meaning of the whole without understanding the parts and cannot, ultimately, know the meaning of the parts unless we comprehend the whole context. "By general agreement, from which there has been virtually no dissent, the question of priority is decided in favor of the whole."[17]

In a letter whose authenticity remains in doubt, Mozart describes this sensation:

> . . . my subject enlarges itself, becomes methodised and defined, and the whole, though it be long, stands almost complete and finished in my mind, so that I can survey it, like a fine picture or a beautiful statue, at a glance. Nor do I hear in my imagination the parts *successively,* but I hear them, as it were, all at once (*gleich alles zusammen*).[18]

Although Sessions cites a work on mathematical creativity[19] when he refers in *Questions About Music*[20] to Mozart's letter (in a different translation), the letter undoubtedly came to his attention in *The Creative Process*. There a reprint of Sessions's "The Composer and His Message" begins on the same page as the Mozart letter. Sessions does not doubt the letter's authenticity; as a fellow creator he recognizes the experience Mozart describes.

In an analogy Sessions explains that if he thinks of someone, he can conjure up an image of that person without necessarily remembering the color of his eyes, or smile, or voice. When he thinks of the *Tristan* prelude, he can reconstruct every detail from memory, filling a classroom blackboard. Likewise, he can "see" the whole of his own piece before him; what remains is to fill in the details with the deliberation of one who knows exactly how it should go.

Symphony No. 2   1944–1946
(Score Marked Princeton, Gambier, Berkeley, 1944–1946)

Commission: Alice M. Ditson Fund of Columbia University
Dedication: Franklin D. Roosevelt
Published by G. Schirmer, 1949. Manuscripts at Princeton University Library.
I. Molto Agitato—Tranquillo e misterioso
II. Allegretto capriccioso (No Pause)
III. Adagio, tranquillo ed espressivo
IV. Allegramente

The Second Symphony, chosen in 1949 for the Walter W. Naumburg Foundation American Composition Award, was dedicated to the memory of Franklin D. Roosevelt, who died while Sessions was writing the third movement. "In a very real sense I think a great many people, including myself, felt the death of Roosevelt as a kind of personal loss."[21] In addition, Sessions's mother died a few days before the completion of this Symphony.

Although "in contrast to the First Symphony, the Second does not allow for aural perception of a stable key center for any duration longer than five or six measures,"[22] D minor was a point of departure for the first movement rather than an explicit tonal area. The movement can be divided into five contrasting sections, ABABA. The A is Molto agitato and the B is Tranquillo e misterioso.

Four main ideas are introduced at the opening of the movement. The first idea is a held woodwind and horn chord with a string arpeggiation. This chord acts as a unifying device by reappearing at or near the beginning of each of the five sections. This device, always connected with an upbeat gesture, is not literally repeated at each juncture. The second idea, a horn theme, appears first at m. 3 and then in the trumpet at m. 5. The third, a chordal fragment played by trumpet and horns, repeats with slight changes (beginning m. 10). Last is an oboe theme beginning with two leaps of major sixths, m. 16. The instrumentation helps to distinguish texturally the two sections: Molto agitato (A)—muted trumpets, stopped horn, piano, xylophone, unison horns and trombones, unison doubling of two woodwinds, and high string virtuosic writing; and Tranquillo e misterioso (B)—solo muted strings, solo flute, oboe, clarinet and bass clarinet, French horns and other brasses muted. The last section, Agitato, acquires the colors and textures of the Tranquillo section with the music of the Agitato. Precedent for this ingenious formal design was found on a smaller scale in the fourth piece of Pages from a Diary.

Comparison of the two B sections reveals an imaginative view of structure as recurrence, a recurrence not in any given order of musical ideas, but rather in an almost random, dreamlike manner. In the second B section, ideas occur with accompaniment figures of other B ideas. Form here is a result of a free play of the imagination that has pervaded all recurrent sections in Sessions's music.

Both the fast tempo and the texture of the first movement are reminiscent of the Violin Concerto. The violins in the Second Symphony play unrelenting sixteenth notes similar to the solo line in the last movement of the Violin Concerto. The clarinets and solo violin texture reminds one of the Romanza of the Violin Concerto, for example at rehearsal letters Ee to Ff in the first movement of the Symphony, at Hh for two bars, and from Qq to the end of the movement. One of the main differences between the two pieces is that in the Second Symphony Sessions wanted "a very massive sound."

Sessions discusses the second movement: "I wish I had called the second movement 'intermezzo,' because that's really what it is. It's not a full-fledged scherzo at all. It's very short and a somewhat light interlude between a somewhat stormy first movement and a very dark slow movement." As mentioned above, it had been originally conceived as one of the Pages from a Diary. The remainder of the dancelike movement is derived from the oboe and English horn theme that introduces it.

The monothematic scherzo is the least diatonic of the movements. Henderson describes it as "a sort of 'wrong note' march which by means of rhythmic and thematic character, melodic contour, and phrase structure, suggests a whimsical parody of a traditionally tonally oriented march."[23] The movement is in F major (and F Lydian) and divides into five sections: A, B (m. 56), A (m. 78), B, and A. The work includes quartal harmonies, whole-tone sonorities, pandiatonic combinations, and tertian triads, seventh chords, and ninth chords. Stravinsky was apparently very fond of this movement; he whistled it often.

No pause separates the second movement from the third.[24] Sessions wrote these two middle movements first. The movement begins in B-flat minor, goes through A-flat minor, F-sharp major/minor, E-flat minor, D major, and ends in B-flat minor. Juxtaposition of minor and major is one of the familiar characteristics of Sessions's tonal music. Three themes appear: 1) in the muted violas at m. 3; 2) in a theme carried by the oboe accompanied by clarinet and bassoon at A; and 3) in the solo clarinet line accompanied by piano at F.

The fourth movement can be regarded as a sonata or as a rondo with two principal themes—ABACADBA. Sessions calls the climactic passage "the atomic bomb," a catastrophic moment connected in his mind with the Second World War, although a "victorious mood" predominates. It is the most diatonic movement, clearly in D major. The fourth movement is set in $\frac{5}{4}$ throughout. (The third movement of the Divertimento is also set in quintuple meter.) The rhythmic pattern—eighth, two sixteenths—repeats throughout the movement. Like the first movement, the quarter note equals 126. A few bars after P the brass writing is momentarily reminiscent of *Le Sacre du Printemps*.

Sessions remarked, "Every time I write a new work for orchestra, I think I have a different conception of the orchestra."[25] The end of the last movement is a coup of orchestration. Woodwinds stagger in, each entry marked with a staccato and then sustained. The pitches fall successively in thirds, and the cumulative effect is that of harp arpeggiation, although no harp appears in the score. Despite the magical effect, Sessions worried that the ending was not "logical and inevitable." He asked Schnabel about it, who expressed his positive view. Nevertheless, Sessions took the score home after a performance and scrutinized it carefully. Fortunately, he did not change anything (see ex. 4.4).

The work represents an excellent example of the intermediate stage between tonality and serialism in Sessions's music. At times it is unmistakably tonal, for example in the D major ending of the last movement. Twelve-tone features appear in the melodies and accompaniments of the major themes. As in the First String Quartet, each of the movements begins with what might be considered a row. The initial accompanimental fourteen notes of the violins in the first movement contain the chromatic scale. It is transposed intact to the inversion up a perfect fourth, I-5, mm. 13–14 (see ex. 4.5). The openings of the other movements also contain all twelve pitches, which are presented differently and take varying lengths of time to unfold (see ex. 4.6, 4.7 and 4.8). Intermediary shades between tonality and twelve-tone procedures are also found in the ambiguity of key, as in the third movement. Imbrie writes, "The role of key in the determination of structure has become subsidiary; it is one kind of reference among others whose interaction is needed to produce a musical syntax."[26] Sessions was reluctantly and unconsciously approaching serialism.

Example 4.4. Symphony No. 2, IV, last three measures, full score.

Princeton-Gambier-Berkeley, 1944-'46

Example 4.5. Symphony No. 2, I, row: m. 1 and inversion mm. 13 and 14, violins.
© 1949 by G. Schirmer. Used by permission.

Example 4.6. Symphony No. 2, II, mm. 1–4, oboe, English horn, and cello, and implied row.
© 1949 by G. Schirmer. Used by permission.

The premiere performances of this symphony were not well received. *Musical America* reported that the audience was "offended" and "verbally vindictive." To the reviewer "it seemed to express the epitome of all that is worst in the life and thinking of today."[27] Sessions's former student David Diamond presented another negative view of the work:

> The first movement is far too long—far, *far* too long—and too busy for its materials. The recapitulations seem to be the result of calculation rather than inevitability for fulfillment of the structure. The second movement is entirely too short, and of a charm bordering on the banal, a quality heretofore not recognizable in Sessions' music. The third movement is the best, most convincing, but again, too long. And the last movement fails mainly for its inferior material (a kind of Shostakovich ráh-ta-ta, tá-ta-ta finale, but in a more dissonant harmonic idiom). As a matter of fact, there is too much of this rhythm thumping throughout the movement which obscures any subsidiary material one had hoped would emerge from the incessant din. The last measures fail to bring the work to a conclusive termination . . . . The orchestration of the entire work lacks variety, especially in textures and sonorities.[28]

Sessions remembers Mitropoulos and Monteux each conducting two movements beautifully, but it was Jean Martinon's performance of this work that led Sessions to dedicate his Seventh Symphony to the conductor.

Example 4.7. Symphony No. 2, III, violas, mm. 1–10, and implied row.
© 1949 by G. Schirmer. Used by permission.

Example 4.8. Symphony No. 2, IV, flute, bassoons, piano, and trumpets, m. 1, and implied row.
© 1949 by G. Schirmer. Used by permission.

Piano Sonata No. 2

1946
(Score Marked Berkeley, Nov. 1946)

Dedicated to Andor Foldes (on Holograph Only)
Published by Edward B. Marks, 1948. Manuscript at Princeton University Library.

Premiere: March 1947, New York City, Andor Foldes, Piano.
I. Allegro con fuoco
II. Lento
III. Misurato e pesante
(Played without Pause)

Six years after the completion of this Sonata Sessions wrote:

> I started it as the result of a suggestion by Andor Foldes, for whom I intended to write a short piece. The principal ideas of the various movements, including that which begins at measure 34, all occurred to me at the same time, and I hoped to make out of them a piece that would be not only short but easy to play—the latter is a constant ambition of mine which I have never yet succeeded in fulfilling! As the work progressed I started at one point referring to it as a sonatina; and only later and with some surprise and genuine reluctance did I realize that it would have to be a real sonata . . . . It was the first of my works [after the Duo] however in which I used no key signature. . . . The Sonata itself is not based on the 12-tone system, though adepts of the system [Milton Babbitt] have remarked, and pointed out to me, that it is really very close to it. The work that I have written since then, especially my Second Quartet, is still closer. I have now arrived at the point where I feel that in all likelihood I shall some time go the whole way; but I am very glad that this evolution has been gradual and genuinely subconscious and absolutely undogmatic.[29]

Henderson describes the sonata as "a work of restless rhythmic complexities in mixed meter, written in relentlessly dissonant contrapuntal style."[30] The first movement closely resembles a sonata-allegro form. It contains two distinct themes from which all else derives. The second theme begins at m. 34, the development at m. 69, and a recapitulation at m. 114. "Thematic tonal suggestion is markedly vague or ambiguous throughout the movement."[31]

The second movement is in an ABA form with divisions at Un poco più mosso (B) and Tempo I° (A). Sessions describes the final section as either a coda, transition, or very short recapitulation. Typical of his music, none of the "recapitulations" exactly restates the original material.

The contrasting themes in the third movement are related by mood: "I think of this as a nasty movement. I was thinking of everything I hated and how much I hated it. I hated the Nazis—I feel there's a little of the German Army in this. I feel there's a mechanical view of things in this."[32] A lighter, personal association with the movement is in the low D♭s at mm. 306–8, which remind Sessions of the foghorns in San Francisco Bay. Tempo I° and m. 360 mark the sections of the movement, and a coda begins at m. 394. (The tempo marking quarter note equals 88–92 should read quarter note equals 60–66).

Referring to the piano sound, Sessions says his music was not written for a Steinway, but for a Bechstein, whose upper register is more sonorous and the bass lighter than a Steinway's. "Steinways are for Liszt's music," Sessions says.

Unity is achieved among the movements by intervallic and rhythmic elements first established in the Allegro (see ex. 4.9). The B, E, F, E♭ in the right hand is both an individual motive and a building block toward an overall gesture. The interval of a minor third, the pulse of repeated sixteenth notes, and the motion of individual motives help generate the entire work.

Example 4.9.   Piano Sonata No. 2, I, mm. 1–2.

Repeated seconds (major and minor), fluctuating rapidly, characterize not only transitional sections of the first movement (see mm. 67–69), but also the transition to the second movement. The notes C♯, D♯, D♮, E in mm. 164–68 lead the listener's ear to the opening F, F♯, G of the Lento in which the D♯ resolves to E.

In the original sketch the opening motive of the third movement began on C;[33] in the final version Sessions saved that pitch until m. 233 because it was already prominent in the last measure of the Lento. Although the work ends in C major (Sessions avoided reference to that key until the final two measures), B major also could be its central tonality. The preservation of crucial intervals—major second, minor second, minor third—forecast serialism. Consequently, the work is difficult to analyze as tonal. In recognition of this Sessions said: "Whether it's C major or A minor, I wouldn't know. The whole principle of tonal structure was dissolved by the time this was written, for me certainly."[34]

An examination of the second movement indicates adumbrations of serialism.[35] The initial trichord, E, F♯, G, operates as an order-preserving collection whose resultant hexachords are not incorporated as a twelve-tone row. However, order is maintained within this collection, and it generates inversions, retrogrades, and retrograde inversions (see ex. 4.10). The ascending E, F♯, G and descending G, F♮, E♭ derive from the melodic minor mode, a pattern "so deep in one's consciousness."[36]

The F♯, G, F are inverted immediately to E♭, D, E♮ and form the all-combinatorial six notes, D–G. This hexachord transposed a tritone will generate the remaining six unused notes—combinatoriality. The lower two voices, initially separated by a tritone, present inversions and retrogrades of the initial three-note collection. The first two phrases contain both vertical and linear statements of the minor third. The first theme returns at m. 225, producing the complement hexachord G♯—C♯.

Example 4.10.   Piano Sonata No. 2, II, mm. 1–10.
        © 1948 by Edward B. Marks Music Company.
        Copyright renewed. Used by permission.

The second theme is also built from major and minor seconds. Sessions states that the ''alteration of whole tone in one direction and a half tone in the other direction, or vice versa, is very much a part of this whole thing.''[37] At m. 200 the theme is stated a step higher perhaps because of the voice leading from the preceding measure: C, D, E♭, E♮. Schoenbergian registral displacement is found several times, for example in the expanding gesture F♯, E, D♯ (an inversion of the original trichord at m. 188. The Second Piano Sonata forecasts Sessions's adoption of the twelve-tone method.

The Trial of Lucullus   1947

One-Act Opera in Thirteen Scenes
Libretto by Bertolt Brecht, Translated by H. R. Hays
Dedication: Henry and Lili Schnitzler
Not Published. Score and Parts Available at Edward B. Marks Music Company. Sketches at the University of California at Berkeley Library.
Premiere: 18 April 1947, Berkeley, California, Roger Sessions Conducting.

In 1947 Henry Schnitzler, son of the novelist Arthur Schnitzler and head of the Drama Department at Berkeley, asked Sessions to write a one-act opera to share a bill with Stravinsky's *L'histoire du soldat* for their spring production. Schnitzler proposed contacting Bertolt Brecht, then living in Los Angeles, to ask for a new or suitable text. Brecht more than obliged; his wife sent both the German original and the Hays translation of his radio play, *The Trial of Lucullus (Das Verhör des Lukullus)*. The Sessions opera is the first opera to be based on the new medium of a radio play.

Copyright problems explain why the work has not been published.[38] Since its premiere *The Trial of Lucullus* has been performed three times: at Princeton in 1955, at Northwestern University in 1961, and at The Juilliard School in 1966. Unfortunately, no scores or recordings are commercially available. The opera, however, is Sessions's most successful dramatic work. John Sessions once remarked that the best way to get to know his father's music was to begin with *The Trial of Lucullus*. Of his affinity to the play Sessions writes:

> What attracted me most deeply to it in the beginning and what still moves me profoundly is its insight into and its vision of human nature, not in schematic or oversimplified terms but in all its complex sublety, and its firm insistence on those values which are necessary not only for a decent human life but, ultimately in terms of today, for our very survival as a species.[39]

The Trial of Lucullus was written in great haste. The sketch was completed between 13 January and 13 February 1947; the complete vocal score between 13 February and 13 March; and on 14 March the orchestral score was begun. Rehearsals began a few days later. At each rehearsal performers received a few more scraps of the music. The frantic activity surrounding the composition and rehearsals of this opera is fancifully portrayed in a drawing by S. Earl Saxton, who played first horn in the orchestra (see fig. 4.1).

Spacial considerations at Berkeley dictated that no more than 32 performers could be used. Sessions eliminated second violins and doubled up the woodwinds. The minimum number of players possible is 30, the maximum 46.

Sessions considers that "fundamentally *The Trial of Lucullus* and *Montezuma* are about the same thing—the futility of conquest."[40] Although in both operas identifiable motives appear, in neither "of these works do you have a leitmotif system; the figures do not appear in the orchestra and they aren't transformed."[41] Sessions continues, "*The Trial* is of a less lyrical character than *Montezuma*. I was writing *The Trial* for students. *Montezuma* is more like my *Idyll of Theocritus*."[42] Edward T. Cone compares it with Stravinsky's *Oedipus Rex*.[43]

Sessions says of operatic writing, "When I write dramatic music I keep the picture very much in mind. I visualize the whole scene and how the characters are standing and acting. It's the vocal part which is the most important to me. I'm a Verdi-ite and a Mozartian rather than a Wagnerian."[44]

As have composers for generations, Sessions pays special attention to word painting. Regarding this he frequently mentions Orlando di Lasso, whose music he learned from Bloch. "It's clear in Orlando di Lasso, if you say 'ascended into Heaven,' you don't have a scale going down. You have a passage going up."[45] Such word painting appears in abundance in *The Trial of Lucullus*. For example, in scene 1 the Herald describes the return to normal after the funeral procession (see fig. 4.2) has passed: "the drivers come forth with their oxcarts, the crowd returns to its business, chattering, busy Rome goes back to work." At m. 88 the tempo increases on the word "business." All the parts become more musically active, portraying "busy Rome." From mm. 205–30, during the Hollow Voice's

Figure 4.1.   "The Trial of Lucullus or A Session with Sessions."
Cartoon by S. Earl Saxton, April 1947. Each character in the drawing
is identifiable as a member of the orchestra for the premiere.

description of Lucullus's motionlessness and soliloquy on waiting, the music un-
dulates a half-step in even eighth notes, the continual back-and-forth motion a
metaphor for waiting. In m. 230 the music speeds up when the Hollow Voice says:
"But the newcomer does not seem to have learn'd how to wait."

A classic madrigalism appears in the Old Woman's soliloquy in mm. 310–12.
At "especially with those who have sent a fellow man *down here in the Realm
of the Shadows* before the appointed span of his life was over," the contralto part
descends to its lowest notes—a G♭ below middle C—on "shadows" and hovers
below the treble staff for all the italicised words. When Lucullus calls his witness
"Alexander of Macedon," mm. 437ff, warlike accented chords punctuate his name.
(The motive of Alexander returns at m. 441 in the chorus.) When, in mm. 472–73,
the slaves are called, "they step from the world above/Down to the Realm of the
Shadows." Sessions purposely avoids a melodic leap here because the step
"is . . . a short one."

The main characters are pictured in figure 4.3. The jurors were formerly a
farmer, a teacher, a fishwife, a baker, and a courtesan. The witnesses are figures
from a gravestone frieze depicting Lucullus's triumphs: a captured king, a strange-
eyed queen, a man with a cherry tree, a golden god, a girl with a tablet that names
53 cities, a dying legionary, and a cook.

During the fishwife's inquiry of the two Warriors, she asks, "What have you

got there [in your outstretched hands]?'' One replies, ''I have nothing,'' the only measure (883) of the opera that contains no music. The fishwife's soliloquy is the emotional peak of the opera and has been sung separately.

In an instrumental postlude (mm. 1155–65) two flutes, B-flat clarinet, and solo violin accompany the description of the cherry trees that ''shall in spring flutter its white and rosy twigs in the wind from the hills.'' The fluttering in the wind is portrayed in these instruments. Sessions is particularly fond of this farmer's song.

The musicologist Manfred Bukofzer, a Berkeley colleague with whom Sessions rarely agreed, advised the composer to delete the C♯ in the final A-major chord; he wanted to hear an open fifth at the conclusion. Sessions did not take his advice; instead, he relishes a clever trick of orchestration the C♯ accomplishes: While the two trumpets play the root (A) and fifth (E) of the chord, the flute's C♯ gives the aural impression of a third trumpet.

Sessions waited nineteen years for *The Trial of Lucullus* to receive its first (and only) New York performance. The Juilliard School's performance in 1966 gained the work critical acclaim. Michael Steinberg, of *The Boston Globe,* wrote:

> In every way Sessions' score is beautifully worked. Declamation is accurate and sensitive. That also means it is clear. Not a word is lost, and that indicates virtuosic handling of the small, but richly suggestive orchestra. The writing is evocative, poetic, but essentially spare. The strokes are bold and firm, but they are exactly outlined and precisely placed.[46]

Figure 4.2. *The Trial of Lucullus*, Juilliard American Opera Center Production, 1966. The body of Lucullus is carried through the gate. Courtesy of the Juilliard American Opera Center.

Figure 4.3. *The Trial of Lucullus,* Juilliard American Opera Center Production, 1966.
The freize is brought to life; the judge and jury sit at right.
Courtesy of the Juilliard American Opera Center.

Steinberg states simply that the opera is "a masterpiece. Nothing less." Irving
Kolodin also comments:

> What Sessions provided in 1947 as musical comment on the illusions and emptiness of Lucullus
> remains appropriate to the subject still, possibly because it does not bear a date stamp of style.
> It works with a vocabulary that is neither eccentric nor unsuitably pretentious, mostly in a spirit
> of commentary on the words and action.[47]

Unknown to Sessions, Brecht had also given the German text of *The Trial
of Lucullus* to Paul Dessau. Comparing the Sessions opera with Paul Dessau's,
David Drew writes:

> Sessions for his part has conceded nothing to Brecht's half-baked ideas about music in the theater.
> He has simply, or rather complexly, taken what is by any standards a superb play, and set it
> as the musician he is. . . . The first serious American composer to have achieved mastery in
> Schoenberg's sense has written an opera that towers above the American operas favoured by
> the Met. . . . Musically and dramatically there is great diversity, and its integration is nowhere
> more apparent than at the conclusion. The affirmation of a "better world" is a valid part of
> the American dream, and yet in the hands of lesser composers it has often proved an embarrass-
> ment. Not so with Sessions. . . . It works on every level to ends that were denied Dessau and
> Brecht by external events.[48]

It is important to know the external events to which Drew alluded and to know
something of the history of the play in order to understand the direct effect these

events had on Brecht's and Dessau's opera. According to the editors of Brecht's collected plays, "*Lucullus* was commissioned by the Stockholm radio and completed in a fortnight; Hilding Rosenberg was due to write the music but it never got done and the broadcast did not take place."[49] In 1937 Brecht had written the pro-Soviet Lenin Cantata with composer Hanns Eisler. Brecht wrote the first version of *The Life of Galileo* (November 1938) prior to *Lucullus* and *Mother Courage*, also set to music by Dessau, just after it. "The play itself can be seen as a by-product of [his] Caesar novel, or at least Brecht's reading for it, which had included Plutarch, Dio Cassius, Suetonius and Sallust, now reviewed in the light of the Nazi invasion of Poland and the Anglo-French mobilization."[50] *Lucullus* was first broadcast by the Bern studio of the Swiss-German radio in May 1940, while Norway and Holland were falling to Hitler. There is no recording of this performance.

Brecht invited Dessau to Hollywood, where he gave him the *Mother Courage* songs and *Lucullus*, leading Dessau to conclude that he wanted *Lucullus* turned into an opera.[51] However, Brecht seemed to have had Stravinsky in mind; he asked Dessau if he could interest the Russian in the work. Stravinsky was too busy. In 1949 Dessau persuaded Brecht to make textual changes. Dessau wanted *Lucullus* described as an opera, whereas Hermann Scherchen, the conductor, envisioned a "musical play." The Brecht scholar Eric Bentley gives his opinion of the results: "Dessau's two Brecht operas . . . are indeed *called* operas. But the more effective of them, *The Trial of Lukullus,* the one on which BB collaborated, the music is pretty much reduced to percussive accompaniment of the text. Sublime sound effects!"[52]

The authorities in East Berlin allowed a closed performance for Party members and Free German Youth on 17 March 1951, the day when the central committee passed a resolution "Against Formalism in Art and Literature." They objected to Dessau's Stravinskian music and the fact that the opera was not decidedly pro-Soviet. Brecht and Dessau met with members of the government, who persuaded them to add passages exempting defensive wars from the general condemnation. Responding to continued political pressure, Dessau eventually produced four revised versions of the play, in 1949–1950, 1951, 1957, and 1960.

In Dessau's opera, *The Condemnation of Lucullus (Die Verurteilung des Lukullus)*—the title leaves little to the imagination as to the verdict—one of the major differences from the text Sessions set lies in the last scene. Here each of the jurors and the judge himself jump up to shout "Send him to nothingness!"; even the warriors from the frieze and the slaves who hauled it cry out "To nothingness!" A comparison of the two composer's librettos leads to the conclusion that Sessions's is the finest version of the play.

After *The Trial of Lukullus* Sessions spent the next decade and a half writing a second opera. These years, 1947–1963, mark the boundaries of his next creative period. *Montezuma* was not commissioned, nor was the composer aiming for a specific performance, as he had been in *The Trial of Lucullus*. The obsession with *Montezuma* runs like a leitmotif through his fourth creative period. In it the seeds of total chromaticism planted in his earlier music now bloom to a full-fledged acceptance of Schoenberg's twelve-tone method. As a teacher in the 1950s Sessions encountered and influenced some of his most gifted students.

Notes

1. Conversation with Milton Babbitt March 1975.

2. Taped interview 11 December 1974.

3. Edward T. Cone, "In Defense of Song: The Contribution of Roger Sessions," *Critical Inquiry* 2, no. 1 (Autumn 1975): 97.

4. Columbia University Oral History Collection, pp. 206, 208.

5. Columbia University Oral History Collection, p. 240.

6. Taped interview 18 December 1974.

7. Taped interview 23 October 1974.

8. Allen Forte, *Contemporary Tone Structures* (New York: Bureau of Publication of the Teachers College, Columbia University, 1955), pp. 48–62.

9. Andrew Imbrie, "The Symphonies of Roger Sessions," *Tempo* 103 (1972): 25–26.

10. Taped interview 8 January 1975.

11. Roger Sessions, "Duo for Violin and Piano," *Columbia* ML2169 liner notes.

12. Ibid.

13. Ibid.

14. Ibid.

15. Taped interview 19 March 1975.

16. E. D. Hirsch, Jr., "Carnal Knowledge," *The New York Review of Books* 26, no. 10 (14 June 1979): 18.

17. Ibid.

18. W. A. Mozart, "A Letter," *The Creative Process*, ed. by Brewster Chiselin (New York: New American Library, 1952), p. 45.

19. Jacques Hadamard, *The Psychology of Invention in the Mathematical Field* (Princeton, N.J.: Princeton University Press, 1945), pp. 16–17.

20. Roger Sessions, *Questions About Music* (New York: W. W. Norton & Co., 1970), pp. 28, 86–87.

21. Columbia University Oral History Collection, p. 273.

22. Ronald Duane Henderson, *Tonality in the Pre-Serial Instrumental Music of Roger Sessions* (Ph.D. diss.: Eastman School of Music, 1974), unpublished, p. 319.

23. Ibid., p. 331.

24. There is a mistake in the Schirmer study score: The opening of the third movement is played by double basses, not contrabassoon.

25. Taped interview 19 February 1980.

26. Imbrie, "Symphonies," p. 26.

27. Marjory M. Fisher, "Sessions Symphony Has Premiere," *Musical America*, 25 January 1947.

28. David Diamond, "Roger Sessions: Symphony No. 2," *Notes* 7 (June 1950): 438–39.

29. Letter to Beveridge Webster 28 November 1952.

30. Henderson, *Tonality*, pp. 381–82.

31. Ibid.

32. Taped interview 5 February 1975.

33. Taped interview 7 May 1975.

34. Taped interview 19 February 1975.

35. I am indebted to Milton Babbitt for his help with this movement.

36. Taped interview 25 January 1978.

37. Taped interview 19 February 1975.

38. The firm that published the Hays translation is now defunct, further complicating matters. Another edition is Bertolt Brecht, *Bertolt Brecht: Collected Plays*, 9 vols., ed. by Ralph Manheim and John Willet (New York: Pantheon Books, 1972). *The Trial of Lucullus* is translated by Frank Jones.

39. Roger Sessions, Program notes for Juilliard's production May 1966.

40. Taped interview 25 April 1979.

41. Ibid.

42. Taped interview 2 May 1979.

43. Columbia University Oral History Collection, p. 255.

44. Taped interview 2 May 1979.

45. Taped interview 2 April 1975.

46. Michael Steinberg, "Sessions' 'Lucullas' [sic] Impresses at Juilliard," *The Boston Globe*, 29 May 1966.

47. Irving Kolodin, "Murder, to Music, at the Juilliard," *Saturday Review* 49 (4 June 1966).

48. David Drew, "Out of Limbo," *New Statesman* (24 June 1966): 937.

49. Bertolt Brecht, *Collected Plays*, p. x.

50. Ibid., pp. x–xi.

51. Quoted in ibid., p. xiii.

52. Eric Bentley, "Mahagonny: Notes in the Margin," Lincoln Center Metropolitan Opera Program notes, 1979, p. 18.

5

Adoption of the Twelve-tone System: 1951–1960

Sessions as a Teacher

Sessions taught composition for more than 62 of his 88 years, at Princeton University (for 33 years), at The Juilliard School (for 16 years), and at the University of California at Berkeley (for 8 years). Due to these and other academic credentials—he has 14 honorary doctorates—and to the fame many of his students achieved, the press has tended to view him as an Ivory Tower composer.

A 1976 *New York Times* review describes him: "Mr. Sessions . . . is . . . one of the gurus of American music and some of his pupils at Princeton turned out to be America's most important musicians."[1] A review in *Time Magazine* continues this "Sessions myth": "[Sessions has the] reputation of a Zeus on a cloud-cloaked Olympus doing his own thing, virtually daring the multitudes to like it."[2] And from *The New Yorker*'s Winthrop Sargeant:

> Roger Sessions has for some time now occupied the position of elder statesman of the academic establishment in American musical composition. From his throne in Princeton, he reigns over the fashions taught at countless university music departments, where tyro composers learn to compose more or less like him. . . . His realm is the college composition classes of America, and these have somehow become divorced from the needs of people who go to hear music.[3]

Ironically, considering this popular view of him, Sessions is ambivalent toward academia. This began as early as his experience teaching at Smith College and shows in these comments: "The academic world is a very, very strange place. It's not my world at all."[4] He goes so far as to describe the Ivory Tower as really a "snake pit" peopled by "vipers and slugs."

Exactly what has Sessions's influence as a teacher been? And what is his attitude toward teaching? We learn the answers from interviews with his students, who testify about their experience of Sessions as a teacher, and from Sessions's writings.

Sessions tackled the thorny subject of what and how much a composition teacher can teach in his article "To the Editor."[5] Here he "finds it important for the composer to have at least some experience as a performer."[6] About teaching twelve-tone procedures Sessions states simply, "I don't feel that this is a part of a composition teacher's business. In this I am in full agreement with the point of view of Arnold Schoenberg, who always insisted that such methods are for the composer, young or old, to discover for himself."[7] For Sessions "the ultimate goal of a composer's musical training is to liberate his talents and his creative personality, not to indoctrinate him to or from any specific point of view."[8]

Sessions's writings about teaching show him unafraid to try to clarify the delicate area surrounding the teacher-student, composer-apprentice relationship. He believes "that the best training a composer can have, certainly at the 'advanced' but quite possibly at every level, will be that derived from close association with a single teacher."[9] His desire to form warm relationships with his students is transparent and bears a striking resemblance to his own relationship with an "older colleague," Ernest Bloch.

> But a young composer who is in the early stages of his development is almost certain to derive more benefit from association with an older colleague who takes a real interest in him, and with whom he can talk freely and informally about his own problems, about music and musical questions in general, and about many other matters not so obviously connected with music, than from almost any other single source.[10]

Sessions spells out his credo for classroom teaching in *Harmonic Practice,* written in the late 1940s:

> The problem is, then, to provide the student with the opportunity for abundant experience, and to encourage him, on the basis of this experience, to trust himself. I believe I have learned that students—the average as well as the exceptional—respond most readily when confronted with real challenges, and that, in a general way, even unsuccessful efforts to meet such challenges are incomparably more productive of worth-while results than the relatively easy fulfillment of carefully graded tasks.[11]

Former students were asked what they learned from Sessions, how he affected their careers, and to what extent they agreed with the "Sessions myth"—the idea that he reigned over university compositional life. Their responses are presented chronologically according to when the composer studied with Sessions.

One of Sessions's earliest private students was Lehman Engel, newly graduated in 1924 from The Juilliard Graduate School, where he had studied with Rubin Goldmark. Despite his thorough training, Engel felt that there were aspects he did not understand and he sought help from Sessions. At their first meeting Sessions opened randomly to a page of the vocal score to *La Bohème* and asked Engel to tell him everything about the music on that page. Engel analyzed the harmony, the melody, bass progressions, and modulations. Then Sessions asked, "What about the dynamics?"

I instantly understood that what he was trying to say was the harmonic and rhythmic thrust propelled the dynamics or vice versa and that there was this other element that I simply had never thought about. So we talked, I don't know how long. We discussed *a page* of Puccini, of all people. The next week he pulled out a madrigal of Monteverdi—couldn't have been more different. We went through the same thing. He was literally always saying to me, "You see, you *do* understand. You see the Monteverdi and the Puccini are not that different. They're based on the same fundamental principles."[12]

Through Sessions Engel gained confidence in his training and an ability to examine music.

The qualities that made Sessions a memorable teacher differed, of course, for each student. For David Diamond, Sessions's "analytical attitude" and "total concern with craftsmanship and integrity in composers" stood out. In general, Diamond's class studied "matters of proportion and structure"; specifically, students examined, for example, modulations in late Schubert sonatas. Beethoven piano sonatas Op. 101 and Op. 109 were also taught. This music was given a harmonic analysis, inner parts and variances in the recapitulation were examined, and Schenkerian analysis was applied for one of the first times in this country. Bach's C-minor Passacaglia was dissected bar by bar. Beethoven's Op. 59 No. 1 and Op. 131 quartets were given complete Schenkerian breakdowns. In the composition class Haydn's quartets frequently appeared, partly so that Sessions could point to their varied recapitulations. Diamond remembers Sessions saying that "Haydn had the best sense of recapitulation because it's always a surprise."

In an article for *Perspectives of New Music,* Edward T. Cone relates his experience at his first lesson with Sessions in 1935.[13]

Carter Harman studied with Sessions at Princeton from 1936 to 1942. Harman recalls spending an entire semester of classes on the *Tristan* prelude and Sessions's playing from memory at the piano the first movement of the *Eroica*. To Harman Sessions communicated

standards: a belief in the future of music; a sense of an ideal that he presented. . . . He is lofty in the way he talks and the way he thinks about music. [I saw Sessions as a] hero, a rock of Gibraltar both compositionally and politically. He could trace his musical heritage back to Beethoven. His music was, compared to his contemporaries in the thirties, powerful, inevitable, and credible.[14]

Marion Bauer had recommended Sessions to Milton Babbitt. In September 1935 nineteen-year-old Babbitt went to Princeton to study privately with Sessions. The studies continued until 1938, when he became a member of the faculty. Later, in 1942, he became Sessions's assistant. Babbitt arrived at Sessions's studio with a piece he called *Generatrix,*

the most obvious imitation of Varèse that you've ever seen in your life. . . . So he looked at these [works] and said, "You know, I'm not quite sure you know what you want to study."

And so I said to him what was totally true, that one of the many reasons I came to study with him was not only because of his music but because he had written on Schenker. . . . I said, "I want to really reconsider everything." So we agreed that what we would do would be to take species counterpoint from scratch from sort of a Schenkerian point of view. I did it. We started with the cantus firmus, we worked our way through everything. I also did exercises out of a German book called Knorr. [Ivan Knorr, a pupil of Brahms, had been Bloch's teacher. Knorr's book, *Aufgaben für den Unterricht in die Harmonielehere,* consists solely of musical exercises.] We did exactly that. We never looked at any contemporary music. We never looked at my music. We didn't look at Roger's music. We looked at *Der Wein* together a little bit. I was already so involved in looking at twelve-tone things that Roger thought it would be more diplomatic if he didn't look at my music. But what we *did* do in enormous detail was imitation pieces. Look at a first movement of a Mozart quartet and then write a first movement which would attempt to capture what I considered the most salient analytical features of the piece without imitating the piece, without any of its foreground details. Minuets and trios by the carload. Slow movements. Imitations. Mainly the models were Mozart and Beethoven. We looked at some Wagner; we looked at the prelude of the third act of *Parsifal.* And that, believe it or not, is what we did for three years.[15]

Vivian Fine describes her experience with Sessions:

R. S. was unbelievably generous to me in my student days. He taught me for years for practically nothing and gave his concentrated attention to the exercises and compositions I brought in. Perhaps what I learned from Sessions can be described as a greater awareness of consistent musical thought. This was part of what I perceived as his overwhelming musical intellect and knowledge. Sessions did not go in for fulsome praise. "I like it" was for him quite a compliment. However, he was much taken by the opening of a piece of mine for string quartet: He said he wished he could have written it and said I had "aural vision." This remark sustained me for many years.[16]

Dika Newlin wrote to Sessions as a second choice, after Bartók. From 1941 to 1945 she attended Columbia University and studied privately with Sessions. From Sessions she received a "reinforcement" of what she had learned from Schoenberg, "that one should work from inner necessity." She describes Sessions as a teacher:

An open-minded teacher who aided me further (after three years' study with Schoenberg) to express what I wanted to express in the most well-crafted way possible. Not as strict as Schoenberg. To a young person, he was—like Schoenberg—a good example of independent tough-minded spunky attitude. No popularity-courting for him.[17]

Acting on David Diamond's advice, Mark Schubart studied privately with Sessions from 1941 to 1945. Schubart feels that Sessions's greatest gift as a teacher was his ability to put his finger on what was wrong, to suggest other ways to obtain the musical gesture—a term Schubart particularly remembers—and to clarify and to organize material. Schubart also learned that the only joy in writing music is writing music; there is very little joy from the glamour of a premiere or other trappings. Schubart describes Sessions as very "convivial, who liked to eat and drink, not a fashion plate, with a tremendous ego—very concerned about his own music—but not egocentric."[18]

Leon Kirchner had studied with Arnold Schoenberg in California. He then asked Dika Newlin's advice about whom he ought to study with. She suggested Sessions, and the two met for six or eight months in 1942 in Miriam Gideon's Central Park West apartment. Kirchner felt that he learned from Sessions by his serving as an example, "an intellectual reservoir with a vast knowledge of the repertoire."[19] Perhaps most beneficial for Kirchner was direct contact with Sessions's own music. Sessions played works in progress for his students, especially sketches of *Montezuma*. Sessions also taught by bringing his students into a performance. When *The Trial of Lucullus* was premiered in California in 1947, the young composers were intimately involved with the performance; it was a "family affair," according to Kirchner, who conducted the chorus. Kirchner felt Sessions "made space for others to shine" as a composition teacher.

Warned not to study at Princeton because he would be told how to compose in a very strict way, Eric Salzman met with Sessions and decided to enter the University. He remained from 1954 until 1956. Sessions was "everybody's musical daddy" and as such communicated a sense of "seriousness, tolerance, and humanism" and stressed the "connections between American and European music and an equal responsibility to art, self, and public."[20] Sessions carried out in America the central European tradition, a foil to the widely French-oriented and nationalistic Americanism that prevailed here. Contrary to what Salzman had been told about Princeton, he remembers it as being the only place in this country in which one could get that kind of musical education then.

Harold Schiffman studied with Roger Sessions at Berkeley from 1948 to 1951 and at Princeton from 1955 to 1956. He describes what he learned from Sessions: "Patience—confidence in my own ideas—high standards—not to rely on tricks. Timing. Also, he warned against too much reliance on 'sonority,' color, etc., for its own sake—in contrast to many 'advanced' composers today."[21] Schiffman relates a wonderful anecdote: "During the loyalty oath controversy in the early '50s at the University of California, [Sessions] was asked if he believed in 'private enterprise.' He replied, 'Of course—Composing is the most "private enterprise" there is.'"

Five of Sessions's University of California students—Earl Kim, Leon Kirchner, Spartaco Monello, Leonard Ralston, and Leonard Ratner—had founded the Composers' Forum in 1946, a concert series devoted to contemporary music that endured for twenty years. The Forum introduced to San Francisco what are now classics by Bloch, Dallapiccola, Hindemith, Křenek, Milhaud, Schoenberg, Sessions, Stravinsky, Bartók (the First San Francisco performance of the Sonata for Two Pianos and Percussion), and many others. This series originated in Sessions's composition class.

Paul Turok's view of Sessions as a teacher contrasts sharply with that of many of his contemporaries. He attended Berkeley in 1950–1951 and studied privately with Sessions at Princeton in 1956–1958. Although he loved the man, he felt Sessions was "very constipating as a teacher, terribly concerned with detail without explaining why a certain note was wrong. [He] taught by osmosis.''[22] Turok describes Sessions as ''a man committed totally to his music and terribly absorbed in himself.'' He learned more from Sessions as a person than as a pedagogue. The ''rarefield atmosphere'' surrounding Sessions was one, he felt, of unspoken agreement that everything Sessions said and wrote was right.

Donald Martino studied at Princeton with Sessions from 1953 to 1954. For Martino Sessions's most valuable contribution was ''his ability to perceive a music-work in terms of its overview. His advice that we do so too . . . . From him we can all learn courage.''[23] Martino sums up Sessions's qualities, as well as those of his other teachers: ''Each added an important piece in the puzzle. Babbitt emphasized the detail and its relation to the whole; Roger emphasized the overview; Dallapiccola, the value of nuance and color.''

David Lewin studied with Sessions at Princeton from 1955 to 1958 along with Michael Sahl and Eric Salzman. He learned from Sessions: ''1) to listen carefully and critically to my music on its own terms, 2) to persevere and work hard; to find the essential idea and motivation, in musical terms, underlying even banal or awful sketches.'' Responding to the questions about whether Sessions ''reigns over university compositional life'' and whether Sessions's own music is ''academic,'' Lewin has this to offer:

> (1) How is teaching *not* ''academic''? (2) His music is carefully thought out, and it shows. The music projects a personality which includes a strong intellectual component. There is nothing either good or bad about that, and it has nothing to do with academicism, which does not correlate with intelligence in any case. (3) He certainly does *not* ''reign over . . . university compositional life today''! His direct influence seems amazingly (and unfortunately) small to me, at any rate. He *has* attracted, though, a large number of students who *have* risen to positions of prominence in university life; I think it would be fair to say that his *in*direct influence, in that regard, has been very large.[24]

John Eaton, now a member of the Composition Department of Indiana University, studied with Sessions from 1955 to 1958, as well as with Edward T. Cone, Milton Babbitt, and Earl Kim. The general seminars that Eaton and his classmates took were ''at times incredibly boring,'' but in retrospect what Sessions said rang with ''such truth, such rightness, such aptness.''[25] Eaton felt that Sessions's ''love and complete devotion to music along with his humanity and compassion'' constituted Sessions's greatest legacy to his students.

John Harbison studied with Sessions at Princeton from 1961 to 1963 along with Mark DeVoto, Donald Sur, and Peter Maxwell Davies. In their composition class they analyzed Beethoven's Piano Sonata Op. 10 and his Symphony No. 3. Harbison recalls the discussion of the symphony as ''the most powerful revelation of the function of each detail in the large purpose of the sonata-design that I have encountered.'' Harbison is explicit about what he learned:

> 1. It is essential to write what you love very much. 2. You never go backward. 3. You can't predetermine or choose your style, it is the sum of what you are. 4. Strive to render in the

Figure 5.1.   Roger Sessions.
Date unknown.
Courtesy of David Diamond.

most creative posture possible, what is in the ear. 5. Don't worry about how it fits with what is going on. 6. Come out with it. (Unlike some teachers, he really wanted his students to do well.)[26]

Young composers at Juilliard benefited from Sessions's long years of teaching experience, for instance from his view that "you must write music you love yourself, not something you think somebody else will approve of."[27] Any who impatiently desired to learn everything immediately had to learn to wait until mutual trust and affection had been developed. Sessions still employed the back-to-scratch approach. One eager rock composer wound up studying counterpoint for two years. Another student said: "When I came to Juilliard, I was completely blocked. I couldn't compose anything. Sessions helped me get over it. He loosened me up."

Sessions's Juilliard students of the 1970s have included Matthew Harris, Ken Frazelle, Tod Machover, Ellen Taaffe Zwilich, Daniel Brewbaker, William Komaiko, Joel Feigen, Joseph Tamosaitis, and George Tsontakis. These students feel that they have gained enormously from their study and confirmed much of what had been said of Sessions by older students.[28]

Conspicuous by their absence were positive responses to the question of how Sessions affected his students' careers. In no case did the students interviewed mention Sessions's practical help, that is, getting them a teaching job, writing recommendations for grants, or engineering performances or recordings. His high ideals as a composer and as a teacher appear to be at odds with practical necessity, and some students experienced frustration. To the degree that composers in America need to help each other solve "business-related" problems, Sessions was not so much a failure as he was a nonparticipant who lifted himself above "business."

The similarity of these reactions to Sessions as a teacher has possibly contributed to the "Sessions myth." But the implications of that myth are not borne out in fact: Sessions never attempted to force students to compose as he does. Instead, he reinforced in them his high ideals, common sense, and passionate love of music.

String Quartet No. 2   1950–1951

Dedication: Lorna and Rudolf Kolisch
Published by Edward B. Marks, 1954. Sketches at Princeton University Library.
Premiere: 28 May 1951, Madison, Wisconsin, Pro Arte Quartet.
I. Lento
II. Allegro Appassionato—Tranquillo
III. Andante tranquillo
IV. Presto
V. Adagio
(Played without Pause)

This work, immediately preceding the Violin Sonata, is possibly Sessions's first twelve-tone work. Strong resemblances to twelve-tone techniques are evident, although, as Henderson pointed out, "the second string quartet utilizes a twelve-tone row melodically although the row is not employed extensively as a pitch-organizing principle,"[29] and as Eugene Schweitzer observed, "this quartet rarely has a pure twelve-tone sonority, as many tones recur prematurely . . . . Thus, the presence of the twelve tones is not for a serial purpose but for the purpose of providing fresh material for tonal movement."[30] Indeed, "there is a tendency is listening to this work not to concentrate on the tonal counterpoint, but to hear the work as in one key with added dissonant tones."[31] The "tonality" of the entire piece is B.

As in many twelve-tone works of the Second Viennese School, principal and secondary voices are indicated by brackets (analogous to Schoenberg's *Hauptstimme* and *Nebenstimme* brackets) in the Second String Quartet, for the first time in Sessions's music (for instance, see ex. 5.9 in the section on the Quintet). However, these markings were supplied *after* one performance as a convenience to the players. Sessions justifies the symbols: "If you play everything on the same level, it kills everything else. Individual voices are the biggest problem, because each is like a solo."[32] Sessions later abandoned these indications.

Markings given in parentheses are meant to convey the shape of the phrase. Always concerned about what he wanted from performers, Sessions here has explicitly indicated his desires. Later, in the publications of *Montezuma* and the Cantata, Sessions included a glossary of musical terms and markings as he defined them. It may be that Sessions overreacted to his experience with the First Piano Sonata and decided not to trust details of interpretation to performers; hence, his later scores contain multiple markings. He is vulnerable to the charge that his scores are overmarked.

The pitches of the opening viola solo that begins a "quasi-double fugue" in the first movement (see ex. 5.1a) provide more evidence of an inclination toward twelve-tone thinking. Of the fourteen notes in its subject, all twelve available pitches are included. The chromatic nature of this fugue produces a dissonant texture. The theme appears transposed at various intervals for the four entries. At a formal division, m. 45, another fugue begins that contains all twelve notes as its subject (see ex. 5.1b). Although not every note in the first movement is a clear transposition of one of the two rows or their two countersubjects (see ex. 5.1d and 5.1e), the movement is saturated by these statements and their inversions. Section A of the tripartite movement uses only row I and countersubject I; section B and the return of A employ both rows and the inversion of countersubject II. The second movement divides into two sections: fast and quiet. The fast section returns three times, finally in the guise of a coda. A variation set makes its only appearance in Sessions's music in the third movement. Five variations follow the general contour of the characteristically long theme. The da capo fourth movement has a trio (mm. 650–769). The return, m. 770, is not quite exact until m. 812, after which the da capo proceeds faithfully until m. 939. The last movement, dominated by the opening first violin phrase, which contains all twelve pitches among its first thirteen notes, has the character and length (58 measures) of an epilogue.

Examples 5.1a–e.   String Quartet No. 2, I, two implied rows, inversion of row 2, and two countersubjects at no. 7ff (viola) and no. 47ff (cello).
© 1954 by Edward B. Marks Music Company.
Copyright renewed. Used by permission.

Sessions may have subconsciously modeled this work on Beethoven's C-sharp
minor quartet. Among Opus 131's seven connected movements are a free fugue,
a theme and variations, and a da capo scherzo with trio. Originally, Sessions had
planned seven movements in his quartet. Three (I, III, IV) correspond formally
to the Beethoven work.

Schweitzer writes:

> The key to the understanding of the quartet is the realization that the basic generational force
> lies in the tonal drive produced in the individual line by tonal functions within the line.[33] . . . In
> the absence of functional tonality or of a serial system, the use of thematic material is basic
> in the development of form.[34]

Motives also serve as nonthematic and accompanimental material as well as
forecasters of upcoming music. Sessions ends each movement with a form of the
motive that will begin the next movement.

Herbert Livingstone, who reviewed the work for *Notes*, wrote: "Unquestionably this is one of the finest string quartets by an American composer and I
suspect it is the finest work Sessions has written."[35] Edward T. Cone discussed
the work in *The Musical Quarterly*.[36] This quartet was performed in celebration
of Sessions's eightieth birthday. Although the critic for the *New York Times* called

the quartet superb, he criticized the slow movement: "This is a piece of great concentration and weight. There are times, as in the slow-movement variations, when some varying textures might be welcome, yet the single-minded manipulation of ideas throughout the work is its strength and beauty."[37] Interestingly, the composer agreed with the criticism of the variation movement.

Sonata for Violin   1953

Dedication: Robert Gross
Published by Edward B. Marks, 1955. Manuscript at Library of Congress.
Premiere: 1953, San Francisco, Robert Gross, Violin.
I. Tempo moderato, con ampiezza e liberamente
II. Molto vivo (attacca)
III. Adagio e dolcemente (attacca subito)
IV. Alla marcia vivace

This work is believed to represent Sessions's switch to twelve-tone writing. One dictionary states: "Beginning with the Violin Sonata (1953) he adopted the twelve-tone technique."[38] The change, however, was not as abrupt as reported. While writing this work Sessions only gradually discovered that he was unconsciously incorporating rows. The original idea, the first seven notes, could not bear repetition; consequently, he used the other five. Sessions comments, "It was at this point [m. 7] that I realized that I was using the twelve-tone system"[39] (see ex. 5.2).

Example 5.2. Sonata for Violin, I, mm. 1–10.
© 1955 by Edward B. Marks Music Company.
Copyright renewed. Used by permission.

Contrasts achieved in Sessions's previous works by changes of key and texture are not possible in a twelve-tone work for a basically monophonic instrument. The need for contrast must be met on another level, in this case in the relative space of intervals. The manifestation of space in time can be heard in the opening phrase of the first movement (see ex. 5.2). The pitches of the row are given in specific registers so as to expand the gesture not only upward but outward: minor second, perfect fourth, minor sixth, minor seventh, and finally a minor ninth. Measures 123–32 demonstrate in retrograde form this intervallic space becoming elongated in time (see ex. 5.3).

Example 5.3.   Sonata for Violin, I, mm. 123–32.
          © 1955 by Edward B. Marks Music Company.
          Copyright renewed. Used by permission.

The row combines with itself at the level of I-₅ (see ex. 5.4), presented in the second twelve-tone grouping at mm. 3½–4½, after which the original pitches of the row return (see ex. 5.2). At this point the intervals contract vertically, as opposed to their expanding initial linear statement, achieving the needed contrast. This texture of double stops is continued in the presentation of the retrograde. In the first ten bars are concentrated the essential information the ear requires to comprehend the rest of the work.

Example 5.4.   Sonata for Violin, row (P-₀) and inversion (I-₅)

Strict tempo indications preclude the taking of liberties until a performer knows the work well. Variety is achieved through the exploration of space, as it were. It can also be found on a rhythmic level: Phrases are freely declaimed resulting in new subdivisions and groupings. The rhapsodical first movement's rhythmic nature is carefully marked in the score. M. 54 divides the movement and reiterates the upward gesture of the opening. At m. 11 the "bass line" appears on the top of the double stops—B , F , B, and C. The descending and ascending major second (see, for instance, m. 57) plays a characteristic role. M. 95 marks the concluding section.

Only the B section of the ABA second movement is twelve-tone. This is one of Sessions's few strict da capos—the A section returns without any alteration. The onset of serialism in Sessions's music is accompanied by a return to stricter forms.

The music of the third movement fluctuates between the material of its opening and recitative sections. These inexact repetitions recall the textures and rhythms of preceding sections.

Sessions sees the last movement, marked Alla marcia, as more a waltz than a march. It contains three sections: A until m. 534; B to m. 574, where A's texture and character return; and a coda at m. 607. Unconscious motivic and rhythmic references to the second movement occur in mm. 512 and 513.

Sessions's friend Luigi Dallapiccola admired this Sonata but told Sessions that "it will never be played in your lifetime." Fortunately, Dallapiccola was wrong. Skilled performers of the Sonata have included Matthew Raimondi, Paul Zukofsky, and Curtis Macomber.

Idyll of Theocritus   **1954**
(Score Marked 24 May 1954)

Text: *Idyll No. 2* by Theocritus; translated by Robert C. Trevelyan
Commission: Louisville Orchestra
Dedication: "To Luigi Dallapiccola"
Published by Edward B. Marks, 1957. Manuscript at Princeton University Library.
Premiere: 14 January 1956, Louisville, Kentucky, Audrey Nossaman, soprano, Robert Whitney
    Conducting.

Robert C. Trevelyan, the *Idyll*'s translator, thought it the greatest love poem in the whole of literature. What appealed to the composer about the poem was its immediacy and temporal universality. The emotions explored in the *Idyll*, like those in *The Trial of Lucullus*, transcend time. The composer's empathy extends toward Samaitha, the first-person narrator. He dislikes the male character Delphis and has often said the moral of *Theocritus* is "cast not your pearls among swine."

Seventy years ago Sessions heard Charles Martin Loeffler's *A Pagan Poem*, Op. 14, based on a poem by Virgil. Virgil's poem was based on an earlier poem by Theocritus, who lived in the fourth century B.C. Interested in setting the text, Sessions found a disappointingly unspecific Victorian translation (the lovers only got as far as holding hands); he then attempted his own translation. Finally, in 1952, Sessions discovered the translation by Trevelyan, his old friend from Italy.

Sessions originally titled the work *The Sorceress* but unfortunately decided against it. Dallapicolla suggested the present title rather than simply *Idyll*, and it was adopted. Musical inspirations also stemmed from Dallapiccola and from Schoenberg.

There again, I was very much inspired to do this by getting to know Dallapiccola's works for voice. Of course, they are in Italian and my treatment of the voice isn't like his at all, partly because I'm using the English language because the English language is my native language. But knowing his music gave me the courage to cultivate a much freer vocal line.

I think if Schoenberg hadn't written *Erwartung*, I wouldn't have had the courage to write this. Not that there's the slightest resemblance there in either story or the music, but the idea of a big piece for a single voice gave me a kind of precedent for a solo vocal work of 40-odd minutes' duration.[40]

Sessions's twelve-tone approach in the *Idyll* was not as rigid as Dallapiccola's or Schoenberg's in their twelve-tone music.

The twelve tones [E, F, Eb, Db, Ab, G: C, B, F♯, A, Bb, D; see ex. 5.5, first "O Magic Wheel" occurrence] are there all the time, but they're not always there in the same order. I mean there are a lot of liberties that have to be taken, especially in a piece of large design.[41]

The first main refrain, "O Magic Wheel draw hither to my house the man I love," occurs ten times and the second, "bethink thee of my love and whence it came, O holy Moon," recurs twelve times. Intervallic resemblance in the refrains is not exact. The contour is retained, but the rhythm and sound vary on each return according to Samaitha's state of mind at the time (see ex. 5.5 and 5.6). In addition, the contour and orchestration of the contrapuntal line written against these refrains vary. For example, harp and violin tremolos always distinguish the opening of the invocation "O Magic Wheel." In the first two occurrences a bassoon solo accompanies the vocal melody. This counterpoint is next given to the English horn, then to the bass clarinet and oboes. It becomes dispersed among several instruments and finally disappears altogether.

Sessions says:

I didn't try to follow the row absolutely through at all. It's really a motive, rather than a row. I think there are certain places where it becomes a row, but it isn't real twelve-tone writing in any sense of the word. I was going about that very carefully and gingerly, and this has to be rhapsodic. And I couldn't possibly have used the twelve-tone series strictly in a rhapsodic way then.[42]

Searching for twelve-tone aspects provokes the remark from the composer that "probably one has to do it in order to prove it's not very important."

Sessions describes the work as a monodrama. Despite its operatic and descriptive elements (the music accompanying the Magic Wheel, for instance), the *Idyll* would be impossible to stage since only one character narrates the entire story.

In composing the piece Sessions gave the vocal line total primacy as he had done in all his vocal music. He explains:

This is the first work in which I really went to town with the voice. I always wrote the vocal part first, in this and in almost everything I've written to varying degrees. Because in a vocal work the singer is the boss, so to speak. When I write for the voice I always sketch out the vocal part before working out the accompaniment in detail.

Example 5.5. *Idyll of Theocritus*, soprano refrain "O Magic Wheel draw hither to my house the man I love." Ten occurrences.

Example 5.6. *Idyll of Theocritus*, soprano refrain "Bethink thee of my love, and whence it came O holy moon." Twelve occurrences.

The vocal writing contains no *Sprechstimme* even though the temptation to use it must have been great (for instance at "whispered sweet words"). Sessions used this vocal technique in *Montezuma*. He does, however, incorporate vocal glissandi in the *Idyll*, as in *Montezuma*. Unlike *Montezuma*, Sessions calls for an unusually small orchestra. He restricts the violins to eight players and asks for six violas, five cellos, and four double-basses. If more strings are used, the soloist "drowns in a sea of violins."

In a measure-long interlude (m. 449) near the end of the work the oboe at one time accompanied the sad farewell to the goddess. Sessions recalls changing the orchestration after completing the work. "I conceived it for the oboe, but when I got there the oboe seemed very much out of place—much too intense somehow." He gave the melody to the flute.

Sessions made a four-hand version for himself and Mathilde McKinney, pianist of the Pittsburgh Symphony under Reiner, in order to accompany the singer Martha Long, who was one of Sessions's students. It was performed as such at a Juilliard lecture in the mid-1950s. Sessions also made a single piano arrangement for its premiere in Louisville, Kentucky. This piano version is "somewhat mechanically done—it couldn't sound in the least like the piece if played."[44] Four other sopranos have braved this demanding role: Claire Watson, Eleanor Steber, Janice Harsanyi, and Heather Harper.

Mass for Unison Choir   1955

Commission: Kent School
Published by Edward B. Marks, 1957. Manuscripts at Princeton University Library and the Library of Congress.
Premiere: April 1956, St. John the Divine, New York City, Roger Sessions Conducting.

The *Mass* is not a particularly representative work because Sessions was restricted by the abilities of the choir (at the Kent School) and by the use of an organ ("not my instrument"[45]).

> I wrote it in a much more diatonic and tonal style than I usually do. If you take a boy's prep school [with boys] who go to church and sing hymns a fifth above without very good intonation, you don't go in for very much part writing. And unison chorus was perfectly good. No, this was an occasional piece, definitely.[46]

Sessions's own religious background had instilled in him the English version of the Mass before he became acquainted with the Greek and Latin texts. An ease of flow of vocal writing and a careful adherence to linguistic features results from the fact that English is the composer's native language. It is, in fact, the only language that Sessions has set to music.

Concerto for Piano and Orchestra   **1955**

Commission: The Juilliard School of Music for its Fiftieth Anniversary
Dedication: "To the Memory of Artur Schnabel'"
Published by Edward B. Marks, 1959. Manuscript at the Library of Congress. Sketches at Princeton
   University Library.
Premiere: 10 February 1956, The Juilliard Orchestra, New York City, Beveridge Webster, Piano,
   Jean Morel Conducting.
I. Tranquillo
II. Adagio
III. Allegro
(Played without Pause)

It was apt that Beveridge Webster should have premiered this piece both because
of his having performed so much contemporary music (including Sessions's two
piano sonatas) and because he was a pupil of its dedicatee, Artur Schnabel.

The first movement is in sonata-allegro form with two themes; the second theme
begins at m. 58. Sessions quarrels with the standard definition of "theme." "A
theme really is an associative element. Whatever part of a piece contains that which
awakens your sense of memory, or sense of connection, that's what a theme really
is. It doesn't have to be a musical phrase at all."[47] The development begins m.
95, and the recapitulation occurs at m. 130.

Sessions comments about one particular spot:

> A very amusing thing that I did here. You see this passage in octaves [see ex. 5.7]. Well, that's
> the highest note on the piano, but the C♯ with the C♮ sounds like a perfectly good C♯ that way,
> like a perfectly good octave way up there. Of course it's reinforced below.[48]

The slow introduction to the second movement resembles an argument between the soloist and the orchestra: The orchestra and piano rarely play together.
The main body of the movement begins at Un poco più mosso, m. 229. Benjamin Boretz has described the theme as "a single dramatically expressive phrase

Example 5.7.   Piano Concerto, I, piano solo mm. 117–18.
                © 1959 by Edward B. Marks Music Company.
                Used by permission.

centering around one wide melodic skip [of a major seventh, A–G#],"[49] a description that applies to more than one of Sessions's themes.

Sessions remembers that the rondolike last movement was written in extreme haste in the weeks between late December 1955 and 9 January 1956. Most of the music on the first page, however, was conceived long before. Letters—more accurately scraps of paper—received by the performer during this time reveal the frantic brinksmanship Sessions so frequently engages in. Two examples follow:

> Dear Beveridge,— [no date]
>
> Here are six more pages, which bring you up to nearly half of the Allegro movement. I suppose there are some rhythmically difficult places, notably m. 89. In regard to the latter, the main thing is that the general movement be easy and natural—I don't expect it or want it to be in any way mechanical; the outer parts steady and the inner voice, mainly, not together with them except in the places where the notes (A sharp, G natural, B) coincide. This is identical with what Alban Berg told E. Steuermann years ago in regard to a similar passage and I am convinced the principle is right. I only mention this because I know people who work these things out mathematically and give themselves a lot of extra trouble in this way; and that is not the idea at all, as I am sure you know.
>
> More later—good luck
> R— S—

> Dear Beveridge,— Fri. A.M.
>
> Here you are—the nuances are only sketched in—and there are 13 more measures, which however contain nothing very problematical; just the conclusion of the phrase begun on p. 32 and a short transitional passage—and the beginning of the Finale. I can send it the first thing tomorrow, but will try and get you a pencil copy off tonight. I simply had to go to bed last night—was quite tired out. But you have here enough, I am sure, for these days.
>
> Everything is set for the final delivery Thurs. afternoon. The very best to you all for 1956.
> Roger[50]

When the piano is in the foreground the music is dominated more by the row than when the piano retreats. After a foreshadowing the complete row appears for the first time at the pickup to m. 23 in the right hand of the piano: G, F#, B, C#, F, C: Bb, Eb, E, A, G#, D. Although the work is considered twelve-tone, Sessions feels that his music

> does not lend itself to note-counting very easily. I think rules are made to be disobeyed. They're made to be disciplined by, but then disregarded—in the interests of a higher morality, so to speak. Rules have a certain coordinating purpose, if you have your materials firmly in mind, can be served in independence of the rules.[51]

In review of the premiere performance Paul Henry Lang wrote:

> In his concerto Mr. Sessions offers study and art, connection with musical culture, and superiority over and freedom from passing view and tendencies. His music is hard and sober, mind and

experience speak from it. No false tones, manufactured pathos, or sentimental weeping anywhere, it is always serious and the style is consequent . . . some of [Webster's] best playing occurred in the delicate two-part writing that makes this work so attractive.[52]

Despite its considerable beauty, the Piano Concerto, like the Violin Concerto, languished unperformed for decades. It has only recently been performed in the U.S. by Monique Duphil and the Cleveland Orchestra (Yoel Levy, conductor, 1983) and Rebecca LaBreque and the American Composers Orchestra (conducted by Larry Newland, 1984).

Symphony No. 3   **1957**
(Score Marked Princeton, 25 Sept. 1957)

Commission: Boston Symphony Orchestra for its Seventy-Fifth Anniversary
Dedication: "To the Memory of Serge and Natalie Koussevitsky"
Published by Edward B. Marks, 1962. Manuscripts at Princeton University Library and the Library
    of Congress.
Premiere: 6 December 1957, Boston Symphony Orchestra, Charles Munch Conducting.
I. Allegro grazioso e con fuoco
II. Allegro, un poco ruvido
III. Andante sostenuto e con affetto
IV. Allegro con fuoco

The Third Symphony, the longest of Sessions's symphonies, was a "reaction to the warlike and somewhat grim"[53] Second Symphony. The work was commissioned by the Boston Symphony Orchestra, the orchestra Sessions grew up with and subconsciously writes for. The dedication, one of the conditions of the commission, is somewhat ironic since there had been a "kind of breach" between the composer and the conductor. The unpleasant business surrounding the abortive Boston Symphony premiere of Sessions's Violin Concerto was never forgotten by either, and Sessions's music was not played for many years by the Boston Symphony Orchestra. However, Koussevitsky's memory *did* have an effect on Sessions's inspiration for the work:

> The place where Koussevitsky is buried is in the churchyard at the top of the hill in Lenox. It's really quite a lovely place with trees around it. Well, I thought of this movement [the third] up there. . . . It's a very personal work, and at the same time it's the nearest thing to an orthodox symphony that any of my symphonies are, except perhaps No. 1.[54]

The initial idea for each movement came to Sessions in the fall of 1950 in California while he was working on the Second String Quartet. He sketched out these ideas, as well as ones for the Fourth Symphony, leaving them aside with the knowledge that they would be his next symphonic works. He sketched the beginnings of all four movements at one sitting in 1956, eventually revising the first and third, but keeping the second and fourth as written. The third movement,

originally to be called Elegy, was conceived in 1955 in Tanglewood but not written until the *Mass* and Piano Concerto were finished. To Sessions it contains quasi-
funereal passages, reflects human existence, and recalls memories of the landscape
at Lenox.

Sessions feels he used the row more thematically than otherwise "because I
was approaching the twelve-tone system easily and naturally."[55] The row, E, F,
D, Gb, Bb, Cb: A, G, Ab, Eb, C, Db, appears complete first in mm. 27–31 in
the oboe and at the very end of the work (see ex. 5.8).

Example 5.8.   Symphony No. 3, IV, strings, mm. 328–30.
              © 1962 by Edward B. Marks Music Company.
              Used by permission.

Sessions describes the movements in the program notes from its first performance and on the liner notes for its recording.

> The first movement is in three large sections, which may be compared approximately to the three sections of a classic "sonata" form. The first and last of these sections are composed with a melody for oboe. These two groups are varied, though readily recognizable, in the "recapitulation." The middle section introduces new elements, is stormier[56] in character and less concentrated in pace. [Mm. 57 and 106 begin the sections.]
>
> The second movement is likewise in three sections [A the opening, B m. 76, and A m. 115]—corresponding to the three sections of the classic minuet or scherzo. Here again, however, the third section is a variant, not a repetition, of the first. The middle section, or "trio," is quite simple in conception; it is essentially a dialogue consisting . . . of florid and agitated declamatory passages for violins, over trombones in unison, answered by much quieter phrases in the woodwinds and horns. ["Un poco ruvido" means "a little rough." Sessions thinks of this movement as a "sardonic scherzo." Others have pointed out that it resembles a parody of "Yankee Doodle."]
>
> The third movement is based on two contrasting themes—(1) clarinet, harp, and muted horns; (2) violins, answered in imitation by cellos—connected by a passage, given at first to muted trombones, which assumes each time a different character and greater importance in the two variations which follow. The first of these variations leads to a big climax. The movement ends with a return of the music and the coloring of the opening measures.
>
> The final movement is built of five sections, separated clearly by quiet and relatively static passages, in which various orchestral colors are played off against each other, and the persistent recurrence of short motifs, of sometimes purely rhythmic character, maintains the pulsation. Once again variation is the guiding principle; the third and fourth sections are extended variations of the first and second, respectively. Each of the two main sections contains a number of elements proper to itself. The final section is a kind of "coda" which brings back in summary form the various elements of the opening section.[57]

Sessions exhibits a sense of humor about the unintentional results of composition:

> Cross my heart and hope to die that not until the very end did I realize that it ends in a sort of tonic and dominant, dominant and tonic. And I had a lot of fun writing those last measures, because at the very end that comes out. Not that the tonic has been prepared tonally at all, but that's the way the Symphony ends, so you have A♭, and D♭ in the timpani and trombones, and so you have a descending fifth at the end. That was not a joke exactly, but it was fun[58] [see ex. 5.8].

String Quintet   1958
(Score Marked Princeton, April 1 1958)

Commission: Music Department of the University of California at Berkeley
Dedication: Albert Elkus
Published by Edward B. Marks, 1959. Manuscript at Princeton University Library.
Premiere: 1958, Berkeley, California, Griller Quartet with Ferenc Molnar (First Two Movements);
   23 November 1959, New York City, Lenox Quartet, J. Fawcet, Viola (Entire Work).
I. Movemento tranquillo
II. Adagio ed espressivo
III. Allegro appassionato

The Music Department at Berkeley requested from Sessions a chamber piece. Sessions dedicated this viola Quintet to his friend, the department chairman Albert Elkus. Sessions's love for Mozart's G-minor and C-major quintets and Schubert's C-major quintet "tempted as a stimulus and challenge to adopt this medium for the new work."[59] "The first four notes [see ex. 5.9] were the first idea I had. I thought of that beginning for several years before I wrote the Quintet. I remember I was walking in Berkeley one day, and I decided this was going to be the way my next chamber piece should begin."[60]

Example 5.9. String Quintet, I, first violin, mm. 1–2.
         © 1959 by Edward B. Marks Music Company.
         Used by permission.

Formally, the first movement resembles three stanzas with intervening material, "a little like Beethoven's A-minor Quartet, Opus 132, with three expositions." (The first movement of Sessions's String Quartet No. 1 also follows this scheme.) The first stanza opens the work and the first interruption occurs at m. 25. The initial tempo published in the score, quarter note equals 126, is incorrect; the tempo ought to be quarter note equals 104. "You're always apt to make it much faster, because you can hear it much faster in your mind."[61] The second stanza begins at m. 59, the intervening material at m. 92. M. 136 begins the third stanza. An entire dissertation has been devoted to the triadic analysis of this movement. Wheeler writes of its form: "The movement can be divided in half, and each half divided into four sections, as follows: Section A (mm. 1–25), Section B (mm. 25–34), Section C (mm. 34–47), Section D (mm. 47–58); Section A′ (mm. 59–90), Section B′ (mm. 90–106), Section C′ (mm. 106–129), and Section D′ (mm. 129–158)."[62]

The arialike second movement divides into A, B (m. 180), and A (m. 240). Sessions has sometimes thought of this movement as his favorite slow movement; certainly it is the most appealing movement of the work. He wrote:

> The second movement, . . . is composed of three clearly defined sections, of which the first consists of three phrases, separated from each other by quasi-improvisational passages in plucked or tremolo execution, followed by a second idea in two short phrases, interrupted by the second violin, and continued with increasing animation and intensity to a strong climax beneath the high C♯ and E of the first violin. The latter note is held as the lower instruments subside, leading to a broad contrasting section, in which the melody, now in ¾ time, changing soon to ⅝, descends gradually and quietly to the middle register, eventually returning quietly to the ¼ meter and leading to a return of the idea which opens the movement. This is followed by references to the other ideas in the movements. The final measures contain fragmentary references to all that has preceded, leaving the "last word" to the cello, in its lower register.[63]

The third movement, called a rondo,[64] follows a sonata-allegro plan, a "development" beginning at m. 356 and a "recapitulation" at m. 454.

Repetition is crucial to formal categories. Equally crucial to Sessions's style is inexact repetition: "I recall an idea very plainly and specifically without repeating it literally. I very rarely repeat anything literally because that doesn't seem to be in the nature of this vocabulary."[65]

In a review of the incomplete premiere, Andrew Imbrie pinpoints some of the work's salient characteristics:

> Here is music of deeply original personal expression, devoid of eccentricity or strain. The complexities of detail are so clearly related and necessary to the movement of the whole that the listener receives the impression only of richness and luminosity. . . . The design of the [first] movement, as in a number of other Sessions movements, depends upon the interplay of two slightly contrasting tempos: the second in this case being a little faster, and characterized by jerkier rhythms, shorter note-values, and a more agitated general character. The movement closes in the quieter tempo with which it began. The second movement ranges itself alongside those other highly unified slow movements from Sessions's pen, which have as point of departure a single dramatically expressive phrase centering around one wide melodic skip—one thinks in this connection of the last movement of the Second Quartet and the slow movement of the Third Symphony. Here the subordinate contrasting material, appearing pizzicato, sul ponticello, and in various other forms, takes on a quality of a commentary, an interruption and articulation of the flow, but never assumes precedence. As in the previous movement, the unfolding and blossoming of the melody is the real cohesive force.[66]

A few years later, after Imbrie heard the completed Quintet, he undertook a lengthy discussion of this piece and the Violin Concerto.[67]

Sessions's brackets for primary and secondary lines remain in use in the Quintet, aiding an analysis of phrase structure.[68] The first phrase, in the first violin, corresponds to the first statement of P-$_0$. The original form of the row is F♯, D, C♯, D♯, C, E: G♯, G, A, F, B♭, B. It is combinatorial at I-$_{11}$. The first hexachord (phrased in 4+2 notes) forms the antecedent and the second hexachord (phrased in 3+3 notes) the consequent halves of this typically long Sessions melody.

Sessions's careful attention to the relationship between pitch units and rhythmic units can be seen in the second movement. The first statement of the row takes three measures to unfold; the second unfolds in one-third the time, four triplet divisions of a single $\frac{4}{4}$ bar (m. 162); and the third in one-sixth the original time, two twelve-note statements in sixteenths in m. 163. With five instruments at his disposal Sessions can vary the rate a row unfolds and can overlap it with other row forms. These stretches where metric and pitch content are closely allied delineate the internal subdivisions of phrases and sections. The second movement ends with a retrograde statement of the row, a typical feature of Sessions's twelve-tone writing.

As was stated earlier, the third movement contains three similar sections with contrasting material in between. Here again meter helps to delineate form. The opening section, like the sections beginning at m. 356, m. 454, and the coda (m. 489), is in a comfortable $\frac{3}{4}$ meter. The three contrasting sections that also serve as transitional material leading back to the main sections are each in the more unsteady meter $\frac{10}{8}$. The first such episode lasts from mm. 336–56; the second from mm. 440–55; and the final three short measures, mm. 486–89.

When the work was premiered in New York, critic Paul Henry Lang seemed surprised to find himself liking the Quintet. His insights capture some of its essence: "The first thing that attracts the listener is the true chamber music quality of the work. . . . the conversation among the instruments is intimate, interesting, and urbane. This is a major work and a very significant one."[69] Richard Franko Goldman found it one of Sessions's "most immediately appealing, accessible, and delightful works."[70]

Symphony No. 4   1958
(Score Marked Princeton, 31 December 1958)

Commission: In Celebration of the Minnesota Centennial
Dedication: "To my Wife"
Published by Edward B. Marks, 1963. Manuscript at Princeton University Library.
Premiere: 2 January 1960, Minneapolis, Minnesota, Antal Dorati Conducting.
I. Burlesque—Allegro giocoso
II. Elegy—Adagio
III. Pastorale—Andante tranquillo e grazioso

Mitropoulos asked Sessions for a short orchestral work he could perform often. Sessions had already written parts of an elegy and thought he could combine other pieces with it to form a set. It occurred to him that three pieces might represent the three types of Greek drama: comedy, tragedy, and pastorale. When commissioned, he offered three pieces that now seemed to go together—Burlesque, Elegy, and Pastorale. Only afterwards did he realize he was writing a big work and "why not call it a symphony? I hadn't thought of the movements as differing in terms of tempo, but of character and mood. Actually, they are different in tempo."[71]

While discussing the term "symphony" Sessions recalls a conversation he once had with Dallapiccola. They talked about Robert Schumann's symphonies, which they both loved very much, although Dallapiccola questioned whether they strictly constituted "symphonies." Sessions then asked, "What's a symphony?" Dallapiccola replied, "Of course, you're right." Later in the same conversation Dallapiccola mentioned how much he liked Sessions's Fourth Symphony and Sessions replied that he was not sure it *was* a symphony. Dallapiccola protested, "But of course it's a symphony!" Sessions smiles and remarks, "I still don't know exactly what a symphony is."

Not long after writing the work Sessions revealed that natural sounds influenced his musical thinking: a bullfrog, an ovenbird (at the beginning of the first movement), a whippoorwill (at its end), and a hermit thrush that recurs three times in the woodwinds.[72] Sessions is something of an expert regarding birds. He distinctly remembers the nightingales' singing behind his house in Rome. Clarinet passages preceding nos. 65 and 80 in the third movement possibly represent other birds.

For Sessions comedy usually takes the form of parody; here he pokes fun at himself. He parodies his Second Symphony in the violin line at the beginning of the coda, m. 144ff. The first movement is in a general sonata form.[73] The opening music of the movement introduces all the main sections of the work. The first section starts in the horns at m. 4. The main contrasting section begins on the violins at m. 30 and is flavored with descending leaps of major ninths. This theme contains most of the row (Ab, Gb, D, C, F, Db: Bb, E, D#, G, A, B), although "at that time I didn't want to depend on the row for any thematic material. The row plays a very secondary role in this piece."[74] As usual with Sessions's music, "the music is God and the twelve-tone technique is just a parish priest."[75]

The chords that open the second movement also contain all twelve notes. As was mentioned above, this movement was written first; the beginning and the Funebre section (m. 178ff) were the first sections composed. This Elegy represents "an idealized, or conventionalized, musical biography of a tragic life."[76] The tragic life is that of Sessions's brother John. "My brother had just died a terrible death [in 1948], a lingering death of tubercular meningitis. I've never been affected so much by somebody's death before. I was devoted to him."[77]

The slow opening of the second movement speeds up and in general has "the character of an exposition."[78] The form is: introduction, Adagio (to m. 26); exposition (A, Allegro impetuoso, m. 26, B, second idea, m. 56); development of A (m. 89), third idea (m. 111), development of B (tranquillo, m. 132), development of A (Tempo animato, m. 152); closing section (m. 172), and m. 184 brings a recapitulation of the opening adagio. "I don't think of these things [the musical ideas] exactly as themes. I think of them as sections which are built up in different ways."[79] The last chord is ppp and marked morendo (dying), the same marking as at the end of the Second String Quartet, the *Idyll of Theocritus,* and *Montezuma.*

"The last movement was a poem to nature; nature in the widest and deepest sense."[80] Marked Un poco indolente, this movement, like the first, has a tongue-in-cheek character. He began the movement while on a month-long (mid-September to mid-October 1958) trip to Russia for the State Department, where *The Black Maskers* Orchestral Suite was performed. The last movement was composed extremely quickly. He was informed that the commission would not be fulfilled unless he completed the work by the end of the year. The score is marked "Princeton 31 December 1958."

Boretz sums up the work: "The entire symphony, in fact, could be called an essay in the problem of large-scale musical characterization, if that description did not belie the deeply expressive nature of the work."[81]

Divertimento for Orchestra   1959–1960
(Manuscript Marked 24 February 1960)

Commission: Portland Symphony, in Commemoration of the One-Hundredth Anniversary of the State of Oregon
Dedication: "To Carl Haverlin"

Published by Theodore Presser, 1982. Manuscript at Princeton University Library.
Premiere: 9 January 1965, Honolulu, Hawaii, Honolulu Symphony, George Barati Conducting. (Performed Incomplete by the Portland Symphony)
I. Prelude—Allegro un poco maestoso
II. Aria—Andante tranquillo
III. Toccata—Allegro giocoso
IV. Perpetuum mobile—Presto (no pause)
V. Epilogue—Lento e grazioso

Sessions's close friend and editor, Felix Greissle, recommended using a smaller orchestra for this work. This five-movement work is shorter and more lighthearted than his symphonies, hence the name Divertimento. Fewer changes of time signature distinguish this from other Sessions scores. When time signatures are changed, it is often for a structural purpose. Characteristic, however, are the long lines, colorful orchestration, and dissonant harmonies.

Only four movements had been completed by the time of the scheduled first performance in July 1959. So, as in the case of the First Piano Sonata and the String Quintet, the premiere was a performance of an incomplete work. After the score was completed, conductor Lukas Foss eliminated the third movement because its quintuple meter proved too difficult for the Hamburg Radio Orchestra. The Hawaii performance was its only complete performance until the New York premiere on 5 December 1977 by the American Composers Orchestra conducted by James Dixon.

The Prelude is in tripartite form. The theme of the first section, A, is given at the outset in bassoons and violins and is characterized by its dotted figures and an aggressive, yet light, spirit. The B theme, tranquillo m. 30, consists initially of even-valued eighths in the clarinet. This section builds animato to a climax at m. 50, after which a calmando molto takes the listener back to tempo primo, m. 56, where the A material returns. At m. 76 the second idea is recalled in the flute. Insistent quarter-note trumpet calls hide in the background of the A sections and sometimes steal the foreground.

The second movement, entitled Aria, can also be analyzed as an ABA form. The A theme is given to the violins accompanied by a muted trumpet theme. Simultaneously, sixteenth-note quintuplet figures scurry in the background. The section divides at m. 10 after which the clarinet resumes, leading into m. 14 where the violins again take over the main thematic material. A rallentando leads to a cadence in the middle of m. 18. The B section of the second movement begins with the oboe melody. The color of the line changes within the same family, from the to the English horn and back to oboe, accompanied by triplets in the strings. The violins take over and the music builds animato to a climax at m. 30. At m. 33 the oboe returns, now playing the melody originally given the clarinet in the A section. The piano leads back to the final A section. One of Sessions's famous "long lines" begins in the violins at m. 42. It stretches, at the original andante tempo, all the way to m. 55, marked morendo, the end of the movement.

The Toccata's ABA form is delineated by changes in dominating time signatures. The excited pandemonium of both As is in $\frac{5}{8}$; the B section in which woodwinds predominate is in $\frac{3}{4}$. Both transitions are accomplished by means of metric modulation.

Alternations between instruments to produce a *Klangfarbenmelodie* is here taken to an extreme. The theme of the Perpetuum mobile, in even eighth notes, alternates each measure between strings and xylophone, repeating its eighth notes. Repeated trumpet notes recall the first movement. This movement is the fastest Sessions ever wrote. "I was challenged by writing something as near to a presto movement as I could. It's really sort of perpetuum mobile."[82] The tempo is quarter note equals 252. The excitement subsides four times; the last time the note values slow to halves and lead without pause into the Epilogue.

The Epilogue's theme is given to the cellos, which are accompanied by pizzicato strings. The movement ends with a bass clarinet solo.

Although, naturally, the composer "lived" each work he composed during his fourth period (the 1950s), in the back of his mind was the dream of completing the work he already considered his "magnum opus." It took Sessions from 1947 to 1963 to write *Montezuma*. *Montezuma*'s librettist, G. Antonio Borgese, had died in 1952, but the enthusiasm the Sicilian transmitted to Sessions and Sessions's own never abated. The next decade was to produce only a partial fulfillment of Sessions's dream, for he never considers a work completed until he hears it performed well, and the premiere fell short of what he intended. Sessions was to wait another dozen years before a production satisfied these long-frustrated desires.

Once the time-consuming *Montezuma* was completed, Sessions's fluency accelerated dramatically. During the remainder of his fifth creative period (the 1960s) and into the beginning of the sixth (the 1970s), Sessions wrote more music in less time than ever before. He produced five large orchestral pieces in six years—after he had reached the age of 70.

Notes

1. Harold C. Schonberg, *New York Times,* 5 March 1976.

2. *Time*, 10 May 1968.

3. Winthrop Sargeant, *The New Yorker* 44 (11 May 1968).

4. Taped interview 26 November 1975.

5. Roger Sessions, "To the Editor," *Perspectives of New Music* 5 (Spring–Summer 1967): 81–97. In *Roger Sessions on Music; Collected Essays* this article appears as "What Can Be Taught?"

6. Ibid., p. 84.

7. Ibid., p. 96.

8. Ibid., p. 94.

9. Ibid., p. 95.

10. Ibid.

11. Roger Sessions, *Harmonic Practice* (New York: Harcourt, Brace, & World, Inc., 1951), p. xvi.

12. Taped interview with Lehman Engel 24 August 1979.

13. Edward T. Cone, "In Honor of Roger Sessions," *Perspectives of New Music* 10 (Spring–Summer 1972): 139–40.

14. Taped interview with Carter Harman 4 October 1979.

15. Taped interview with Milton Babbitt 6 November 1979.

16. Letter from Vivian Fine to the author 11 September 1979.

17. Interview with and letter from Dika Newlin 2 November 1979.

18. Taped interview with Mark Schubart 5 March 1980.

19. Taped interview with Leon Kirchner 26 September 1980.

20. Letter from Eric Salzman to the author 8 March 1980.

21. Letter from Harold Schiffman to the author 16 September 1979.

22. Taped interview with Paul Turok 17 October 1979.

23. Letter from Donald Martino to the author 10 February 1980.

24. Letter from David Lewin to the author 2 October 1979.

25. Telephone call from John Eaton to the author 24 September 1979.

26. Letter from John Harbison to the author 23 October 1979.

27. Taped interview with Roger Sessions 17 January 1979.

28. I talked informally with each of the students mentioned.

29. Ronald Duane Henderson, *Tonality in the Pre-Serial Instrumental Music of Roger Sessions* (Ph.D. diss.: Eastman School of Music, 1974), p. 315.

30. Eugene Schweitzer, *Generation of String Quartets of Carter, Sessions, Kirchner and Schuller* (Ph.D. diss.: Eastman School of Music, 1965), p. 80.

31. Ibid., p. 72.

32. Taped interview 11 January 1978.

33. Schweitzer, *Generation of String Quartets*, p. 69.

34. Ibid., pp. 83, 85.

35. Herbert Livingstone, "Roger Sessions: Second String Quartet," *Notes* 13 (June 1956): 524.

36. Edward T. Cone, "Sessions: Second String Quartet," *The Musical Quarterly* 43 (January 1957): 140–41.

37. Raymond Ericson, "A Sessions Retrospect," *New York Times*, 24 March 1977.

38. John Vinton, ed., "Roger Sessions," *Dictionary of Contemporary Music* (New York: E. P. Dutton, 1974), p. 675.

39. Taped interview 12 March 1975.

40. Taped interviews 8 and 15 October 1975.

41. Taped interview 8 October 1975.

42. Taped interview 15 October 1975.

43. Taped interview 8 October 1975.

44. Untaped conversation 13 May 1980.

45. Taped interview 5 November 1975.

46. Ibid.

47. Taped interview 5 November 1975.

48. Ibid.

49. Benjamin Boretz, "Current Chronicle," *The Musical Quarterly* 47 (July 1961): 386–96.

50. Roger Sessions, letters to Beveridge Webster December 1956.

51. Taped interview 5 November 1975.

52. Paul Henry Lang, "Juilliard Orchestra," *New York Herald Tribune,* 12 February 1956.

53. Untaped class lecture, New York, 12 March 1980.

54. Taped interview 12 November 1975.

55. Ibid.

56. In the Columbia University Oral History Collection interview, 1962, Sessions admits to portraying "a storm" in the middle section of the first movement and "rustlings and chirpings of whippoorwills" at the end of the movement.

57. Roger Sessions, "Symphony No. 3," *RCA* LSC-3095 liner notes.

58. Taped interview 12 November 1975.

59. Roger Sessions, The Juilliard String Quartet Program notes, 21 October 1980.

60. Taped interview 19 November 1975.

61. Conversation 14 October 1980.

62. William Scott Wheeler, *Harmonic Motion in the Music of Roger Sessions* (Ph.D. diss.: Brandeis University, 1984), p. 9.

63. Sessions, Program notes.

64. Richard Franko Goldman, "Current Chronicle," *The Musical Quarterly* 46 (January 1960): 71–73.

65. Taped interview 19 November 1975.

66. Andrew Imbrie, "Current Chronicle," *The Musical Quarterly* 44 (July 1958): 370–71.

67. Andrew Imbrie, "Roger Sessions: In Honor of His Sixty-fifth Birthday," repr. in *Perspectives on American Composers*, ed. by Benjamin Boretz and Edward T. Cone (New York: W. W. Norton & Co., 1971), pp. 59–89. The article first appeared in *Perspectives of New Music* 1 (Fall 1962): 117–47.

68. Sessions soon gave up the use of these signs "because it oversimplifies the picture so much." Taped interview 16 October 1979.

69. Paul Henry Lang, "Modern Chamber Music," *New York Herald Tribune* (24 November 1959).

70. Goldman, "Current Chronicle," p. 71.

71. Taped interview 26 November 1975.

72. Columbia University Oral History Collection, p. 316.

73. *See* Benjamin Boretz, "Current Chronicle," *The Musical Quarterly* 47 (July 1961): 391–93.

74. Taped interview 3 December 1975.

75. Ibid.

76. Taped interview 26 November 1975.

77. Ibid.

78. Taped interview 3 December 1975.

79. Ibid.

80. Taped interview 26 November 1975.

81. Boretz, "Current Chronicle," p. 393.

82. Taped interview 26 November 1975.

6

The Futility of Conquest:
The Music of the 1960s

Montezuma   **1947–1963**
                                        (Score Marked Princeton, N.J., 1 July 1962)

Opera in Three Acts
Libretto by G. Antonio Borgese
Dedication: "To Felix Greissle"
Published by Edward B. Marks, 1962. Manuscripts at Princeton University Library.
Premieres: 19 April 1964, West Berlin, Heinrich Hollreiser Conducting; 30 March 1976, Opera Company of Boston, Sarah Caldwell Conducting.

Montezuma represents a stylistic change in Sessions's music, a dividing point in his total oeuvre. Of this John Harbison writes:

> The second crucial moment in Sessions's career involves accession to fluency and a coincidental cultivation of compression, extreme variety of phrase shape, and more frequent and pronounced contrast. The catalyst and crystallizer is *Montezuma*, a natural arena in which these new forces work themselves out under the stress of the drama. . . . *Montezuma* stands on the divide, with its prime-of-life, middle-period vitality and its late-style compression and swiftness of transition.[1]

Sessions describes the implications of the story:

> It's the high-level relationships between human beings—that's what it's about. And it has a sort of deeper implication, too. Because when it was written Borgese was a refugee from Mussolini. And I wasn't exactly a refugee from Hitler, but I'd been in Germany and seen Hitler come in and seen what he was doing to Germany and by implication the world. And we had those things on our minds very much as the text developed.[2]

He continues:

> The general idea, I think, is pretty clear: That conquest is a very problematical matter.[3] The essential catastrophe of *Montezuma* is that Alvarado, but Cuauhtemoc also, really ruined the whole thing. Alvarado and Cuauhtemoc on their respective sides were the hawks, and

they kept reacting violently to everything and take what seems a shortcut, which is, alas, a very common failing of the human race.[4]

And finally:

Cuauhtemoc really thought Montezuma was unwise in his view of the situation. Montezuma really saw it very realistically. He realized the Spaniards had resources behind them and technology, so to speak, modern technology—horses, which the Mexicans had never seen, and they had artillery and guns, which the Mexicans had never seen—and that in the end the Aztecs had no choice except to learn to live with them and give them what they wanted and learn from them. Cuauhtemoc wanted to try to stand up to them and throw them out, you see. That in a way is the theme: How futile the hawks really are in the long run, the futility of conquest. We're still up against that problem in the world today. If you write an historical drama about the past, you're bound to interpret the past, not reproduce it, I'm sure. Because nobody knows what *really* went on, ever.[5]

The history of the collaboration between Borgese and Sessions is traced in my article "The Plum'd Serpent" in the March 1985 issue of *Tempo*. The article also discusses the story and the poetry and compares *Montezuma* with *The Trial of Lucullus*. Charles Mason's dissertation, *A Comprehensive Analysis of Roger Sessions's Opera Montezuma*, contains detailed chapters on the musical depiction of the scenery, and a technical analysis.[6]

Sessions describes the music of *Montezuma*:

In planning the music I kept, of course, three distinct levels constantly in mind; first of all, the coherence and emphasis of the drama as a whole; secondly, the underlying character of each individual scene or episode; and finally, the individual characters and their reciprocal relationships. The problem, so to speak, was to delineate all of these as sharply as possible at all levels, the larger levels serving as framework for the smaller.[7]

The first act of *Montezuma* is the most straightforward of the three acts and the easiest to analyze. Its five scenes are relatively self-contained, and each is preceded by an introductory passage and followed by an interlude or a codalike section. The title character does not appear in act 1, but allusions ("No one, no one ever dared to look him in the eye. Forbidden is his threshold, hallowed, awful.") intensify our anticipation of meeting him.

Due to the necessity of cutting down the text, Sessions found himself in act 2 relying on stage pictures to an unparalleled degree. This act stands out from the first and the third because of its visual and somewhat ritualized nature. The first two tableaux represent known historical events, the meeting of Cortez and Montezuma and ritual human sacrifice. In some ways the remainder of the act corresponds to its opening. Almost no action takes place; the main characters reflect on the associations they have with actual pictures—portraits of Don Carlos of Spain and of the Virgin and Child. The central point of the act is Malinche's aria in Montezuma's gardens; its conclusion is Cortez's (somewhat forced) logic for taking Montezuma prisoner. As in the first act, Sessions shows the stridency of Alvarado and Cuauhtemoc by increasing the tempo whenever one of them sings. Conversely, Montezuma's speeches are almost always labeled Tranquillo.

The third act is musically and formally more complicated than the other two. The last 400 measures (scene 11) constitute its largest through-composed chunk, building inexorably to Montezuma's death (m. 863) and to the end. Both the vocal counterpoint and the meters and rhythms become more complex. One obvious reason for this is that Sessions wrote this music much later in his career than the music of the first two acts; by then his style had changed.

Ostinatos, pictorialism, and *Sprechstimme* function in *Montezuma* to illustrate and enhance the text. In Sessions's opera, as in Berg's operas, a *Hauptrhythmus* is used to propel scenes of violent death. In *Lulu* a *monoritmica* appears in act 1, scene 2 to underline the suicide of the Painter, and in *Wozzeck* it represents Marie's murder in act 3, scene 2. Ostinatos underscore deaths by violence throughout *Montezuma*: the Aztec sacrifice (act 2, mm. 242–74); the *auto-da-fé* (act 3, mm. 33ff, 69ff, and 162–66); and Montezuma's plea before being stoned (act 3, mm. 762–76). Not only do ostinatos play an important role in the onstage deaths, but *monoritmicas* also accompany murderous thoughts: of revenge (act 3, mm. 69–77), of conspiracy (act 3, scene 7), and of Alvarado's power-hungry ravings, "What lives must die!" (act 3, mm. 278–303). In addition, both composers carefully distinguish tempos in various sections of music as a way to unify large structures. They both "modulate" rhythmically from one section to another to achieve a smooth flow.

Sessions subconsciously parallels Schoenberg's *Moses and Aron* in the way he differentiates the two male leads. Aron sings eloquently, while Moses is confined to *Sprechstimme*. Cortez, a baritone, sings in poetry and, in the main, animando. Montezuma, a tenor, sings andante tranquillo and in prose. With regard to the level the operas address, Sessions feels that *Montezuma* is closer to *Moses and Aron* because it deals with "public figures" in a "sort of world situation" as opposed to Berg's more personal operas.

In *Montezuma* ostinatos serve several other functions. They describe the action, achieve unity, and build drama. They also assume an allegorical role by representing in music a situation on stage. Through association and repetition they can take on a meaning of their own. Sessions uses the device in all of these ways. For example, whenever horses appear or are discussed, a trotlike $\frac{3}{8}$ pattern occurs. Bernal's description of the wreckage of battle, beginning in act 3 at m. 503, is accompanied by an ostinato that ends the interlude preceding the next scene, the soldier's homesick song, and continues until the stage brightens again at m. 529. Here the ostinato effectively unites the end of one scene with the beginning of the next by underlining their mutual theme, the pain of being in an absolutely hopeless position. Ostinatos allegorically represent the trance that the Aztec priest Netzahualcoyotl enters while endeavoring to unravel the mystery of the Virgin birth (act 2, mm. 597–624), Montezuma's impeded movement once shackled (act 2, mm. 888–98), and Cortez's desire that Montezuma remain stationary during the *auto-da-fé* (act 3, mm. 106–14).

In the second tableau, the Aztec sacrifice, the violence is underlined by a bass drum figure, mm. 242–65, picked up by the Teponaxtli pattern in m. 265 and continued through m. 274, up to the beginning of scene 6. The drum beating was part of Aztec ritual; it summoned the Indians to the sacrifice. Eleven victims meet their deaths during this music. In act 2, mm 587–624, Netzahualcoyotl's trance is underscored by a Teponaxtli $\frac{5}{4}$ ostinato associated with the Aztecs. Again, rhythm serves Sessions to portray allegorically both the motionless state of a trance and the infinitely unsolvable Mystery.

The climax of act 2, the shackling of Montezuma, mm. 882–83, is audibly represented by a rapidly alternating diminished third (in the bass) while Cortez utters, "Oh! Unwelcome to my ears tinkle of irons!" After Montezuma's helpless cry (m. 884), Olmedo's prayer in Latin (mm. 886–88) and Cortez's last line of the act ("Caps down Caballeros! Caps down! The King passes." at mm. 888–93) are accompanied by an ostinato in $\frac{5}{4}$.

Most of scene 7, the *auto-da-fé*, is underscored by an insistent rhythmic ostinato. At the moment of each mention or indication of the pyre a repeated eighth-note figure appears, mm. 33f, mm. 69ff. The offstage pyre is thus made real to the audience. Montezuma is restrained by Cortez from leaving this unpleasant scene, mm. 106–14; a $\frac{5}{8}$ ostinato represents Cortez's desire that Montezuma remain physically in place. The final shrieks of the victim (m. 164) interrupt a brief ostinato begun at m. 162 and continued through m. 166.

Another rhythmic ostinato begins in act 3, scene 7, a scene of conspiracy, spoken in "undertones" at dusk and marked Misterioso ed inquieto. The ominous quality of an ostinato is particularly apt here to express the plotting by the two Mexicans to overthrow the Spanish. Timbales reinforcing the piano's $\frac{5}{8}$ pattern (mm. 216ff) lend it an exotic flavor. Because the pattern itself is duple, it sets up to the ear larger two- and four-bar units. Sixteenth-note triplets flutter, and against the regular $\frac{5}{8}$ pattern the two voices sing continuously in $\frac{3}{4}$. The resulting sensation is three against (the implied) four against five. The effect accumulates as more complicated layers are added.

When Alvarado convinces himself of his need to take control, which occurs shortly after the conspiracy scene, a similar ostinato passage begins (m. 278), this time occasioned by the appearance of drummers in the action. A large battery of percussion—Chinese drums, guiro, claves, maracas, tam-tam—play an ostinato that breaks up every few measures only to return, finally ending at the climax, "What lives must die!" (m. 303). At m. 762, during Montezuma's plea to his people, stage drums begin a pattern in $\frac{5}{8}$ that varies but remains through m. 776 where the Indians interrupt him.

As can be observed in his other vocal works, Sessions portrays emotions and words with analogous pictorial music. For example, the orchestra trills while Bernal the Old sings, "I wave my cap with trembling hand" (act 1, mm. 46–47). The shriek of the Aztec sacrificial victims is portrayed by a long cello glissando (act 2, m. 271); the Indians' greedy rush to obtain their remains is portrayed by a rapid ascending chromatic scale in the next measure. When Malinche sings to a bird, the xylophone answers (act 2, m. 298). A fortississimo cluster under the bass staff roars like the Spanish cannon (act 1, m. 523). After Cortez's tongue-lashing of Alvardo the latter says, "Check your temper, sir" (act 3, m. 387), the texture lightens suddenly, and a subito molto rit. is marked, effectively "checking" the music. In the soldier's song (act 1, mm. 660–90) the man's drunkenness is portrayed both in the vocal line and in the accompaniment. Appropriately, "very low" (act 3, m. 648) is sung on the lowest note of the range. Within one measure (act 2, m. 398) sounds indicative of a storm and of peace appear. A vocal glissando occurs at appropriate words: "swoon" (act 2, m. 629), "frightens" (act 2, m. 750), "fiery" (act 3, m. 40); the line "What lives must die!" (act 3, m. 303) incorporates both the glissando and *Sprechstimme*.

Sessions uses *Sprechstimme* not only for words that evoke a dry, raspy sound, but also at places where the speaker is overcome by emotion. Words whose meanings are literally portrayed are: "O my shackled tongue!" (act 2, m. 39); "Thus stupor ultimate parches the tongue of the narrator" (act 2, m. 123); "Oh! Unwelcome to my ears tinkle of irons!" (act 2, m. 883); "from scepter to fetters, from throne to dust" (act 3, m. 12); "shrouds" (act 3, m. 359); and "ugly" (act 1, m. 751). Examples of overwrought emotions generating this recitativelike style of singing are: "thou frenzied child. An omen runs in my veins, fear moistens the lock" (act 1, m. 503); "no god's is this man's countenance" (act 1, m. 521); and "Defend thine own, fight!" (act 2, m. 786). Sessions graduates the effect between unmeasured *Sprechstimme* and singing in one place (act 1, mm. 695ff).

In addition to standard orchestral instruments Sessions incorporates two piccolos, English horn, E-flat clarinet, bass clarinet, contrabassoon, celeste, harp, and six percussion players who play Mexican and Chinese drums, maracas, rapeguero (scratcher or guiro), cymbals, claves, and Teponaxtli (an authentic Aztec percussion instrument that has a narrow slit on the top, in the form of a letter H, whose two tongues produce different pitches).

Sessions's score is more than usually specific regarding accents and dynamics. He provides a descriptive key, which has been incorporated at the head of each orchestral score since *Montezuma* at the suggestion of Felix Greissle.

The row for *Montezuma* is compact and used trichordally. The relation between the original and the inversions is very close: Upon inversion at least one pitch of each trichord remains the same (invariant) (see ex. 6.1). These trichords function independently from one another, and they account for vertical and horizontal structures in which, through applying semi-Schenkerian voice-leading analysis, Edward Laufer discovers a "subtle tonal organization and association of specific referential sonorities."[8]

Although the total chromatic collection of pitches is always present, "set usage becomes at times so free as to be abandoned altogether," Laufer writes. Mason agrees: "However, there is no discernible pattern of progression from one set [of

Example 6.1. *Montezuma*, row (P) and its inversion (I).

trichords] to another.'"[9] Naturally, some reference points are necessary to maintain unity over such an extended period of time. These sonorities become associated with certain events and, upon repetition, serve to bind together both local and large-scale designs in the opera. Ten easily recognizable motives are given in example 6.2. Referring to these melodic associative fragments, Sessions writes:

> The fragments themselves are used sparingly and are not "developed" in the usual technical sense of the word. In this respect my classical models could be said (with humility!) to have been Mozart—in my mind the supreme master of characterization—and Verdi, especially in his later works, rather than Wagner. This does not imply a lack of admiration for the latter, simply a difference of approach, based on many factors.[10]

Example 6.2. *Montezuma*, motives.
        © 1962 by Edward B. Marks Music Company.
        Used by permission.

Laufer has found that pairs of specific pitches recur at similar points in the drama. His two most important pairs are B-B♭ and F-F♯, and to a lesser extent E-D♯. "The B-B♭ [used both horizontally and vertically] sonority seems to recur at moments portending or portraying doom and sacrifice." However, Mason finds this "purely coincidental."[11]

Unquestionably, *Montezuma* presents many challenges to the operagoer as well as to the stage director. Peter Maxwell Davies suggests the best approach to the opera is first to digest the Fifth Symphony, "the stylistic key to the most difficult section of the opera, the third and final act."[12]

> However, if one can take the music as a whole, its enormous gestures and long articulations begin to fall into place, and Sessions emerges as a great lyricist with a full and virile melodic sweep. The "total melody," often arising from the weaving together of related threads, conceived as a large melodic gesture in several parts rather than as "counterpoint" as such is, when one begins to hear how this most original concept works, even direct and straightforward.[13]

As Davies pointed out, analysis of Sessions's Fifth Symphony helps us to understand better the structure of *Montezuma*. The Fifth Symphony is Sessions's first in which the movements are not separable, just as the sections of the third act of *Montezuma* are also glued together musically. By the time he was working of the Fifth Symphony and *Montezuma*, Sessions's writing had become so concise and sweeping that interrupting the flow became difficult. Ostinatos helped him to bridge the breaks between scenes so as not to relax the mounting tension. In this way Sessions allows the flow of the drama to guide the music.

To take another example of formal complexity, the love "duet" between Cortez and Malinche at the end of act 1 can barely be called a traditional duet since Cortez does most of the singing, Malinche sings only a few lines, and never do they sing together. John Harbison compares the act 1 love duets of *Montezuma* and *Otello*.[14] Considering Sessions's passion for late Verdi and his acknowledged debt to him, it is certainly possible that the Verdi opera influenced Sessions subconsciously.

Unusual also is the fact that entire scenes are not sung at all, but are vividly portrayed on stage and in the wildly dramatic music (like those in Weber's Wolf's Glen Scene in *Der Freischütz*). These occur in the second act, where the auspicious meeting of Cortez and Montezuma is completely mimed, and the human sacrifice, the most violent music of the whole opera, is presented in tableau. This reliance on the visual is unmatched elsewhere in opera.

Finally, the evenly balanced situations and characters—for example, for the Aztecs' human sacrifice, the Spaniards create an *auto-da-fé*, Montezuma's warlike second lieutenant is counterbalanced by Cortez's, as is Montezuma's priest by the Spanish Father Olmedo—establish a symmetry that makes it difficult for the audience to take sides. Cortez's reverent treatment of Montezuma while the latter is being shackled at the end of act 2 is characteristic of the opera's overall ambivalence. Since each faction is given equal weight—humanity, sympathy, agressiveness—any attempt to assign blame for the tragic end of Montezuma is doomed to frustration. In constructing a symmetrical story and opera the author and composer deliberately built in this level of ambiguity. The lack of formal demarcation, the density of the vocal and orchestral writing, the number of visual events, the nonliteral musical repetitions, and the precarious balance set up between good and evil all contribute to the carefully complicated design. This ambiguity doubtlessly contributed to the variety of reactions the productions of the opera received.

Figure 6.1.   *Montezuma*, Berlin Production, 1964.
The Mexicans present a ritual dance. Malinche (Annabelle
Bernard) and Cortez (William Dooley) are in the center.

In Berlin Heinrich Hollreiser conducted the premiere, Rudolf Sellner directed, and Michel Rafaelli designed the stage. William Dooley sang Cortez, Annabelle Bernard played Malinche, and Helmut Melchert was Montezuma. The opera was performed in a German translation on 19 April 1964.

On the opening night *Time* magazine reported that "when Sessions appeared with his cast for curtain calls, a chorus of boos rose violently from the balconies."[15] Sessions recalls the scene: "Half the audience was cheering and half booing."[16] Sarah Caldwell and her mother were sitting next to a booing man; the elder Caldwell engaged him in a fist fight. A couple of days later Caldwell informed Sessions of what she considered the problems of the production, problems Sessions was not ready to deal with at that time. "And it took me a long time to realize how bad it actually was. That's still a sore spot with me."[17] In retrospect Sessions views the problems: There were often too many people on stage; Montezuma and Alvarado were "grossly miscast," and Dooley did not have time to learn his part; the director misunderstood opera and music (at one point he called for the character Tranquillo to appear); Martti Talvela was also miscast as the Aztec priest, a minor role, when he "would have been wonderful as Bernal."

The American premiere, in 1976, was both staged and conducted by Sarah Caldwell. The scenery was designed by Herbert Senn and Helen Pond. Donald Gramm sang Bernal the Old, Brent Ellis sang Cortez, Phyllis Bryn-Julson was Malinche, and Richard Lewis sang Montezuma. The alternate cast included John Moulson as Montezuma and Pamela Kucenic as Malinche. For the two tenor roles Sessions envisioned voices who could sing Otello (Montezuma) and Siegfried (Alvarado).

Immediately after the Boston performance Sessions said:

> I was uncomfortable about *Montezuma* until I heard this performance done the way it should be done. In Berlin the whole idea of the opera was wrong. I mean it's not a big mass spectacle at all. The most telling thing about this production was that there were never too many people on the stage. That makes so much difference, because it focuses on what's really going on.[18]

Printed reaction spanned the range from disappointment to enraptured respect to noncommitment. John Harbison wrote of it in glowing terms: "I hope it is clear that I regard *Montezuma* as one of four or five great operas of this century."[19] The *Saturday Review* was somewhat less enthusiastic:

> But this would have required a dedication to the kind of theatrical purpose which Delfina Vargas brought to one set of costumes (Aztec) and Mabel Astarloa to another (Spanish), but which was lacking in Sessions's consistently non-vocal, continuously overweighted score.[20]

Time's pronouncement was simple and direct: "*Montezuma* is indisputably twelve-tone music's finest hour on the operatic stage."[21] Leighton Kerner's *Village Voice* review also praised the opera: "Minute by minute, the musical and dramatic

Figure 6.2. *Montezuma*, Opera Company of Boston Production, 1976. From left to right: Bernal (Donald Gramm), Malinche (Phyllis Bryn-Julson), and Cortez (Brent Ellis). Used by permission of the Opera Company of Boston

Figure 6.3. *Montezuma*, Opera Company of Boston, 1976. Bernal the Old (left, Donald Gramm) describes the Mexican market. Used by permission of the Opera Company of Boston.

diamonds and daggers that had leapt out from the score were attacking and amazing me from the Orpheum's . . . stage.''[22] But the *New York Times* did not agree: ''That said, the evening was not a triumphant success. It was eminent, respectable, but that couldn't compensate for the boredom. And the librettist, G. Antonio Borgese, Mr. Sessions and Miss Caldwell all deserve their share of the blame.''[23] Finally, *The New Yorker* had this to say:

> This account of the Boston ''Montezuma,'' though not altogether enthusiastic, should at least close with enthusiastic expressions of gratitude to Miss Caldwell and her colleagues for bringing the work to the American stage, and of appreciation for the immense labors of musical preparation that must have gone into it. Such phrases always sound flat. I had hoped that I would be adding, ''and at last the glory of the work was revealed!''[24]

In February 1982 *Montezuma* was finally performed in New York, its third production. The Juilliard American Opera Center production was conducted by Frederik Prausnitz, the director was Ian Strasfogel, and Ming Cho Lee designed the sets. James Dietsch sang Cortez, Robert Grayson played Montezuma, and Hei-Kyung Hong sang Malinche. Strasfogel changed some of the wording and cut one aria. The production was extravagant, sets and costumes were again beautiful and expensive, but quite different from those in the Boston production. Although hastily rehearsed, the performances went well, and many of the dramatic moments were truly effective. Unfortunately, the press did not agree. The reactions were almost unanimously negative, worse than previous reviews. For example, Peter G. Davis wrote in a review entitled ''Montezuma's Revenge'' that ''Sessions has written a terrible opera, a tragic waste of a valuable composer's precious time . . . the opera's flaws only become more apparent and aggravating with each hearing . . . the ear becomes lost in a sea of gray monotony.''[25]

Alone in defending the work, Andrew Porter compared the difficulty of *Montezuma*'s achieving public success with that of Berlioz's *Les Troyens*, and insisted that more rehearsal and attention to the composer's intentions will ultimately reveal the masterpiece:

> Any fool, as Brahms might have said, can hear what is ''wrong'' with ''Montezuma'': it is too densely and busily composed and too heavily scored . . . ; and G. Antonio Borgese's libretto is ''impossible,'' mainly but not only because of the syntactical torment it inflicts on natural English word order . . . . It [the libretto's diction] seems to me now an awkwardness that, since Sessions accepted it, we, too, must accept—as an integral part of his opera.[26]

Montezuma succeeds despite these problems chiefly because the music, to borrow Susanne Langer's phrase, ''swallows'' not only the poetry but also the drama. Colorful and evocative, descriptive and vehement, the music propels this epic drama with its ''commanding form.''[27]

Figure 6.4. *Montezuma*, Juilliard American Opera Center Production, 1982. Act 2, scene 4, Cortez (James Dietsch) and Montezuma (Robert Grayson) discuss a portrait of King Carlos. Courtesy Juilliard American Opera Center. (*Beth Bergman*)

Psalm 140   **1963**
                                         (Score Marked Princeton 2 June 1963)

Commission: Princeton Theological Seminary in Commemoration of its Sesquicentennial Anniversary
Dedication: "To Janice Harsanyi"
Published by Edward B. Marks, 1964, Organ Version. Orchestral Score not Published. Sketches
    at Princeton University Library.
Premieres: 1963, Princeton Theological Seminary, Janice Harsanyi, Soprano, with Organ; 11 February
    1966, Boston Symphony Orchestra, Anne Elgar, Soprano, Erich Leinsdorf Conducting.

Although the commission called for organ and the published work is scored for
organ, in Sessions's mind the unpublished orchestral version of this work is the
definitive one. Sessions's opinion about the organ has not changed since he wrote
the Chorale: "You hear the notes on the organ and an organist can make them
sound quite nicely. But I've got to have an accent—you can't make an accent on
the organ."[28]

About writing the piece Sessions says:

> They wanted a religious text. And this is a Presbyterian institution [the Princeton Theological
> Seminary]. I'm *not* a Presbyterian at all, of any kind. I'm a Catholic fellow-traveler in a way.
> And I was very upset by what was going on in the world. I wanted to find something that would
> say something that meant something to me. The first part of the Psalm is about Senator Goldwater
> and people who wanted to go right to town with the bomb. The last part of the Psalm is about
> Pope John. Well, Pope John died the day I finished it and I thought of him.[29]

He thought of dedicating the work to Pope John but reconsidered, thinking it might
be construed as odd because of the denomination of the Princeton Seminary.

In the program notes for the Boston Symphony Orchestra performance Sessions wrote:

> I had in mind from the beginning a certain kind of biblical text, which, as conceived musically
> by me, would require the full resources of a dramatic solo voice. I chose the text of this Psalm
> after much searching in the Bible for exactly what I wanted. The text is that of the King James
> version . . . it is this version [the orchestral] that I consider definitive. There is very little dif-
> ference in the actual notes of the two versions, but the orchestra yields more flexibility of nuance,
> more transparency, and more sharpness of outline.[30]

Psalm 140 was begun while Sessions was still working on the orchestration
of *Montezuma*. "I feel that *Montezuma* had a very, very strong influence on all
the music I've written since."[31] The element of exoticism in *Montezuma*'s orchestration affected the orchestration of subsequent works, and his instrumental vocabulary
had also grown. In *Psalm 140* Sessions incorporates a heckelphone for an effect
at m. 26, the pedal E below middle C, on the words "Keep me, O Lord." "I
wanted a tone somewhat like the English horn. But the lowest note on the English
horn is that E, and it's almost impossible to play it very softly."[32] Orchestras lacking
heckelphones could assign the note to bassoon.

The row is fairly obviously stated in the opening vocal line, m. 4: F♯, E, C, D♯, G♯, D: G, C♯, B, A, F, B♭.

The writer of the review for the *Christian Science Monitor* pointed to a contradiction in mood, which might be attributed to the angry attitude Sessions expressed above.

> But Mr. Sessions' piece also went contrary to the mood of the psalm itself. "Deliver me, O Lord, from the evil man," sang David: "preserve me from the violent man; which imagine mischiefs in their heart; continually are they gathered together for war."
> Whereupon the composer unleashes his atonal energies in stabs of violence, in stirrings of mischief, in explosions of war. Mr. Sessions has set a prayer to music as if it were an angry prayer. But the petitioner is not angry. He is asking to be saved from the effects of anger.
> Yet how many composers could resist the meaning of such words as violence, mischief, war? They fall right into an expressionist's hands. And Mr. Sessions displayed his usual skill in manipulating the orchestral forces to stunning effect. His writing for the voice, too, was intelligently done; it was at least singable by the right kind of singer.[33]

Symphony No. 5   1964

Commission: Eugene Ormandy
Dedication: "To Eugene Ormandy"
Published by Edward B. Marks, 1971. Sketches at Princeton University Library.
Premiere: 7 February 1964, Philadelphia Orchestra, Eugene Ormandy Conducting.
I. Tranquillo—Allegro molto
II. Lento
III. Allegro deciso
(Played without Pause)

H. Wiley Hitchcock writes of the Fifth Symphony:

> The Fifth Symphony seems the most accessible of recent works by Sessions. That density of texture which we have come to expect from him, and which has led to so many comparisons between him and Schönberg, is here offset by clean-limbed, sharply profiled foreground melody.[34]

He also points to the rhythmic relationship between the two melodies of the first movement and the iambic (eighth-quarter-eighth-quarter) rhythms of the background material of all the movements.

While Sessions composed the Fifth Symphony and *Psalm 140*, he was orchestrating *Montezuma*. The orchestral color that he had achieved in *Montezuma* was to influence all successive works, especially in the writing for percussion. In the first movement of the Fifth Symphony, for example at m. 105, Sessions writes a section for alto flute, an instrument he has loved since *The Black Maskers*. What shows *Montezuma*'s influence, however, is the counterpoint written for it—on marimba. This produces a new texture in Sessions's music.

The first movement can be analyzed generally as an introduction (Tranquillo), A (Allegro molto), B, and A—a kind of arch form. A bass drum roll connects the second movement to the first. Above this the trombones spell out the row (F, A♭, E♭, A, D, E: C♯, C, B♭, F♯, G, B), mm. 140–43. Sessions was to later use the trombone to connect movements again: A trombone melody opens the third movement of the Ninth Symphony, serving as a transition from its second movement. After the opening of the second movement of the Fifth Symphony,

> there are three different episodes: first, brass, trumpet, and horns are almost choralelike [mm. 143–46]. An interlude [m. 149] is much more rhapsodic. Then [m. 150] the chorale comes back, longer. The second time this expands. Then the choralelike episode returns, which is really a trumpet solo with accompaniment. This episode becomes more elaborate. In the course of this another idea, on the oboe, accompanied by alto flute [Un poco meno mosso e tranquillo] occurs. Finally [m. 183], it comes in the last time, more subdued. It ends up, instead of the trombone, you have the trumpet muted answered by the oboe and cello [mm. 190–96].[35]

(The third movement of the Ninth Symphony also contains a brass choralelike idea.) The third movement of the Fifth Symphony operates in a regular $\frac{7}{4}$ time.

> There is a little episode with rather short phrases in the middle. The $\frac{7}{4}$ comes back and this comes in on the tuba [m. 244]. The climax begins at m. 263 and quiets down with a very quiet, very nice ending [from tranquillo, m. 273, to the end], if I may say so, which is a kind of variation of the very beginning.

This episode acts as an alternating idea on the woodwinds. The trumpet theme at mm. 265ff foreshadows the trumpet theme of the first movement of the Sixth Symphony. Both the Fifth and the Eighth Symphonies have prologues and epilogues and are played from beginning to end without pause. (The Seventh Symphony and the Divertimento also have epilogues.)

In order to provide a sense of conclusion Sessions generally ends his loud and vigorous works on a downbeat. However, in his works that end quietly, he usually prepares for the conclusion by sustaining one low pitch while the melodic material peters out above it, the "Sessions ending." Such is the case, for example, with the Fifth Symphony, *Montezuma*, the Eighth Symphony, and the Concerto for Orchestra, and the Cantata (see ex. 7.4).

Andrew Imbrie sums up Sessions's style in his symphonies with the following remarks.

> It is, then, a general sense of hierarchy that imparts to Sessions's music so much of its structural durability. Not only the accents, but also the relative lengths of phrases, the relative complexity, duration, and dynamic force of climaxes, and the manner in which they are approached and dissolved, the alternation of tempi, the development, recall, and dissolution of motives—all these are adjusted so that the resultant distribution of weight is unequal. And this inequality permits us to make the necessary distinctions between events of local and general import, of foreground and background. Yet even this sense of hierarchy can be, and is, subjected to strain, as in the cases we have seen, where the controlling meter becomes irregular, and is threatened by the pulse of the surface detail; or where a transitional figure appears to take on an expressive significance beyond its function, before acknowledging that function; or where, indeed, any

musical element can become something other than what it seems at first to be. The ever-present potentiality of flux is checked by the will of an artist whose sense of musical perspective allows him to create the most various and uncannily convincing solutions.[36]

Also convincing is the immediate awareness that each new orchestral work of Sessions is not only a vital continuation of the symphonic tradition, but also one in a succession of works that could have only been written by this composer. From *The Black Maskers* Orchestral Suite to the Concerto for Orchestra Sessions has developed a unique and recognizable orchestral profile: the strident sonority of violins in their highest register refusing octave doubling; the blurred warmth of the brass interweaving in a dense counterpoint that cannot be untangled; the black laughter of woodwinds, which breaks off into florid bel cantolike solos of intense expression played by piccolo, alto flute, bass clarinet, even contrabassoon; the brittle foreground of xylophone and marimba; and the ominous drums and maracas. With utmost resolve Sessions seems to be continually writing one great work that, to paraphrase Paul Valéry's words, is never finished, only temporarily abandoned.

Piano Sonata No. 3   1965

Commission: Eugene Istomin
Published by Edward B. Marks, 1969. First Movement Manuscript at the Princeton University Library.
Premiere: March 1969, Berkeley, California, Jacob Lateiner, Pianist.
I. Adagio e misterioso—Sostenuto
II. Molto allegro e con fuoco
III. Lento e molto tranquillo (*In Memoriam: November 22, 1963*)

The third movement of the Third Sonata is Sessions's elegy to John F. Kennedy. Sessions learned of the President's assassination in Berlin.

> I came down in the morning to have breakfast. The waitress [at the Berlin Academy] said, "We've heard about what happened to your President. He was assassinated in Dallas." This was all in German. And I wouldn't believe it. But obviously . . . she showed me the newspaper and it was obviously true and I had this idea and I went up to my room and thought of that [pointing to the music in ex. 6.3].[37]

Example 6.3.   Piano Sonata No. 3, III, mm. 1–4.
          © 1969 by Edward B. Marks Music Company.
          Used by permission.

Lento e molto tranquillo ($\downarrow = 44$)

Example 6.4. Piano Sonata No. 3, I, mm. 1–3.
© 1969 by Edward B. Marks Music Company.
Used by permission.

For years Sessions had an idea in mind that he planned to use in a piano work some day. The first sketch of the third movement was that idea; it is related to the opening melody of the first movement as an inverted expansion of its whole-tone gesture. The opening of the piece (see ex. 6.4) is mirrored by the ending of the last movement: F#–A, E#–G#.

The through-composed first movement expands upon three gestures: the whole-tone descent, a dotted figure plus a syncopated figure, and a repeated-note passage. The development of this sonata movement begins at m. 24 and the recapitulation at m. 60. A unifying feature of the work is its trichordal use of the row (Ab, F, A, Gb, E, C: G, Cb, Db, Eb, Bb, D). The last two measures bring the retrograde of the row, ending therefore on a minor third, F–Ab.

The second movement can be described as a rondo, the opening accented eighth-note upward sweep providing the rondo's articulation points. In Campbell's dissertation on the three sonatas, the form of this movement is described as a sonata with retrograde recapitulation.[38] Cone writes of the second movement's più tranquillo section: "Not only is the accompaniment more independently conceived throughout [than the accompaniment in the Lento of the Second Sonata] but it develops the same material as the melody, although in individual fashion."[39] The row is stated in trichords in the original form at the end of the movement.

The third movement proceeds in free variation form. Campbell describes it as "three large sections each delineated by a recurrence of the opening theme of the movement," which he calls a "monothematic ternary design."[40] The variation technique pervades the movement at a fundamental level: "Each phrase has to add something; it has to get more interesting as it goes on," Sessions says. Cone writes of the third movement:

> The harrowing climax is a broad plateau rather than a peak. It is built on a succession of chords each of which is presented with sufficient emphasis—by repetition or by isolation—to allow it to make its own point tellingly. At the same time each is bound to its neighbors by a progression that is made to seem all the more relentless by the consistent development of an easily discernible three-note motif that permeates the texture.[41]

Intricate rhythms and polyrhythms have been mentioned as a characteristic of Sessions's style. Of this Campbell writes:

> Sessions shapes time more directly in the third sonata than either of the [two earlier sonatas]. The rhythmic texture refers much more to the immediate context; it imparts an almost rhetorical quality to gestures at all levels. It is as if Sessions combines the rhythmic freedom and spontaneity of the recitative with the coordination and culmination of the aria.[42]

Discussing the rhythmic aspect of this work, Sessions revealed:

> Of course, I think *always* my tendency has been to get rid of rigid regular meter, be free of it, which doesn't mean never having it. But it means letting a melodic line, for instance, develop as naturally and as expressively as possible.
> I think music has gradually left behind the structure of rigid bar lines, for instance. I think in no first-class composer does the bar line mean that the first beat of the measure should be accented, except in waltzes, of course.[43]

Rhythm plays an important role in articulating phrase structure. Sessions says, "If music isn't clearly articulated, it's for me a great weakness. And things have to have a definite beginning and a definite ending. I think of rhythm in terms of phrase structure first of all, rather than simply in terms of note values." To Sessions bars consist of small musical units within these phrase substructures. "A measure to me means a certain section of music that really goes together as one unit. But very often I will have an ⅜ measure in which I have one beat of two eighths and two other beats of three eighths." Irregularity is maintained within the bar as well as within the individual beat. The result is as much mobility, free movement, and avoidance of regular accents as possible. Bar lines are frequently the last detail Sessions writes in his music.

As in Pages from a Diary and the Divertimento, Sessions again uses meters and rhythm to illuminate form. Contrast of rhythmic freedom with rhythmic regularity helps to distinguish formal articulations in, for example, the first movement.

Concerning pitch material, Sessions says:

> Freedom can really only exist in a specific given framework. What the row does is to establish a region. And in my music you can move around in the region fairly freely, if it's really definitely

established, you see. . . . But I would say it's the *music* that has to be organized, not simply the notes. Because very often people assume that if you can find *some* kind of organization there, whether it has any relation to what you actually hear or experience in hearing, or should think of in hearing, that then you've disposed of the problem. I don't think you've *approached* the problem in those terms. It has to be organized in terms of the musical ideas. In other words, things have to have connections and if one's ear recognizes those connections—they make sense—that's what's important. But just because you have A♭, F, A♮, C♯ somewhere else, that's not necessarily going to make a recognizable connection.

Despite the fact that Sessions's piano music is idiomatic, pianists nevertheless complain about its extreme difficulty. As a pianist Sessions's own technique improved tremendously with the aid of his friend Arthur Schnabel during a four-hour lesson in 1945. Schnabel coached Sessions and the cellist he was accompanying on Beethoven.

Eugene Istomin, who commissioned the Third Piano Sonata, found it too difficult to play. Sessions presented him with the penciled manuscript. After a four-year delay, Jacob Lateiner gave the work its premiere. Robert Helps has made an excellent recording (see appendix 3). Other distinguished performers of the work include Alan Feinberg and Rebecca LaBreque.

The difficulty of the sonata has given rise to two other dissertations on this work: Duffin's *The Interpretation of Accent Signs in Roger Sessions's Third Piano Sonata* and Merryman's *Aspects of Phrasing and Pitch Usage in Roger Sessions's Piano Sonata No. 3.*[44]

Symphony No. 6   1966
(Manuscript Marked Tanglewood, 5 July 1966)

Commission: The New Jersey Symphony in Celebration of the 300th Anniversary of the State of New Jersey
Published by Theodore Presser, 1975. Sketches at Princeton University Library.
Premieres: 19 November 1966, Newark, New Jersey, New Jersey Symphony, Kenneth Schermerhorn Conducting; 4 March 1977, New York City, The Juilliard Orchestra, Jose Serebrier Conducting.
I. Allegro
II. Adagio e tranquillo
III. Allegro moderato

Only the first two movements of this commission from the New Jersey Symphony were ready by the due date, January 1966. The orchestra performed these two movements of the Sixth Symphony in January. It was not until the following fall that all three movements were first heard.

At that time Sessions apparently saw the Sixth Symphony as a sequel to the Fifth. A review in the Philadelphia *Evening Bulletin* discussed this:

The work is a companion piece to his Fifth Symphony, given its premiere by the Philadelphia Orchestra two years ago. And, as the composer has hinted, his latest symphony is a continuation of his Fifth. It seethes with the same taut, restless energy. It has the same concentration of thought. It speaks the same language of accumulated wisdom and passion.[45]

Whatever Sessions thought of the Sixth Symphony at the time, in retrospect he views it as the first of a trilogy of symphonies (the Sixth, the Seventh, and the Eighth), all written within three years and all related in his mind to contemporary events, particularly the Vietnam war.

Despite its initial success both in the press and with audiences, Symphony No. 6 was destined to join other works that languished years between performances. For Sessions's eightieth birthday in 1976 The Juilliard School gave the Symphony its second performance and New York premiere. Donal Henahan wrote of the infrequent performance of Sessions and other contemporary composers: "This sort of time lag is hard for an older composer to take, unless he has the patience of a Roger Sessions, but for a comparative unknown it can be crippling. Mr. Sessions, serene in the conviction of his music's ultimate worth, has not let neglect cripple him."[46]

The New York performance was to Sessions the real premiere of the work. The original New Jersey Symphony performance was "unrecognizable as my music, except for a bass clarinet solo."[47] The acoustics of Alice Tully Hall helped to reveal the subtleties of the work. What had seemed unconnected and imbalanced in a rehearsal room became crystalline and smooth in performance. It was a lesson in all the intangibles with which a composer has to deal: qualities of orchestration, projection, texture, and conditions of performance. For orchestral players, hearing no one but immediate colleagues, Sessions's sound seemed complicated and disjunct with little inherent meaning out of context. Only when the listener can hear connections among sections can he or she understand the full musical sentence.

The role of a good performance in helping an audience appreciate "difficult" modern music cannot be underestimated. The Juilliard Orchestra fully deserved the following praise:

> The performance seemed almost flawless, which was all the more striking because the writing is so intricate, and it was a great credit to the student orchestra. . . . It is a remarkably transparent score, characteristic in its high degree of activity and beautiful workmanship.[48]

During the 1983–1984 season the San Francisco Symphony performed the work on numerous occasions under the direction of Edo de Waart.

The repeated major ninth interval of the initial idea of the first movement is a characteristic and memorable shape that the listener can identify as a unifying element. It reappears in inversion, most notably at Tempo I°, m. 148.

The third movement's material is treated so freely that it "almost has no theme at all, except the trumpet call at the beginning, which comes back of course." The trumpet line has the row: G, C♯, D, C, A♭, B: B♭, E, D♯, A, F, F♯.

> You have reminiscences, but in quite different form, in all my music from the Third Symphony on. It's a more static recalling of the same ideas. By static, I mean that it isn't moving constantly from place to place, harmonically and otherwise. In this style recapitulation in the old sense of the word would not work at all. There's always movement heard. The movement you might say is planned on dynamic terms.[49]

This led to a discussion of variation:

> Essentially it's always a question of variation. It's the same material, but it's variation within a certain framework. It's not so free as a set of variations, because they all have a certain character in common. The variations are simply the vehicle for the form. It's not Variation 1, Variation 2, and Variation 3. It's a constant process of variation in a certain direction.[50]

Six Pieces for Violoncello   1966
**(Score Marked Tanglewood, Massachusetts,
Berkeley, California, August–October 1968)**

Dedication: "To my Son, John"
Published by Edward B. Marks, 1967. Sketches at Princeton University Library.
New York Premiere: 31 March 1968, ISCM All-Sessions Concert, John Sessions, Cello (Earlier Performances in Northampton, Massachusetts).
I. Prelude
II. Dialogue
III. Scherzo
IV. Berceuse
V. Fantasy
VI. Epilogue

Although Sessions maintains that he named the movements of this work after he composed them, programmatic elements related to familial associations played a role in the composition. And, of course, Prelude and Epilogue are logical names for the first and last pieces of a set.

The participants in the Dialogue, Sessions and his son, neither argue nor question and answer one another; it is a friendly conversation. Sessions describes the movement: "Let's say I start to talk about a certain subject—I couldn't tell you what we'd be talking about—and then my son comments at some length, and then I say, 'But . . . .' (My daughter used to say, when she was a little girl, 'I hate that word—but.')"[51] Assuming the first phrase represents Sessions talking, then the second phrase at mm. 8–13 could be John. M. 14 is a variation of the opening, therefore representing the first speaker. At m. 10 the second speaker begins timidly, pianissimo sul tasto non vibrato, and becomes more animated with an accelerando and a crescendo to fortissimo with note values speeding up to thirty-second notes. The "last word," a reiteration of the opening trichord, is had by the first speaker (Sessions). Because of interpretative problems, this piece is the most difficult of the six to perform.

The Berceuse has very definite associations for Sessions. After his granddaughter (John's daughter, Teresa) was born he saw her lying in her crib and immediately thought of the opening (see ex. 6.5) The minor third and major third derive from the first tetrachord of the retrograde of the row (the original is: B, E, Bb, C, Db, A: G♯, F♯, Eb, G, D, F). The piece ends with the minor third appearing in inversion, reminiscent of its original appearance. The Fantasy provides contrast to the preceding movement and opens with the inverted form of the row.

Example 6.5. Six Pieces for Violoncello, IV, Berceuse, mm. 1–4.
© 1967 by Edward B. Marks Music Company.
Used by permission.

In an interview about twentieth-century cello music one performer of the Six Pieces, Joel Krosnick, offers his opinion: "Roger Sessions's pieces on the other hand are more fascinating music compositions than they are *cello* pieces. The cello writing supports the musical structure, but he shows very little interest in really exploring the instrument's unique timbral possibilities."[52]

A *Village Voice* review commented that the work was

> . . . a superb creation. One has the sense that these short statements were being improvised on the spot. A line is played, then is followed by an imitation of itself in truncated version—as if the original phrase had been forgotten and a new thought came suddenly to the composer. Silences well-timed are another virtue of the work.[53]

John Sessions has also performed the Double Concerto, written for him, in the early 1970s. In 1979 Sessions began a Duo for Violin and Cello for John and his violinist wife, Giovina. The Concerto for Orchestra interrupted that project, which was not resumed.

Symphony No. 7   1967
(Score Marked Berkeley, November 1966; Princeton, July 1967)

Commission: In Celebration of the Sesquicentennial Anniversary of the University of Michigan
Dedication: Jean Martinon
Published by Theodore Presser, 1977. Sketches and Manuscripts at Princeton University Library.
Premiere: 1 October 1967, Ann Arbor, Michigan, Chicago Symphony Orchestra, Jean Martinon
   Conducting.
I. Allegro con fuoco
II. Lento e dolce
III. Allegro misurato

Sessions has called this symphony his favorite. It can be seen as the second member of a trilogy of symphonies about the state of the world, especially the war in Vietnam. Extramusical influences on the symphony were the war and the semipornographic book *The Story of O,* a novel of horror that struck Sessions deeply.

The first movement comprises an ABA form with divisions at m. 90 (B) and m. 158 (return of A). M. 240 begins a coda. The piece ends, predictably enough for Sessions, with a retrograde statement of the row. The row appears at the beginning: G (first chord), E♭ on the tuba and double bass, F and E in the violins, B in the bassoon and bass clarinet, C: A, D, G♯ on trombones, F♯, B♭, and C♯.

The two initial ideas of the slow movement return, m. 63, in reverse order.

The last movement is rather grim. It has a kind of scherzo with dark rumblings underneath. It's the most brutal [movement] except for the very end. The main part of the third movement ends in a sort of impasse with an ostinato on the horns, which gets slower and slower. And then the Epilogue was very slow. And if I may say so, that's about the best ending I ever wrote. Or one of them. It's quite unusual[54] [see ex. 6.6].

Example 6.6.   Symphony No. 7, ending of the third movement, mm. 161–66.
                © 1977 by Merion Music, Inc.
                Used by permission of the publisher.

A contrasting element appears at Allegretto un poco scherzando, m. 35, in the same tempo but a different subdivision. When preparing the score for publication Sessions changed this by bringing the lower instrument's mutterings into more relief against the prevailing ⅜ (m. 38). There he added the pizzicato, made the strings' entrance clearer, and later wrote in quasi misterioso. "This was one score that I really revised before publication, especially the last movement."[55]

Another idea comes in at m. 63 on the E-flat clarinet. M. 86 is a variation of the opening of the movement, with differences evidenced in the use of the row and in the orchestration. A quiet epilogue follows after the music has worked back into ⅜ time. In the epilogue several instruments drop out and never return: contrabassoon, trumpets, trombones, tuba, percussion, xylophone, vibraphone, but not piano (as the score indicates).

Example 6.7. Symphony No. 7, row and its combinatorial inversion.

Example 6.7 shows the row for the Symphony and its inversion at eleven semitones, the transposition of the inversion that produces six new notes in each of the hexachords. This combinatorial relationship is exploited throughout the work.

Symphony No. 8   1968

Commission: The New York Philharmonic for its 125th Anniversary
Dedication: "To My Daughter, Elizabeth"
Published by Edward B. Marks, 1973. Sketches at Princeton University Library.
Premiere: 2 May 1968, New York City, New York Philharmonic, William Steinberg Conducting.
I. Adagio e mesto
II. Allegro con fuoco
(Played without Pause)

The Eighth Symphony, one of the most quickly written of Sessions's pieces, was composed in just four months. By 1968 Sessions was somewhat numb to the war. Of the three symphonies, the Sixth, Seventh, and Eighth, Sessions feels this one represents a resignation in mood to the political events that had before stirred his musical wrath.

Both the Fifth and the Eighth Symphonies have prologues and epilogues and both are played from beginning to end without pause. Sessions describes the slow movement of the Eighth as containing three episodes.[56] The opening theme comes back before the last episode and again at the end of the work. Two main figures—a rhythmic figure of two notes and a four-note (later a five-note) figure—occur twice, interrupted by muted violins and violas (see ex. 6.8). The meter then breaks into irregular groups during which woodwinds and violins carry on a dialogue.

The second episode is begun by an oboe melody whose three entrances mark three sections. The second section reintroduces the five-note figure in the high register of violins. The third section begins with the English horn and moves ahead to a climax. The music in the maracas leads to the final episode, which consists of melodic fragments and of the opening material; this episode ends with a return to the original two-note rhythmic figure.

The second movement's two fast sections are characterized by a three-note motive at the beginning, reappearing frequently in inversion. After the first section a quieter episode follows in which a solo violin appears. The climax in the

Example 6.8.   Symphony No. 8, I, two figures.
            © 1973 by Edward B. Marks Music Company.
            Used by permission.

first fast section is followed by a harp solo. A new three-note figure gives rise
to new material. After this section's climax, a solo violin returns to the descending
idea that began the work.

Andrew Imbrie describes the Eighth as "a study in flexibility."[57] He notes
the large-scale metrical freedom, the malleable beat within the measure, and the
alternating quarter and dotted quarter-note values, all of which produce a flexible,
unpredictable beat in all dimensions of the piece. He describes this as "unequal
distribution of all types of weight."

> Sections vary greatly in absolute size, and the relations among them are at once modified and
> clarified by the presence or absence (and by the kinds and degrees) of connecting ritardandi
> and accelerandi. Sometimes the smallest suggestion of a return, because of its exquisitely calculated
> placement, will serve to recapitulate (as in the first recalling of the prologue idea). Sometimes
> a separate section, possessing enough individuality to render it capable of formal autonomy,
> turns out to be really transitional in nature, because of the gradual way in which the rhythms
> change.[58]

Sessions describes it as " . . . a kind of prose rhythm in a way. People have
said that about the Cantata. The Cantata reproduces the rhythms of Walt Whitman, because I love them and find them congenial."[59] The notion of prose rhythm
suggests a possibility of prose, of a hidden vocal program to the work. Since Sessions was aware of contemporary political events, which had a profound effect
on the writing of this symphony, it is not impossible to imagine an American prose
text underlying these rhythms.

The row is stated more unmistakably than in any other of Sessions's works: at the outset by the violins, accompanied only by the insistent eerie crescendo and diminuendo of the maracas. These sound to Sessions like a "snake in the under-bush." The row's notes are E, F, G, Bb, F#, B: C, A, C#, D#, D, and G#.

Printed reaction to the premiere ranged from outright dislike to the kind of enthusiasm that reviewers feel they should express. For example, the *New York Post* described the work as "easier to admire than love on the first hearing."[60] Harold Schonberg called it "a severe, dissonant, unmelodic piece, beautifully scored and orchestrated. It has almost everything but individuality. . . . It even has melodic contours, or at least as melodic as 12-tone music can get."[61] Audience reaction was only mildly polite. The piece "laid one of the big eggs of the season. At the close few in the audience even realized it was over."[62]

The hostility shown by Winthrop Sargeant in *The New Yorker* is puzzling considering the beauty of this work. Sargeant envisioned two prognoses for Sessions's music: "Either it is a passing disease from which we shall one day recover or music is dead and Mr. Sessions is one of the most enthusiastic pallbearers."[63]

Rhapsody for Orchestra   1970

Commission: Baltimore Symphony Orchestra
Dedication: Sergiu Comissiona
Published by Theodore Presser, 1981. Manuscript at Princeton University Library.
Premieres: March 1970, Baltimore, Maryland, Sergiu Comissiona Conducting; 12 January 1981, New York City, The Brooklyn Philharmonia, Lukas Foss Conducting.

Sessions describes the Rhapsody: "The title implies for me a work of essentially lyrical and quasi-improvisatory character, in which strong contrasts appear on a relatively small scale."[64] Writing the Rhapsody was a reaction to composing the Cantata. This piece was written extremely quickly, in just two months, at the end of the six-year period of work on *When Lilacs Last in the Dooryard Bloom'd*.

The ten-minute work is divided into three sections and an epilogue. The first section, Allegro, presents rhythmic ideas, variants of these, and two episodes; a broad phrase on the violins and woodwinds and a gentler phrase in the oboe are answered by bassoon and clarinet. This rises to a climax, followed by a contrasting episode introduced by the trombones over a staccato bassoon figure. After a second and greater climax is reached the first two episodes are recalled.

A rallentando and pause lead to the second section, Andante e molto espressivo, begun by a long phrase on muted violins accompanied by the English horn. The texture becomes more animated with the appearance of a flute melody and an oboe melody. A tremelo in muted violins and violin melody lead to the Andante.

The Molto vivace e giocoso in $\frac{2}{4}$ is characterized by short motives, lively gestures, and quick changes in orchestration. A contrasting phrase begun in two unison trombones climaxes fortissimo in the full orchestra. A return to $\frac{3}{8}$ precedes a six-octave descent in the orchestra, landing on a low E.

Five chords lead into the recitative epilogue, beginning on the trombone and passing to the cello, violas, and violins, all accompanied by a group of woodwinds and interrupted three times by short passages. The end brings a reminder of the beginning.

The work's performance in New York by the Baltimore Symphony was greeted with ambivalence:

> Mr. Sessions made his new ten-minute work relatively easy to listen to, if not particularly direct in statement. Its twists and turns may conceal more expressive substance than is detectable on first hearing, but it is also possible that the Rhapsody is not top-drawer Sessions.[65]

Such reactions by the *New York Times* have become so regular as to be predictable. Indeed, Sessions has said he would "worry" about his music if he got a good review from *Times* reviewers.

Sessions was retired from Princeton in 1965. That year he began teaching at The Juilliard School. He moved from the house the University had given him at 70 Alexander Street to 63 Stanworth Lane, and until 1983 he commuted to New York, staying overnight once a week.

He spent the academic year 1966–1967 at Berkeley, 1967–1968 at Juilliard, and 1968–1969 as Charles Eliot Norton Professor at Harvard University. From 1969 to 1983 he taught yearly at The Juilliard School, including a graduate seminar on Stravinsky and Schoenberg and a doctoral course on advanced composition and analysis. He usually taught about six private students a year at Juilliard. (During the 1970s he spent many summers in Franconia, New Hampshire, or in Lichtenstein.) In addition to performing his opera, *The Trial of Lucullus,* Juilliard also performed his Double Concerto for Violin and Cello (which it commissioned), his Sixth Symphony, and *Montezuma*, as well as numerous chamber works. Sessions enjoyed returning to a conservatory atmosphere, which he missed after leaving the Cleveland Institute.

The publication in 1970 of Sessions's 1968 Norton lectures brought to an end his long career as a writer. For 41 years—from 1926 to 1967—Sessions had published an average of at least one article a year and produced four books. In the late 1960s Sessions abandoned the elephantine torso of a fifth entitled simply *Music*, relieved when the publishers no longer seemed interested. Writing books had subtracted time from work on his music. Eventually, he felt he had "written more prose than [he] had any business to." *Questions About Music* represents the summation of his musical thought at the end of five creative periods of work.

Another change for Sessions took place at the beginning of the 1970s. After a long association with Edward B. Marks Music Company and despite the fact that his close friend and editor, Felix Greissle, worked for the music publishers, Sessions decided to switch publishers. Composer and colleague Vincent Persichetti persuaded him to let his music be handled by Theodore Presser Company and its subsidiary, Merion Music.

Sessions's move back to a conservatory, his cessation of prose output, his change of publishers, and his return to New York all heralded a new creative decade.

Notes

1. John Harbison, "Roger Sessions and 'Montezuma,' " *Tempo* 121 (June 1977): 3.

2. Taped interview 14 April 1976.

3. Taped interview 21 February 1979.

4. Taped interview 9 October 1979.

5. Taped interview 21 February 1979.

6. Andrea Olmstead, "The Plum'd Serpent: Antonio Borgese's and Roger Sessions's *Montezuma*," *Tempo* 152 (March 1985). Charles Mason, *A Comprehensive Analysis of Roger Sessions's Opera Montezuma* (DMA diss.: University of Illinois, 1982), unpublished.

7. Roger Sessions, Program notes for the Opera Company of Boston, 1976.

8. Edward C. Laufer, "Roger Sessions: *Montezuma*," *Perspectives of New Music* 4 (Fall 1965): 104.

9. Laufer, "Roger Sessions: *Montezuma*," p. 97. Mason, *Comprehensive Analysis,* p. 136.

10. Sessions, Program notes.

11. Laufer, "Roger Sessions: *Montezuma,* " p. 104. Mason, *Comprehensive Analysis,* p. 52 n. 2.

12. Peter Maxwell Davies, " 'Montezuma' Creates a Stir in Berlin," *New York Times* (3 May 1964), p. 2, 11:3.

13. Ibid.

14. Harbison, "Roger Sessions and 'Montezuma,' " p. 5.

15. "The Bland Giant," *Time* 83 (8 May 1964): 50.

16. Taped interview 21 January 1976.

17. Ibid.

18. Taped interview 14 April 1976.

19. Harbison, "Roger Sessions and 'Montezuma,' " p. 5.

20. Irving Kolodin, "Opera and the Power That Corrupts," *Saturday Review,* 15 May 1976.

21. William Bender, "Three for the Opera," *Time* (12 April 1976): 84.

22. Leighton Kerner, "An American Opera Comes Home," *Village Voice,* April 1976.

23. John Rockwell, "Sessions's 'Montezuma' Comes to U.S.," *New York Times,* 2 April 1976.

24. Andrew Porter, "The Matter of Mexico," *The New Yorker,* 19 April 1976.

25. Peter G. Davis, "Montezuma's Revenge," *New York Magazine* (8 March 1982): 89.

26. Andrew Porter, "The Magnificent Epic," *The New Yorker* (March 1982): 128.

27. Suzanne K. Langer, *Feeling and Form* (New York: Charles Scribners Sons, 1953), pp. 122, 149–68.

28. Taped interview 3 December 1975.

29. Ibid.

30. Roger Sessions, "Psalm 140 for Soprano and Orchestra," Boston Symphony Programs, 11–12 February 1966, pp. 984–985.

31. Taped interview 3 December 1975.

32. Ibid.

33. Harold Rogers, "Sessions' Psalm 140," *The Christian Science Monitor,* 12 February 1966.

34. H. Wiley Hitchcock, "Current Chronicle," *The Musical Quarterly* 50 (July 1964): 381.

35. Untaped conversation 14 December 1977.

36. Andrew Imbrie, "The Symphonies of Roger Sessions," *Tempo* 103 (1972): 31.

37. Taped interview 14 January 1976.

38. Michael Ian Campbell, *The Piano Sonatas of Roger Sessions: Sequel to a Tradition* (DMA diss.: Peabody Institute, 1982), unpublished, pp. 165–66.

39. Edward T. Cone, "In Defense of Song: The Contribution of Roger Sessions," *Critical Inquiry* 2, no. 1 (Autumn 1975): 109.

40. Campbell, *The Piano Sonatas,* pp. 166, 168.

41. Cone, "In Defense of Song," p. 104.

42. Campbell, *The Piano Sonatas,* pp. 211–12.

43. This and all subsequent Sessions quotations in this section are taken from taped interview 11 January 1978.

44. Diana Ruth Duffin, *The Interpretation of Accent Signs in Roger Sessions's Third Piano Sonata* (DMA diss.: Ohio State University, 1979), unpublished. Marjorie Merryman, *Aspects of Phrasing and Pitch Usage in Roger Sessions's Piano Sonata No. 3* (Ph.D. diss.: Brandeis University, 1981), unpublished.

45. James Felton, "New Sessions Work Has World Premiere," *The Evening Bulletin* [Philadelphia], 21 November 1966.

46. Donal Henahan, "For Roger Sessions, a Tribute and a Premiere at 80," *New York Times,* 4 March 1977.

47. Untaped conversation. The orchestra then contained many amateurs, while now everyone in it is professional.

48. Raymond Ericson, "Concert: Symphony by Sessions," *New York Times,* 6 March 1977.

49. Taped interview 22 March 1977.

50. Ibid.

51. Taped interview 4 February 1976.

52. Joel Krosnick, Program notes for *The Cello: A Twentieth Century American Retrospective,* 9 January 1984, The Juilliard Theater. Interview with Perry Goldstein.

53. *The Village Voice,* 18 April 1968.

54. Taped interviews 25 February 1976 and 10 May 1977.

55. Taped interview 17 January 1979.

56. Roger Sessions, "Symphony No. 8," *Argo* ZRG 702 liner notes.

57. Imbrie, "Symphonies," p. 30.

58. Ibid.

59. Taped interview 11 February 1976.

60. Harriet Johnson, *New York Post,* 3 May 1968.

61. Harold Schonberg, "Music: Steinberg Leads Philharmonic in New Sessions Work," *New York Times* (3 May 1968), p. 41:4.

62. *Time,* 10 May 1968.

63. Winthrop Sargeant, "Is Music Dead?" *The New Yorker* (11 May 1968): 140.

64. Roger Sessions, "Rhapsody for Orchestra," *Argo* ZRG 702 liner notes.

65. Allen Hughes, "Moderns Arrive from Baltimore," *New York Times,* 23 March 1970.

7

The Last Decade of Composition: 1970–1981

When Lilacs Last in the Dooryard Bloom'd

1964–1970
(Vocal Score Marked Princeton,
2 January 1970; Orchestral Score
Marked December 1970)

Cantata for Soprano, Contralto, and Baritone Soloists, Mixed Chorus, and Orchestra
Text by Walt Whitman
Commission: University of California to Commemorate its Centenary in 1964
Dedication: "To the Memory of Martin Luther King, Jr. and Robert F. Kennedy"
Published by Theodore Presser, 1974. Sketches at Princeton University Library. Manuscript in Composer's Personal Collection.
Premiere: 23 May 1971, Berkeley, California, Helene Joseph, Soprano, Stephanie Friedman, Contralto, Allen Shearer, Baritone, Michael Senturia Conducting.

In 1865, when Lincoln's funeral train made its way to Springfield, Illinois, Walt Whitman wrote *When Lilacs Last in the Dooryard Bloom'd*, published that year in *Sequel to Drum-Taps* and eventually in *Leaves of Grass*. Sessions's Cantata was also written under the spell of another tragic moment in our history:

> I wasn't thinking of anybody's assassination except Lincoln's when I started that second part, but then Martin Luther King was shot and Bobby Kennedy was shot. And his funeral train was passing through while I was writing that part ["Here, coffin that slowly passes, I give you my sprig of Lilac."] and I was affected by it.[1]

Sessions first encountered Whitman's poetry at Harvard during the winter of 1910–1911 when he bought *Leaves of Grass*. Asked why he did not pursue the notion of setting *Lilacs* then, Sessions responded:

> I'm sure I didn't think I was ready to cope with a thing like that. I made some sketches which I suppose I destroyed years ago. But I didn't like the sketches. I didn't think they did justice to the text. So I put it off. And then, years later, in 1964, I got a letter from the University of California asking me to write a choral piece for their anniversary.[2]

Perhaps the idea resurfaced in Sessions's mind when he was at the American Academy in Rome in 1930. His colleague there, Normand Lockwood, wrote an hour-long work for soloists, chorus, and orchestra entitled *Requiem* that illustrated Whitman's poem "Memories of President Lincoln."

Comparison with Hindemith's 1946 Requiem, on the same text, is inevitable.[3] Hindemith's setting was also written as an elegy, for Franklin D. Roosevelt. Sessions uses three soloists, Hindemith two. Both composers distribute the lines between soloists and chorus identically, except that Sessions assigns "Come, lovely and soothing Death" to the contralto soloist, while Hindemith gives it to the chorus. Sessions does not particularly like Hindemith's piece, saying Hindemith has never been one of his favorite composers.

Three themes dominate the poem and music. The lilacs, sung by the baritone, represent springtime. The star, sung by the chorus, symbolizes Lincoln. The hermit thrush, soprano soloist, represents the American countryside at the time of Lincoln's funeral, as well as death itself.

The piece is divided into three parts based on the logical demarcations of the poem. The first section, expository and short, introduces the three themes. The second section describes the pageantry of the progress of Lincoln's funeral train. The third is Whitman's contemplation of death.

An investigation of the marginalia Sessions wrote in his edition of *Leaves of Grass* reveals some of the thought processes of the composer. Many lines of poetry are underlined (like his handwritten copy of the *Idyll of Theocritus*). Brackets delineate omitted portions; for the most part those decisions remained. He assigns stanzas of poetry either to solo or to chorus; changes he later made are striking. For example, the last section of part one, "In the swamp," a soprano solo, was first assigned to chorus. The idea of a baritone soloist came to Sessions later; he is nowhere mentioned in the annotations. His long solo at the beginning of the third part is simply labeled "solo," and his lines in the middle of stanza 15, "And the singer so shy," were originally assigned to the chorus. The Death Carol following put Sessions in a quandary: It is marked "sopr. Contr?" The soprano's last solo, "To the tally of my soul," was first tentatively assigned to the chorus. At this late point in the text the most interesting annotations—music—begin to appear. An arrow is drawn from the words "deliberate notes" to the margin, where the music in example 7.1 appears. In stanza 19 chords were annotated for the "Victorious song" section; however, this whole section of poetry was later eliminated. In the final stanza two annotations appear: "Yet each I keep, and all, retrievements out of the night" (see ex. 7.2); and for the last words, "dusk and dim," Sessions gives each a note (see ex. 7.3).

Example 7.1.   *When Lilacs Last in the Dooryard Bloom'd,* marginalia.

Example 7.2. Marginalia.

Example 7.3. Marginalia.

The cumulative effect of Sessions's editing results in a more direct, immediate, pared-down version of Whitman's original text, less a personal vision than a general expression of sorrow. In addition, Sessions was concerned with the question of length: "I left out quite a lot in the last stanza because it's recapitulative and it would have been too long."[4]

Two solos have been extracted and sung separately: the soprano song of the thrush, mm. 50–80, at the end of the first section and the climactic "Come lovely and soothing death," mm. 391–495, sung by the contralto.

The "Americanness" of the work is inevitable considering the composer's origins and the circumstances under which it was composed. It is also seen in the melodic and rhythmic inflections in the poetry. To speak the poem in the rhythm of the music, as Margaret Hillis imaginatively rehearsed her Chicago Symphony Chorus, reveals the natural accents of Sessions's rhythms. Andrew Porter describes this aspect of the work: "It is remarkable for being a completely natural setting of the words and yet a span of music so shapely and satisfying that those words might have been written expressly to fit the structure of the score."[5]

As in his previous vocal music, Sessions portrays the images in a musically descriptive manner. One of the allusions is the music associated with the hermit thrush (see mm. 62–63). He denies that he is doing anything more than "suggesting the kind of sound Whitman writes about in *Specimen Days*. There's nothing that literal about it."[6] Although claiming this, Sessions is nevertheless able to differentiate among wood thrushes, hermit thrushes, and Wilsons's thrushes; he can sing their various songs and refers to "the very, very special quality that American birds have" over nightingales. Sessions had once before written music to portray a hermit thrush, in his Symphony No. 4. He had heard the bird many times in its natural habitat, the deep woods of northern New England.

The opening rocking tritone figure in the Cantata is the motive of the lilacs. Sessions uses the madrigalism of a melismatic, winding melody to illustrate the words "winding" (m. 116), "song," "dirges" (mm. 122–23), "poured around" (mm. 125–26), and "seawinds, blown from the east" (mm. 214–19). To portray "the thousand voices rising," the four choral voices enter successively, an eighth note apart, and rise over the bar line at mm. 124–25. The "tolling, tolling bells' perpetual clang" (mm. 129–35) is vividly clanged in the orchestra. As in *The Trial of Lucullus*, daily business is portrayed, here by fast, repeated-note passages: "and the fields all busy with labor,/And the infinite separate houses, each with its daily usages" (see mm. 351–55).

The contralto solo, "Come lovely and soothing death," dips to its lowest pitch, G♭ below middle C, on the word "night" (m. 458). The downward leap of an octave and a tritone on "well-veiled" at m. 470 subtly veils the word due to the soft quality that results when a low pitch is approached by leap.

The description of the Civil War, m. 517, and "the debris of all the slain soldiers of the war," m. 535, are both accompanied by appropriate cannon fire. All three of the main themes are brought back at the end at "Lilac and star and bird," mm. 591–93.

The last phrase "does not cease so much as recede out of earshot,"[7] similar in mood and effect to the end of Symphony No. 7. Sessions employs the bass clarinet at the end (see ex. 7.4).

Example 7.4.   *When Lilacs Last in the Dooryard Bloom'd.* mm. 599–600.
© 1974 by Merion Music. Used by permission of the publisher.

The first hexachord of the row for the Cantata is in the opening of the soprano solo, mm. 4–6. The pitches of the second hexachord, mm. 6–8, are those of the inversion at five semitones in the ordering 1, 2, 3, 4, 0, 5. This form of the row, combined with its inversion at the fourth (five semitones) above, forms a symmetrical row (Sessions's term) or, in other words, an all-combinatorial row (see ex. 7.5). Sessions constructs four additional possibilities by exchanging the last pitches of the two original hexachords, C and E♭. When C (5) is in the first hexachord, an all-combinatorial row is formed; when E♭ (11) appears in the first hexachord, an all-interval row is produced (see ex. 7.6). Once having arrived at this ingenious alteration, Sessions negates its importance, stating that although he has used an all-interval row several times, he has "never found that you've gained anything by it. Because if you want an interval, you can get it anyway."[8]

In the Violin Concerto beginnings of sections are clearest in tonal definition and rapidly become more chromatic afterward. In the Cantata sections start with distinct row statements—the orchestra plays pitches of one hexachord, the chorus

Example 7.5.   *When Lilacs Last in the Dooryard Bloom'd*, original (P-₀) row and its inversion (I-₅).

Example 7.6.   Alteration of the original row producing all-interval row.

sings pitches of the other—but analyzable usage of the twelve-tone method soon dissolves. As is usual for Sessions, the major sections of the work end with retrograde statements of the row. The third part ends with both hexachords of the retrograde in the last two measures of the piece (see ex. 7.4).

In the score Sessions states explicitly how the rhythms and inflections ought to be performed:

> The singer should . . . interpret the *rhythmic detail* in terms of the unforced inflections of the English language, which the composer has used as the basis of his vocal conception. He should, therefore, on no account force himself into a mechanical rendition of the exact note-values as written, but rather interpret them freely in terms of natural English diction, respecting the subleties of rhythm and stress which are inherent in the words themselves. It is in this manner that he will best realize the composer's intentions.

He also lists definitions for the musical terminology and accents he employs.

Critical reaction to the Cantata has been mixed, but is generally favorable. Writing of its East Coast premiere on 24 March 1975, David Hamilton observes: "The music is so intimately bound up with, and firmly reflective of, Whitman's sounds, words, lines and stanzas that the communication is extraordinarily direct: nearly all of the words were quite easily intelligible even without the printed text."[9] The performers were Diana Hoagland, soprano; D'Anna Fortunato, mezzo-soprano; and Alan Baker, baritone. The music was conducted by Michael Senturia.

In January 1976 Sir Georg Solti conducted the Chicago Symphony Orchestra and Chorus, performance of the Cantata, with soloists Sarah Beatty, soprano; Josephine Veasey, mezzo-soprano; and Dominic Cossa, baritone. A *Village Voice* review characterized the audience, "as expected, split for the most part between oldsters against and youngsters for."[10] The Boston Symphony Orchestra performed and recorded the Cantata in March 1977 under Seiji Ozawa, with soloists Esther Hinds, soprano; Florence Quivar, contralto; and Dominic Cossa, baritone.

In a record review Andrew Porter exceeded his previous zeal for the work:

> . . . the words are uttered with an American accent, the melodies take shape from the rise and fall of American speech, and the local visions as well as the universal emotions are passionately and vividly present. . . . *When Lilacs Last in the Dooryard Bloom'd* is not "merely" a cantata but a profoundly moving, inspired, and visionary composition.[11]

Concerto for Violin, Violoncello, and Orchestra   1970–1971

Commission: The Juilliard School for its Sixty-Fifth Anniversary
Dedication: "To Paul [Zukofsky] and John [Sessions], the First Soloists of This Work, in Gratitude and Admiration"
Published by Theodore Presser, 1979. Sketches at Princeton University Library.
Premiere: 5 November 1971, New York, Juilliard Theater Orchestra, Paul Zukofsky, Violin, John Sessions, Cello, Leon Barzin Conducting.
I. Allegro moderato ma sempre con fuoco
II. Adagio
III. Molto allegro (doppio movimento)
(Played without Pause)

All three performances of the Double Concerto—the premiere, one at Northwestern, and one at Aspen—were performed by Paul Zukofsky and the composer's son, John Sessions. Sessions writes about the work:

> What I had in mind was a work in which two solo instruments play different and at times, contrasting roles, always distinct from that of the orchestra, and frequently combining with each other in an independent ensemble. The different roles are forecast in the two cadenzas—the first on the violin, the second on the cello, with which the Concerto begins, immediately after two introductory measures in the orchestra; they are also embodied in many dialogue–like episodes in which they, as it were, briefly converse; also in various solo episodes, in which one instrument often plays in support of the other. At other times, of course, the two instruments form a single unit in which neither predominates, although their contrasting roles will, I believe, often be evident here too . . . .
>
> The role of the orchestra is preponderantly that of support, but also that of commentator or, so to speak, master of ceremonies.[12]

Allen Hughes's review of the premiere acknowledged that "the score is a rich tapestry worked in complex counterpoint and glowing colors. Its slow section is quite eloquent, and throughout one is conscious of and affected by the intensity and integrity of the music."[13] However, for Hughes Sessions's desired solo effect did not work: "The biggest problem is that of hearing the soloists through the sonorities of the orchestral score."

As in the Violin Concerto, the Double Concerto opens with a brief fanfare, although here the trumpet call is more condensed and the violin immediately launches into a brief cadenza. The trumpet's four clarion notes reappear (transposed up) to inaugurate a short cello cadenza. The solo string writing involves double stops, alternating subdivisions of beats, and multiple accent marks. The two solo instruments reenter, m. 38, exchanging their versions of the trumpet's four notes. The character of the two is conversational; they "have a little talk together"[14] reminiscent of the recitativelike sections in the Six Pieces. Again an imagined vocal model stimulates Sessions's solo string writing, and again one of the conversation's participants must be the composer's son, John.

The structure of the first movement resembles the triple-stanza expositions of String Quartet No. 1 and the Quintet. The opening material recurs three times, at m. 60, m. 136, and m. 197. The second theme (Sessions pokes fun at the idea that a second theme is "lyrical") appears at m. 110 and at m. 181. At mm. 197–204 the first idea reappears at the original pitch level and functions as a return of the opening idea, a coda, and a transition to the second movement.

As in Sessions's Fifth and Eighth Symphonies, the movements of the Double Concerto are connected without pause. The second movement begins slowly with a statement of the row in the cello and double basses. The addition of the maracas in m. 5 momentarily recalls the opening of the Eighth Symphony. The Adagio movement can be seen as an ABA structure: B begins at m. 224, un poco più mosso, and A at m. 263. M. 272 begins a transition to the third movement.

The third movement's introductory theme consists simply of a repeated note, high B on the violin. When discussing this, Sessions mentions precursors such as Beethoven's Waldstein Sonata and the Fifth Symphony. At m. 205 a second section begins. As in most concertos the cadenza appears before the return of the initial idea. The repeated-note theme reappears at m. 408 and at m. 442, the beginning of the coda.

The original form of the row is stated explicity in the violin five measures from the end of the piece: F♯, B♭, C, A, F, B: E, C♯, D♯, D, G, G♯. The cello has the "last word" with a retrograde-inversion of the row (see ex. 7.7).

Example 7.7.   Concerto for Violin and Cello, violin and cello solos, mm. 464–68.
© 1979 by Merion Music. Used by permission of the publisher.

Canons (to the Memory of Igor Stravinsky)   1971

Commission: *Tempo* Magazine
Published by *Tempo*, 1972.
Premiere: 1972, London.

The editors of the Boosey & Hawkes periodical *Tempo* asked distinguished composers to contribute canons for an issue dedicated to the memory of Igor Stravin-

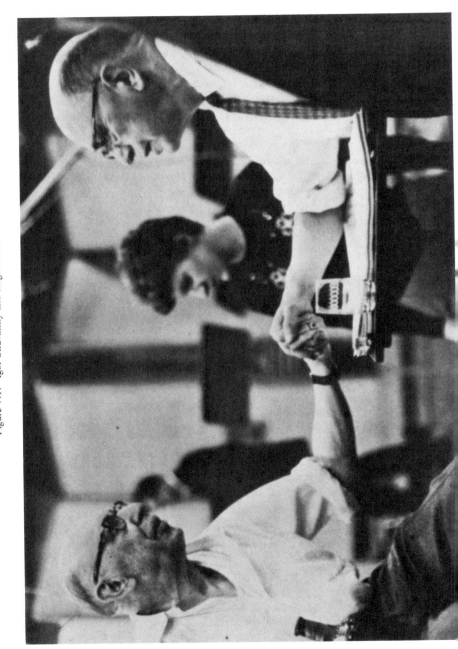

Figure 7.1. Igor Stravinsky and Roger Sessions.

sky.[15] Sessions and Stravinsky had known and admired each other since the 1920s. Stravinsky wrote of Sessions in 1963:

> I imagine that the importance and value of Roger Sessions have been felt by everyone except music critics, even though knowledge of his true stature and achievement have been denied us by too few performances of his music.
>
> Now at sixty-five [*sic*], and honored everywhere as one of our first composers, Roger Sessions will go abroad to hear the first performance of his opera *Montezuma*. I wish him the greatest success for this premiere, as well as for all following performances, in Berlin and elsewhere, including, I hope, the United States. (One would not have to "hope" if he were a German composer living in Munich and published in Mainz.)
>
> Roger Sessions is one of the people I most admire and respect: as composer, scholar, teacher, intellect. But last and most, he is a dear friend.[16]

Sessions wrote this one-minute string quartet on 8 August 1971 aboard a ship bound for Oslo. The inscription at the end of the manuscript reads "On the high seas."

Concertino for Chamber Orchestra   1971–1972

Commission: Fromm Foundation for the Contemporary Chamber Players of the University of Chicago
Dedication: Paul Fromm
Published by Edward B. Marks, 1974. Sketches at Princeton University Library.
Premiere: 14 April 1972, Contemporary Chamber Players of the University of Chicago, Ralph Shapey Conducting.
I. Allegro
II. Lento molto
III. Molto vivo

Edward T. Cone notes in his article in *Tempo*[17] that there are no historical or stylistic associations evoked by the term "concertino." "Nor does the diminutive imply any relaxation of the standards of formal structure and expressive intensity that we expect of its composer."[18] Cone suggests the term "sinfonietta." Sessions does, however, have specific notions associated with the title. In the preface of the score he states:

> The Concertino, as the title implies, is a concerto of relatively small dimensions. I decided on the title, as I often have done, after the work was already under way. It was partly suggested by the fact that Mr. Shapey's organization is composed of players who, especially among the woodwinds, are accustomed to playing several instruments in their chosen categories. Since this work, designed as it is for an orchestra of chamber dimensions, and by conception as well as by the demands of the medium itself, emphasizes solo performance, I decided to avail myself of the players' versatility and give each of the various available instruments a significant role to play. Hence the title Concertino and the composition of the ensemble, in which the flautist plays also the alto flute (in the second movement) and piccolo, the oboist also the English horn, the clarinetist clarinets in E flat and B flat, as well as (briefly in the second movement) the bass clarinet. The bassoon plays also the contrabassoon, which appears only in the second movement, where it plays an important role throughout.

Viewing this orchestration as a "succinct model—a scale reduction as it were—of his ideal orchestral sound,"[19] Cone distinguishes the characteristic sonorities of each movement: E-flat clarinet in the first, dialogue between contrabassoon and alto flute in the second, and piccolo in the third. A pattern of *Klangfarbenmelodien* is achieved through the occurrences of a given color, additions to that color, and returns to a single, although not necessarily the same, color. Violins playing tremolo sul ponticello accompany much of the second movement; in the third movement that texture briefly returns. Formal articulations are marked by detensifications of texture. Cone writes that "it gives the impression not of having been 'orchestrated,' but of having been conceived from the beginning in specific orchestral terms. The instrumentation is the skin of the musical body rather than its clothing."[20] Sessions considers it "the whole anatomy."[21]

The first movement operates in sonata form: introduction at mm. 1–7; exposition at m. 8, first theme at m. 23, second theme at più tranquillo e grazioso; recapitulation at mm. 91ff; coda at mm. 106–20.

The row (B, C♯, D♯, E, F, F♯: G, G♯, A, B♭, C, D) is found in unordered hexachords, "but the accompaniment suggests that Sessions may be working out a concept of twelve-tone 'dissonance.' Some lines and sonorities are apparently derived from neither hexad, but their elements 'resolve' to others that are so derived."[22]

The melodies of the second movement derive from the basic set: D, A♭, B♭, G, C, A: E♭, C♯, E, B, F, F♯. It is, however, "fruitless to attempt to work out [the accompaniment's] derivations."[23] This movement is in song form; the unlikely singers are the contrabassoon and alto flute. Sessions feels that the contrabassoon has the principal role in this movement. A contrabassoonist once told him that with this piece he had increased the contrabassoon repertoire 25 percent. The alto flute line initially inverts the contrabassoon line.

The rondo's set forms and transpositions "seem to be guided by quasi-tonal considerations."[24] Fifths are made available by the ordering: D, G, A♭, C, B♭, A: F♯, E♭, F, C♯, E, B. The cadence, mm. 135–36, moves by fifth to an E. The pulse of this fast movement speeds up from an initial half-note pulse to a quarter-note pulse. In the second half of the movement time signatures such as $\frac{7}{4}$ and $\frac{5}{4}$ occupy most of the bars. Sessions feels as comfortable in meters of seven and five as he does in three and four.

Three Choruses on Biblical Texts   1971–1972
(Score Marked Chicago, Princeton 25 June 1972)

Texts: 130th Psalm "De Profundis" (1); First and Second Chapters of *Isaiah* (2); 147th, 148th and 150th Psalms (3)
Commission: Amherst College in Commemoration of the Sesquicentennial Anniversary of its Founding
Dedication: Amherst College
Published by Theodore Presser, 1976. Piano Reduction by Felix Greissle. Manuscript at Amherst College. Sketches at Princeton University Library.

Premiere: 8 February 1975, Amherst College, Lewis Spratlan Conducting.
1. "Out of the Depths"
2. "Ah, Sinful Nation"
3. "Praise ye the Lord"

An Amherst publication documents the filling of this commission.[25] In it Sessions was asked why he chose a Biblical text. He alluded to his *Psalm 140,* stating:

> I wanted something both, in terms of my own feelings, relevant to the human condition and essentially non-sectarian in its implications, also not ultimately pessimistic—which I am neither intellectually nor temperamentally capable of being, and which also would be entirely inappropriate for a festive occasion![26]

Sessions used the King James version, "a wonderful work of literature." When asked "Do you find that you respond pictorially to textual images or does the evocative character of the music come about in a more or less subconscious fashion?", Sessions answered:

> With me it is a matter of responding vividly and in a wholly spontaneous and unconstrained manner to the text, basically of course in terms of musical sound and movement. That obviously involves occasional "pictorial" elements, and I certainly don't shy away from these.[27]

Pleased with the results of the orchestral sound in *The Trial of Lucullus,* Sessions again omitted the second violin section and brought the other strings, woodwinds, and brass into greater relief. The piano, used in all of Sessions's symphonies except the Third, appears in the final chorus, adding "a certain crispness and brilliance to the texture."[28] The contrabassoon frequently doubles the contrabasses at the unison to support the bass singers. The trombones and trumpets play a vital role throughout.

Always specific about details of instrumental notation, here Sessions has given the singers three directions for nonpitched sounds. In "Ah, Sinful Nation" at m. 17 all four voices are given pitched square-shaped white notes, explained in the score "to be intoned 'parlando'." The text here is: "Why shall ye be stricken anymore?" Diamond-shaped notes direct attention to the articulation of consonants, for example at "Out of the dep*ths* have I cried unto Thee, O Lord." In "Ah, Sinful Nation" diamond-shaped notes further modify the parlando for pictorialism on "faint" (m. 22) at "The whole head is sick, and the whole heart faint." Here Sessions adds "almost whispered."

An example of pictorial usage occurs in mm. 77–80 of "Praise ye the Lord." The words "young men" are given to the tenors, "and maidens" to the altos, "old men" to the basses, "and children" to the sopranos, each in its appropriate voice range for its age.

Pitched notes are also given specific directions: "Notes indicated in parentheses are to be omitted by singers whose range does not permit their full and accurate enunciation of pitch. On no account are they to be transposed to a higher or lower octave."

Sessions imagines the chorus as one voice, a block of sound. This unified compound is harmonically conceived and is set in opposition to the orchestra and its line. Felix Greissle felt that in contrast to most twelve-tone composers since (his father-in-law) Schoenberg, Sessions's use of the twelve-tone method emphasizes its vertical and harmonic possibilities rather than its melodic ones. The row is D, E, C♯, D♯, F, B: A, F♯, B♭, C, A♭, G.

In constructing the text for the second piece Sessions excised local references from the first two chapters of *Isaiah*. "That's the Watergate one. Not only Watergate, but Vietnam, etc."[29] In contrast to the second piece, which deals with the subject of corruption, the third is an optimistic revelation, purifying that which preceded it. "Sort of a general amnesty. I always call that my ecological Psalm. It's the whole of nature, so to speak. Including human nature."[30]

Five Pieces for Piano   1974–1975

Dedication: "To the Memory of Luigi Dallapiccola"
Published by Theodore Presser, 1976. Manuscript in Composer's Personal Collection.
Premieres: May 1977, Davis, California, Robert Miller, Pianist; 24 October 1977, New York City,
  Robert Miller, Pianist.
I. Lento (Score Marked Franconia, August 1974)
II. Con fuoco (Franconia, August; Princeton, 1 November 1974)
III. Andante, leggero e grazioso (Princeton, 23 December 1974)
IV. Molto agitato (*In memoriam L. D., February 19, 1975*) (6 April 1975)
V. Molto adagio (January 1975)

> It started with the first one up in Franconia [New Hampshire]. I was writing some little pieces for my granddaughter, who was eight years old at that time. Then this [see ex. 7.8] was one of the ideas that I had. Well, I decided "That's not for Teresa." I realized this was my own music, which little pieces for eight-year-old girls aren't.[31]

Example 7.8.   Five Pieces for Piano, I, mm. 1–4.
    © 1976 by Merion Music. Used by permission of the publisher.

In these pieces the rhythms alone are formidable. Sessions's playful attitude toward these is illustrated by this segment of one of our interviews.

AO: The polyrhythms give a sensation that the hands, or voices, are moving in different tempi from one another, which is a sort of rhythmic stratification of counterpoint.
RS: Unfortunately that's my disease. It gets worse and worse. [laughter]
AO: It's progressed quite nicely here. It's at an acute stage.
RS: I'm not trying to get over it.[32]

The notational problem such rhythmic complexities present is staggering, one which only years of experience can solve. Perhaps the largest problem in that respect is placing bar lines correctly. A lesson Sessions learned from his Duo was never to extend beams over the bar lines.[33] Sessions tells Eduard Steuermann's story of asking Alban Berg how to perform polyrhythms in his Chamber Concerto. Berg's answer: "I just don't want them to be together."

Another feature of these pieces that strikes the listener is that one never feels a sense of excess, no wasted motion. "That is more and more true of my music as it goes on. This is much more concentrated. I don't mean that there are any extra notes in my First Symphony!"[34]

Accents are very carefully marked and sometimes as many as three different markings appear on one note. Metronome markings give a mean indication of tempo and are "very much a relative matter." For example: "I would mind if this section [mm. 14 and 15 of the Lento] were not accurate here. But I think it should not be any faster than that [quarter note equals 72]."[35] Sessions quotes Felix Greissle: "Markings are for the first five performances." In other words, when a performer really knows the music, he knows what to do.

Characteristic of Sessions's piano writing, transition sections often are identifiable by tremolos, keeping a sustained note in motion. Pedal marks are rare: "A pianist should know when to use the pedal."[37]

> The fourth piece was the most difficult. It was while I was writing that that Dallapiccola died. I was thinking of him part of the time I was writing it, especially in these parts [mm. 13–15]. I wrote the dedication at the top of the fourth movement, and then later I thought, "Why don't I dedicate the whole thing to him, to his memory?"
>
> I found him certainly as congenial a composer as I have ever met. I never think of him as a composer for the piano especially. He played the piano, but he wrote very, very little for the piano. I think of him more as a composer for voice, and for small groups of instruments, aside from his big works. Of course he was extremely good at whatever he did.[36]

Octaves are used only as a reinforcement of an extremely low or high note for "a little extra brilliance." "An octave on the piano is the only way of reinforcing a note. If you want to reinforce a note in the orchestra, you double at the unison. If you have an octave in the orchestra, it just adds more space."[38] Hence, one does not find octave doublings in Sessions's orchestral works after *Montezuma*. "Octaves elsewhere are disturbing because they emphasize one tone and disrupt the texture a little bit."[39]

Figure 7.2.   Roger Sessions with the Author, 1978.
(*Whitestone Photo*)

The element of contrast intensifies as the pieces progress. "The contrasts are less sharp in I and II than in III." In the fourth piece "the diminished fifths need to be brought out." The largest climax is at m. 50. In the fifth piece the climax is "more florid."

Pointing out that "you read music much faster than you play it or listen to it," Sessions indicates that at the beginning of the first piece "the prevailing beat is a half note, not a quarter." In the "very intense" fourth piece Sessions writes a marking he rarely uses, fff, "just ff with a little extra juice." The character of the third measure is not faster than the first. The third piece is "easy and graceful, not too fast."

Waltz   1977–1978

Commission: Robert Helps and Robert Moran
Dedication: Robert Helps
Published by C. F. Peters, 1978. Manuscript in Composer's Personal Collection.
Premiere: 1978, Chicago Art Institute, Chicago, Illinois.

By coincidence, Robert Moran and Robert Helps both found themselves in 1976 writing waltzes for piano. They approached C. F. Peters Publishing Company with the idea of commissioning other composers to write short (four minutes at most) waltzes for the instrument. Sessions, Ross Lee Finney, Ivan Tcherepnin, Lou Harrison, Milton Babbitt, John Cage, Virgil Thomson, Philip Glass, and others responded.

Sessions describes his 63-measure-long Waltz as "twelve-tone without any row."[40] It is technically difficult and speeds along in $\frac{3}{8}$ with the eighth not equaling metronomic marking 159. The piece is ternary with divisions at m. 25 and a return to the opening at m. 46. The climax, m. 46, is typical of Sessions's textures at such places: very high, intense, and loud octaves in the right hand. The climax is also a recapitulation of the opening repeated whole-tone motive, alluded to at the end with the same transposition and harmony as that used in the beginning.

Symphony No. 9   1975–1978
(Score Marked Franconia, New Hampshire, 2 October 1978)

Commission: Syracuse Symphony
Dedication: Frederik Prausnitz
Published by Theodore Presser, 1984.
Premiere: 17 January 1980, Syracuse, New York, Syracuse Symphony, Christopher Keene Conducting.
I. Allegro; Impetuoso—Tranquillo
II. Con movimento adagio—Doppio movimento quasi allegretto
III. Allegro vivace
(Played without Pause)

Writing for the Syracuse Symphony must have given rise to many memories for Sessions. In the first decade of this century he remembers visiting his grandfather, the Reverend Frederic Dan Huntington, who, as the Bishop of Central New York in Syracuse from 1869 to 1904, founded the Calvary Church. After Huntington's death Sessions continued to visit Syracuse because his sister, Hannah, married a native of the city, Paul Shipman Andrews, and lived in Onondaga from the time of World War I until 1962.

In reference to writing the Ninth Symphony, Sessions remarks: "When I'm composing a big work I have to acclimate myself into that world without reference to what I've done before."[41] Years of experience have streamlined the amount of sketch material necessary before Sessions completes the final orchestration. For works like the Violin Concerto and *Montezuma* he had written out a particell before orchestrating. Now sketch books become fewer and smaller and particells unnecessary. In addition, Sessions has never composed at the piano. He wrote the Ninth Symphony directly onto orchestral transparancies, later filling in details such as percussion writing and doublings. Placement of bar lines remained the largest problem; he had to alter some several times.

By Christmas of 1976 Sessions had completed two-thirds of the first movement. Sessions describes it:

> The first four notes were what I started with. These notes come in very slowly at first, then they work up. The oboe and the muted trumpet start the first two notes, and then the horns come in with the second two notes, and then bang!, the rest of the notes come in [see ex. 7.9].[42]

As in the Concertino, the Ninth Symphony incorporates two tone rows. The first row is A, B♭, E♭, F, D, C♯: G♯, B, G, F♯, C, E. This row is combinatorial in that the second hexachord rearranged in descending scalelike order—C, B, G♯, G, F♯, E—is an inversion of the first hexachord, A, B♭, C♯, D, E♭, F. The second row, A, G, F, F♯, D, A♭: B♭, D, B, E♭, E, C♯ was not derived from the first. It appears as an independent idea first at m. 6 and again at m. 25 in the violins. It is "a motive outside the twelve-tone structure of the piece, only in the first movement."[43]

In July 1977 Sessions wrote: "My symphony is going well, I think; I have nearly finished the first movement, and am already well into the second. I'm afraid it will not [be] easy to play, but it has to be what it has to be!"[44] The second movement was finished during April 1978. It begins and ends with trombone solos. The concluding solo overlaps the beginning of the Allegro vivace.

Despite the confidence described above, Sessions still has doubts:

> But my only excuse [for not writing sooner] is that work on my 9th symphony has been musically taxing. I hope this is because it is a big work with unusual problems and not because of the inexorable problems of old age! Actually I am quite convinced it is not the latter; I have plenty of musical ideas, but I set myself a rather special task in this work and it involves both agony and joy in the making of it. That is a fairly (nonsense; *thoroughly*) familiar experience for a composer but it seems more acute than usual this time. I find it comforting to read the score of my 7th symphony [just published] and to discover that it did, from my point of view come out right that time![45]

Example 7.9.   Symphony No. 9, I, mm. 1–3.

The "special task" he alludes to begs the question of inspiration, one of the most imprecise to try to discuss. In a general sense the William Blake poem *The Tyger*, with its problem of evil and images of the tiger and lamb, helped to inspire the writing of this symphony. This poem exemplifies the element of contrast so often discussed in Sessions's prose and always found in his music. The opposition of the violent "tyger" to the lamb, representative of a cooperative and peaceful spirit, constitutes a conflict between brutality and gentleness, in the first movement especially. Sessions has said that the first measures represent the tiger lying in wait (see ex. 7.9). At the end of the first movement, the Blake verse is implied: "Could he who made the lamb make thee?" The movement ends with a question mark. Possibly another line of the poem inspired a technical aspect of the work, its symmetrical row: "What immortal hand or eye,/Dare frame thy fearful symmetry?"

Figure 7.3. Ninth Symphony, First Movement, mm. 100–105.
Manuscript.

In the first movement, the opening fast section is contrasted with the quieter, "slower and more lyrical" B section, only to return to the (much varied) opening material and its unresolved-question conclusion. In the Con movimento adagio a scherzando passage offers a contrast to its surrounding slower music. A fast section begins and ends the third movement, which culminates—unlike the quiet petering out of the Seventh Symphony and the Cantata—with a definite cadence, a sudden bang.

The critical response to the premiere was typical of the reviews that Sessions receives, that is, respect but not love. The *Syracuse Herald Journal* reported: "This was vintage Sessions, music of uncompromising seriousness, rocky in its ideas, toughminded in the way those ideas jostle each other, more flint and sparks than warmth and light."[46] The work's New York premiere came shortly after the premiere, performed by the Syracuse Symphony in Carnegie Hall. The *New York Times* found the piece "knotty." But Nicholas Kenyon wrote that "something compels one to listen, and to listen hard." [47] My own review of this work contrasts the Ninth with Sessions's previous symphonies.[48]

Sessions was "not superstitious" about the portentous number nine in symphonic writing. Nevertheless, his last orchestral work was to be entitled Concerto for Orchestra.

Concerto for Orchestra   1981

Commission: Boston Symphony Orchestra for its One-Hundredth Birthday
Dedication: "To Seiji Ozawa, also in Memory of all His Excellent Predecessors who Built and Maintained the Boston Symphony Orchestra"
Published by Theodore Presser, 1983. Manuscript in Composer's Personal Collection.
Premiere: 23 October 1981, Boston Symphony Orchestra, Seiji Ozawa Conducting.
I. Allegro
II. Largo
III. Allegro maestoso
(Played without Pause)

This commission to write an orchestral work in celebration of the Boston Symphony Orchestra included a performance on a program with Beethoven's Ninth Symphony. Sessions rarely finishes a commission on time, but in this case the incentive of the program sped up his work. During the spring and summer of 1981 he rapidly composed his Concerto for Orchestra.

The title echoed two famous precursor's, Bartók's (commissioned by the Boston Symphony Orchestra in 1943) and Elliott Carter's. But, the title may not be apt since not all sections of the orchestra are given soloistic treatment; for instance, the strings are not featured. As in his Ninth Symphony, a prominent solo role is given to the trombone. "Instead of sharp-cut, distinct, contrasting movements and the effect of spotlights playing upon now one part of the platform, now another, there is a single, intricate, poetic span."[49]

Sessions wrote of the work:

> . . . in the first section, alternately playful and lyrical, the woodwinds play a very prominent role; this is followed by a slow section. . . . In this part, a solemn Largo, the brass instruments play the main role. . . . A contrasting middle section extends the register by introducing the high woodwinds and more movement. After a climax the music of the previous Largo returns. . . . A trumpet call . . . introduces the final section, which is festive in character. A short concluding statement, three phrases long, brings the piece to a quiet end.[50]

The work received rave reviews, including Porter's judgment that "his concerto is the work of a great composer at the peak of his powers."[51] Sessions was awarded a Pulitzer Prize for this piece. A headline on the front page of the *New York Times* read: "A Composer, 85, and a Dead Poet [Sylvia Plath] Among Winners of Pulitzer Prizes."[51] However, Sessions never took prizes very seriously.

The Boston Symphony performed the work again in Tanglewood on 10 July 1981. On the previous day Sessions's 75-year-old wife died after having been hospitalized for several weeks. The couple had been married for almost 46 years and were, in Sessions's words, "very close." Two years previously, Sessions's first wife, Barbara, died.

The *New York Times* issued another of its negative reviews of Sessions's music:

> But on a first hearing, at least, the impression remains that Mr. Sessions is trapped by a borrowed musical language. Time after time, the voices of Schoenberg and Berg seemed to intrude, freighting Mr. Sessions's music with the dated echos of Viennese Expressionism. Perhaps some day such questions will seem less important, and Mr. Sessions's orchestral music will be prized on its own terms. But that seems unlikely right now.[52]

Sessions's music has never met with whole-hearted support in the press. It is in the musical community that the composer is revered and his music prized.

At 86 Roger Sessions was still composing and teaching. A parallel can be drawn between him and one of his favorite composers. His passion for Verdi is not only evidenced by his teaching—a semester on *Falstaff*—and in his music—formal similarity between *Montezuma* and *Otello* can be found—but also in the pattern of his creative career.

Verdi's last work, *Falstaff*, was his only comic opera, written in 1893 when the composer was 80 years old. After Sessions turned 80 he worked on a comic opera on the subject of *The Emperor's New Clothes* in which the emperor is onto the joke but nevertheless continues it. Sarah Caldwell had encouraged the composer to write another opera. In the fall of 1979 Caldwell, Andrew Porter, and Sessions met, and it was suggested that Porter write the libretto. Porter worked on it for several years, and Sessions worked on parts of the music, interrupted by the Boston Symphony commission for the Concerto for Orchestra. The project was permanently interrupted by the lack of a finished libretto and the death of Sessions's wife.

Personality

Sessions once compared himself to one of the trees at Forty Acres, an apt metaphor. Strength, consistency, and assuredness are reflected in his person and in his music. Indeed, it is difficult to imagine Sessions ever changing from this immutable, treelike self.

What initially seems a grim and somewhat formidable veneer disappears with his warm smile and easy laughter. His face is dominated by sympathetic brown eyes, deep wrinkles, a moustache, oversized ears, and a pair of black horn-rimmed glasses that lodges a hearing aid. He is bald, short, and sturdily built. The blandness of the grays and greens of his clothing, usually a tweed or corduroy jacket, vest, and baggy pants, is offset by a perky beret and the distinctive rosette of membership in the American Academy of Arts and Letters.

In excellent health, he has no serious diseases and has endured relatively few minor operations. He states that the older he gets, the less sleep he needs. When one doctor prescribed a pacemaker in the summer of 1979, Sessions consulted another, who told him what he wanted to hear—that he did not need it. He refused the "piece of machinery," but struck a difficult bargain with himself—after 60 years of smoking, he abruptly quit.

Abandoning his pipe meant another sacrifice. The pipe was his favorite implement because of the continual attention required to clean, fill, and light it. This preoccupation appeared to be a nervous habit, replaced by rolling up matchbooks or fidgeting with some nearby object. Since music constantly streams through his head, his feet continually keep the pulse, even polyrhythmically. One can only speculate on the apparent contradiction between this uneasiness and the basic sturdiness of the man; however, he is aware of his nervousness.

He speaks extremely slowly in a quiet, low voice, the profound and the mundane stated with exactly the same emphasis. The pauses in his sentences are so long that the listener wonders if the thought is finished (perhaps now one should say something?). After a long silence he will continue. Not for nothing did his son teasingly nickname him "Flash."

Although he states that discretion is not his middle name ("because it goes badly with my last"), one cannot imagine him being impolite or tactless. His basic integrity prevents dishonesty; he cannot help being himself in any situation, and part of his charm lies in his being unable to keep a secret. He displays a high level of tolerance for other people: "I've come to the conclusion, especially since the war, that I'm not going to judge individuals until I have been in [their] situation myself."[54] Sessions's gentlemanly politeness marks him unmistakably as a product of an older time. On an envelope sent via a student Sessions wrote "by courtesy of Tod Machover." When bidding farewell he says, "Godspeed." He insists on walking on the street side of a woman, while remarking how antiquated the custom is. He never interrupts someone speaking. Always dignified, he is never pompous.

Sessions's personal security and solidarity is evinced in his predictability. He will have lunch at the same restaurant every Tuesday and Wednesday for years, even at the same table. On the other hand, assumptions about him can be misleading. When preparing for a radio interview in 1980, we "rehearsed" in a mock interview; on the air none of his answers were anticipated.

Sessions is a political liberal, a loyal and generous teacher, a devoted family man, and a "closet Catholic." He is more disturbed by what he reads on the front pages of newspapers than by unfavorable reviews of his music in the arts section. In the summer of 1980 he wore a Kennedy button. He is affectionate toward his students and defends them. "My motto, which I've communicated to my students, is that if you don't stick your neck out, nobody will ever put their arms around it. But if you go out on a limb, all your friends sort of fade away, you know."[55] When colleagues congratulated him on his Pulitzer Prize citation in 1974, Sessions excitedly deflected the conversation to a more significant subject—the birth of his first grandson, named Roger after him. Perhaps because of his family's Anglican religious background, Sessions considers himself "a Catholic fellow traveler."

John Harbison describes Sessions's personality:

> He was distracted, affectionate, generous, healthily self-absorbed and inimitable. His slow-spoken, slow moving demeanor was part of a paced personality, as if he was built to endure forever. In everything he did, even just enjoying himself, he seemed to be concentrating on essentials. . . . I have images of him as a tender, passionate and confused father; he had difficult relationships with both his adolescent children, but I remember being very touched then (when I was touched by little) by his very vulnerable efforts to understand and reach them. I also remember his humor, always at the same slow pace, without meanness. I have a strong sense of his strong and supportive bond with Lisl. I also recall his great pride in John's and Betsy's accomplishments, and their fascination-exasperation with him with full awareness of his stature and power. I suspect one of the great happinesses of his life was enjoying the very original rewarding and gifted people that they became.[56]

When coaching performers on his music, Sessions's best traits shine. At once supportive, encouraging, and calm, he defuses fear by confronting it directly: "Perhaps you're a little bit afraid of me." Sessions has learned through years of experience how to treat performers' delicate nerves. He speaks in generalities, for instance, "I feel you're holding back," but often is quite specific, singing the phrase himself, advising on the use of the pedal, or pinpointing an out-of-tune note. All of this is suggested in a positive manner, and his compliments are heartfelt.

Sessions's *Weltanschauung* is formed by cautious optimism, genuine human understanding, empathy for others, and a self-awareness ("I've been a sinner and I've been a fool"). During the lockout of the Metropolitan Opera musicians in 1980, he sympathized with the musicians and worried, "I'm afraid I'm becoming cynical. . . . These people are artists!" He has never shied away from reality, even

Figure 7.4. Aaron Copland, Roger Sessions, and Robert Craft, 1981.
"Homage to Stravinsky" at the Whitney Museum.

the ultimate reality of age, about which he likes jokingly to quote a friend: "Old age is not for sissies." He can mention the certainty of his own death with calmness.

Although Sessions feels a work is not completed until it has been performed adequately, his personality and his New England upbringing would not allow him openly or covertly to engineer performances of his works. His lack of aggressiveness in this regard has undoubtedly hindered his career. His family, friends, and students become irate first at the length of time it takes for his large works to be performed and then at the hostile reactions they often receive in the press. Elliott Carter thinks that the very devotion of people close to Sessions helps him to maintain his serenity.

> In any case, the public neglect of Sessions would be an outright American scandal if such neglect were not so common, especially by the publics and musicians of the thirties, forties, and fifties. That his wonderful opera *Montezuma* had first to be produced in Berlin before a vociferously anti-American audience is only part of the American process of attrition that drives our composers to despair or sullen stubbornness and discourages their development no matter how talented and promising they may have shown themselves. Sessions has been protected from this (the fate of Varèse, Ruggles, Ives, and many others) by his ability to teach and the devotion of his students and colleagues.[56]

Notes

1. Taped interview 2 April 1975.

2. Taped interview 28 April 1976.

3. *See* Andrew Porter, "An American Requiem," *The New Yorker*, April 1977.

4. Taped interview 30 October 1979.

5. Porter, "An American Requiem," p. 139.

6. Taped interview 11 December 1979.

7. Michael Steinberg, "Roger Sessions: *When Lilacs Last in the Dooryard Bloom'd*," Tanglewood Program notes, 1977, p. 21.

8. Untaped conversation 4 December 1979.

9. David Hamilton, "Music," *The Nation*, 19 April 1975.

10. Leighton Kerner, "Sessions Blooms in Chicago," *The Village Voice*, 16 February 1976.

11. Andrew Porter, "Sessions' Passionate and Profound *Lilacs*," *High Fidelity Magazine* (February 1978): 70.

12. Roger Sessions, Aspen Conference on Contemporary Music, Program notes, 1972.

13. Allen Hughes, "Juilliard and Manhattan Present Sessions and Haieff Works," *New York Times* (7 November 1971), p. 8, 3:2

14. Untaped conversation 11 November 1980.

15. Sessions's Canon is published in *Tempo* 98 (March 1972).

16. Igor Stravinsky, in Roger Sessions's BMI brochure, 1965.

17. Edward T. Cone, ''Sessions's Concertino,'' *Tempo* 115 (December 1975): 2–10.

18. Ibid., p. 2.

19. Ibid., p. 3.

20. Ibid., p. 7.

21. Untaped interview 20 May 1980.

22. Cone, ''Sessions's Concertino,'' p. 9.

23. Ibid.

24. Ibid., p. 10.

25. Henry G. Mishin, ''The Genesis of a Commission: Roger Sessions, Three Choruses on Biblical Texts,'' published by the Friends of Amherst College Music, Sesquicentennial Celebration, Spring 1974.

26. Ibid., p. 6.

27. Ibid., p. 7.

28. Ibid., p. 9.

29. Taped interview 18 January 1977.

30. Ibid.

31. Taped interview 30 November 1976.

32. Ibid.

33. In the first movement of the Duo triplets are beamed over the bar lines.

34. Taped interview 30 November 1976.

35. Ibid.

36. Taped interview 23 May 1978.

37. Ibid.

38. Taped interview 30 November 1976.

39. Ibid.

40. Untaped conversation 11 January 1978.

41. Taped interview 4 January 1977.

42. Taped interview 24 May 1977.

43. Taped interview 27 May 1980.

44. Letter to the author 26 July 1977.

45. Letter to the author 7 August 1977.

46. Earl George, ''Symphony's World Premiere Impresses,'' *Syracuse Herald Journal,* 19 January 1980.

47. Nicholas Kenyon, ''Challenges,'' *The New Yorker* (7 April 1980): 132.

48. Andrea Olmstead, ''Roger Sessions's Ninth Symphony,'' *Tempo* 133 (December 1980): 79–81.

49. Andrew Porter, "Celebration," *The New Yorker* (9 November 1981): 164.

50. Roger Sessions, Boston Symphony Orchestra, Program notes, 22 October 1981.

51. Porter, "Celebration," p. 164.

52. Peter Kihss, "A Composer, 85, and a Dead Poet Among Winners of Pulitzer Prizes," *New York Times* (13 April 1982), p. 1.

53. John Rockwell, "Concert: Boston Symphony Opens at Tanglewood," *New York Times* (11 July 1982), p. 39.

54. Columbia University Oral History Collection, p. 152.

55. Taped interview 7 May 1975.

56. John Harbison, letter to the author 23 October 1979.

57. Allen Edwards, *Flawed Words and Stubborn Sounds; a Conversation with Elliott Carter* (New York: W. W. Norton & Co., 1971), p. 65.

Appendix 1

Roger Sessions's Family Tree:
The Porters, Phelpses, Huntingtons, Sargents & Sessionses

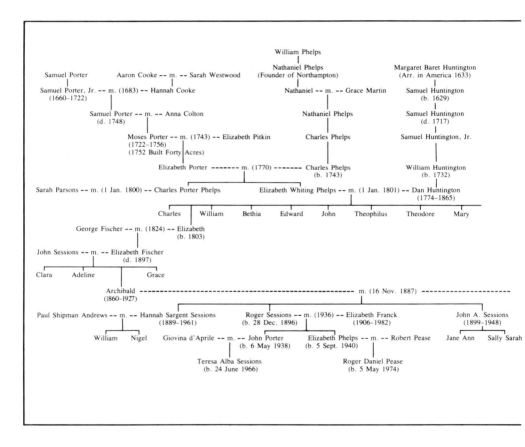

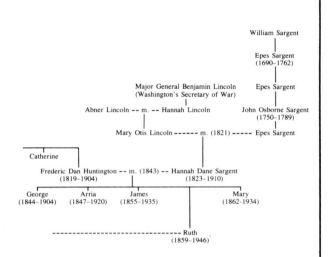

William Sargent

Epes Sargent
(1690–1762)

Epes Sargent

Major General Benjamin Lincoln
(Washington's Secretary of War)

John Osborne Sargent
(1750–1789)

Abner Lincoln -- m. -- Hannah Lincoln

Mary Otis Lincoln ------ m. (1821) ----- Epes Sargent

Catherine

Frederic Dan Huntington -- m. (1843) -- Hannah Dane Sargent
(1819–1904)   (1823–1910)

George   Arria   James   Mary
(1844–1904)   (1847–1920)   (1855–1935)   (1862–1934)

-------------------------------- Ruth
                                 (1859–1946)

Appendix 2

Catalogue of Unpublished and Incomplete Works

1. *Lancelot and Elaine* (1910). Opera based on Tennyson's *Idyll of the King*. Sessions's first composition. (Manuscript at the Princeton University Library)

2. Trio for Piano, Violin, and Cello (1916).

3. Sonata for Piano and Violin (1916). Written for Horatio Parker at Yale; influenced by D'Indy and Franck. On looking back, Sessions recognized that the problem with this piece was that he did not modulate soon enough to the key of the dominant. (Holograph at the Library of Congress; sketches for the Finale at Princeton University Library)

4. Symphony in D Major (December 1917). One movement of this symphony won Sessions the Steinert Prize at Yale. His inability to finish the second movement prompted him to seek help from Ernest Bloch. Dedicated to George H. Bartlett. I. Andante. II. Lento e sostenuto. (Sketches and manuscript at Princeton University Library)

5. Nocturne for Orchestra (1921–1922). Forty-five minutes long. (Manuscript at Princeton University Library)

6. Incidental music for *Turandot* for two pianos and eight percussion instruments. Attempts a Chinese flavor. Written and performed in Cleveland, Ohio, for a production of *Turandot* that took place 8–10 May 1925. Dedicated to Mrs. Joseph Russell. (Manuscript at Princeton University Library)

7. Opera on *The Fall of the House of Usher* (1925). Libretto by Sam Eliot, Jr. of Smith College. Idea came from *The Black Maskers*. Incomplete.

8. Pastorale for Flute solo (1927). Written for and given to Merry Cohu, a flautist married to Barbara Foster's sister, Eleanor. (Manuscript lost)

9. Strophes (1927–1929). Sketches for a work for piano and orchestra, described by Sessions as "a work that had different strophes, somehow connected, a little like variations."

10. Orchestra Suite (1929). Sketches for the first movement, composed in Rome.

11. Waltzes. "I wrote a lot of waltzes when I was in Rome; some of them are rather nice." These displayed a neoclassic trend. (Lost)

12. Symphony (1929). Sessions kept the sketches for this symphony and returned to them in 1948–1949, but he again abandoned them. (Manuscripts at the Princeton University Library)

13. Ballata, illustrative of scenes in Boccaccio's "Decameron" (1929–1930).

14. Three Dirges for Orchestra (1933).

15. Symphony (1934–1935). Sketches. Discarded in 1948–1949.

16. Pages from a Diary. Discards. (1937–1939).

17. Studies in Counterpoint (1938–1941). (Princeton University Library)

18. Miscellaneous compositions (1935–1944). (Princeton University Library)

19. Duo for Violin and Cello (1978). Incomplete.

20. *The Emperor's New Clothes* (1978–1984). Libretto by Andrew Porter. Incomplete.

Sessions describes the works here as belonging "to something I'd really outlived and wasn't interested in anymore." They were projects, holdovers from previous manners of writing, and even completed works that are not considered to be part of his catalogue. The unfinished works were written chiefly in the periods before Sessions's study with Bloch, between *The Black Maskers* (1923) and Symphony No. 1 (1927), and in the late 1930s when he was grappling with career problems and raising children.

Interestingly, his abandonment of works ceased around 1950 when he subconsciously began to adopt the twelve-tone method. Since then Sessions's direction has been precise; he almost never started a work without completing it. He offers a possible explanation for this (during a taped interview on 23 April 1975): "Being precocious is a problem because you develop unevenly. Also being an American composer and finding your own identity was a problem at that time. Sometimes I feel that being precocious makes you develop more slowly later on."

Appendix 3

Chronological Discography

This discography lists records that are reasonably available. A more complete discography is given in: Paul Rapoport, "Roger Sessions: a Discography," *Tempo* 127 (December 1978), pp. 17–20. All recordings are stereo unless otherwise indicated.

The Black Maskers (1928)

American Recording Society Orch./Walter Hendl: *Desto* D 404 (mono), DST 6404, DC 6404

NB: Romualdo's Song is not recorded.

Eastman-Rochester Sym. Orch./Howard Hanson: *Mercury* MG 50106 (mono), SR 90103, MMA 11145 (mono), AMS 16093, MG 50423 (mono), SR 90423, SRI 75049, *Mercury* 75049

Three Chorale Preludes (1924 and 1926)

Marilyn Mason, organ: *Counterpoint/Esoteric* CTP 522 (mono)

Symphony No. 1 (1927)

Japan Phil. Sym. Orch./Akeo Watanabe: *Composers Recordings Inc.* CRI 131 (mono), CRI SD 131

On the Beach at Fontana (1930)

Bethany Beardslee, sop; Robert Helps, pno: *New World Records* NS 243

Sonata for Piano No. 1 (1930)

Robert Helps: *Composers Recordings Inc.* CRI 198 (mono), DRI SD 198

Rebecca LaBreque: *Opus One* 56/7

Concerto for Violin and Orchestra (1935)

Paul Zukofsky/French Radio and Television Phil. Orch./Gunther Schuller: *Composers Recordings Inc.* CRI 220 USD, CRI SD 220

String Quartet No. 1 (1936)

Pro Arte String Quartet: *New World Records* 302 (mono)

Galimir Quartet: *Guild Recordings* set no. RSSI (78 r.p.m.)

Pages from a Diary (1939)

Maro Ajemian: *MGM* E 3218 (mono)

Leon Fleisher: *Epic* LC 3862 (mono); *Columbia* FCX 999 (mono), SAXF 999

Herbert Rogers: *Composers Recordings Inc.* CRI SD 281

Roger Shields: *Vox* set n. SVBX 5303

Duo for Violin and Piano (1942)

Paul Zukofsky, vln; Gilbert Kalish, pno: *Desto* set no. DC 6435 to DC 6437 (record no. DC 6437)

Patricia Travers, vln; Otto Herz, pno: *Columbia* set no. MM 987

***Turn, O Libertad* (1944)**

Gregg Smith Singers/Oresta Cybriwsky and Raymond Beegle, piano duet/Gregg Smith; *Vox* set no. SVBX 5353

Symphony No. 2 (1946)

Phil. Sym. Orch. of New York/Dimitri Mitropoulos: *Columbia* set no. MM 920 (78 r.p.m. records nos. 13095 D to 13098 D), ML 2120 (10'' mono), ML 4784 (mono); *Composers Recordings Inc.* CRI SD 278

Sonata for Piano No. 2 (1946)

Rebecca LaBreque: *Opus One* 56/7

Noël Lee: *Valois* MB 755

Alan Marks: *Composers Recordings Inc.* S-385

Beveridge Webster: *Dover* HCR 5265 (mono)

Quartet No. 2 (1951)

Kohon Quartet: *Vox* set no. SVBX 5305

New Music Quartet: *Columbia* MS 5105 (mono)

Sonata for Violin (1953)

Hyman Bress: *Folkways* FM 3355 (mono)

Robert Gross: *Orion* CRS 73110

Paul Zukofsky: *CP²* 1

***Idyll of Theocritus* (1954)**

Audrey Nossaman, sop./Louisville Orch./Robert Whitney: *Lou.* 57-4 (mono)

Symphony No. 3 (1957)

Royal Phil. Orch./Igor Buketoff: *RCA* LSC 3095, *CRI* S-451

Divertimento for Orchestra (1958)

Louisville Orch./Leonard: *Lou.* 776

Piano Sonata No. 3 (1965)

Robert Helps: *Acoustic Research/Deutsche Grammophon* 0654 086, *New World Records* 307
Rebecca LaBreque: *Opus One* 56/7

Six Pieces for Violoncello (1966)

Roy Christensen: *Gasparo* GS 102

Symphony No. 7 (1967)

Louisville Orch./Leonard: *Lou.* 776

Symphony No. 8 (1968)

New Philharmonia Orch./Frederik Prausnitz: *Argo* ZRG 702

Rhapsody for Orchestra (1970)

New Philharmonia Orch./Frederik Prausnitz: *Argo* ZRG 702

***When Lilacs Last in the Dooryard Bloom'd* (1971)**

Esther Hinds, sop.; Florence Quivar, mezzo; Dominic Cossa, bar./Tanglewood Festival Chorus, Boston
Sym. Orch./Seiji Ozawa: *New World Records* NW 296

Concertino for Chamber Orchestra (1972)

University of Chicago Chamber Players/Ralph Shapey: *Desto* 7155

Five Pieces for Piano (1975)

Robert Black: *Composers Recordings Inc.* CRI S-481

Waltz (1978)

Alan Feinberg: *Nonesuch* 79011 (digital)

Concerto for Orchestra (1981)

Boston Sym. Orch./Seiji Ozawa: *Hyperion* A66050 (digital)

Sessions himself has performed on a recording of Stravinsky's *Les Noces*. Stravinsky, *Les Noces* (*The Wedding*); pianists: Samuel Barber, Aaron Copland, Lukas Foss, Roger Sessions; sop., Mildred Allen; mezzo, Regina Sarafaty; tenor, Loren Driscoll; bass, Robert Oliver; The American Concert Choir, Margaret Hillis, director; Columbia Percussion Ensemble; *Columbia* MS 6372.

Bibliography

The most conspicuous aspect of Sessions's bibliography is its scarcity. No previous books and relatively few articles have been written exclusively about him. Sessions himself has written four books and published numerous articles found in *Roger Sessions on Music; Collected Essays.* In my review of this collection (*Perspectives of New Music*, Spring-Fall 1981) Sessions's writings are discussed. Lesley A. Wright published a valuable bibliography on Sessions in *Current Musicology,* no. 15 (1972).

Most of Sessions's scores and sketches, as well as his lecture notes, have been given to the Princeton University Library. Access to the Princeton archives is gained only by written permission of the composer.

Interviews with Sessions were conducted by Frank Rounds and Edward T. Cone for the Oral History Collection at Columbia University: "The Reminiscences of Roger Sessions" (13 March–24 October 1962). Edward T. Cone also published "Conversations with Roger Sessions" in *Perspectives of New Music* in 1966. A 1975 interview is published in Cole Gagne and Tracy Caras's *Soundpieces: Interviews with American Composers,* Metuchen, N.J.: The Scarecrow Press, Inc., 1982, pp. 355–65. A radio interview with Sessions is at the Rodgers and Hammerstein Collection at the New York Public Library of the Performing Arts. The Opus One recording of the three piano sonatas includes an interview with the composer. My own interviews, taped over six and a half years, and their transcriptions are in my personal collection.

This selective bibliography contains five sections: Writings by Roger Sessions, Reviews of Roger Sessions's Writings, Books Discussing Sessions Among Others, Articles on Sessions, and Articles on Individual Works.

Writings by Roger Sessions Arranged Chronologically

"Wagner's Opinions of Other Composers." *Harvard Musical Review* 1, no. 8 (May 1913): 17–20.
"The Case Against Professional Musical Criticism." *Harvard Musical Review* 2, no. 2 (November 1913): 3–6.
"Our Attitude Towards Contemporary Musical Tendencies." *Harvard Musical Review* 2, no. 4 (January 1914): 3–6, 23.
"Book Review of *Symphonies and their Meaning* by Philip H. Goepp." *Harvard Musical Review* 2, no. 5 (February 1914): 22.
"Parsifaliana." *Harvard Musical Review* 2, no. 6 (March 1914): 13–15.
"Fifty Years of Richard Strauss—I." *Harvard Musical Review* 2, no. 8 (May 1914): 12–19.
"Fifty Years of Richard Strauss—II." *Harvard Musical Review* 2, no. 9 (June 1914): 3–12, 18–20.
"Fifty Years of Richard Strauss—III." *Harvard Musical Review* 2, no. 10 (July 1914): 17–25.
"A New Wagner Essay." *Harvard Musical Review* 3, no. 2 (November 1914): 3–7.
"The Psychological Basis of Modern Dissonance." *Harvard Musical Review* 3, no. 3 (December 1914): 3–10.

"Richard Strauss As a Tone Poet." *Harvard Musical Review* 4, no. 1 (October 1915): 4–8.

"Richard Strauss As a Tone Poet—II." *Harvard Musical Review* 4, no. 2 (November 1915): 11–15.

"Richard Strauss As a Tone Poet—III." *Harvard Musical Review* 4, no. 3 (December 1915): 9–13.

"An American Evening Abroad." *Modern Music* 4 (November 1926): 33–36.

*"Ernest Bloch." *Modern Music* 5 (November 1927): 3–11.

*"On *Oedipus Rex*." *Modern Music* 5 (March 1928): 9–15.

*"Music in Crisis—Some Notes on Recent Musical History." *Modern Music* 10 (January 1933): 63–78.

*"Music and Nationalism; Some Notes on Dr. Göbbel's Letter to Furtwängler." *Modern Music* 11 (November 1933): 3–12.

*"New Vistas in Musical Education." *Modern Music* 11 (March 1934): 115–20.

"Composition and Review." *New York Times* 11 (March 1934), p. 10, 6:7.

Letter on Otto Klemperer's reading of Beethoven's Fifth Symphony. *New York Times* (28 October 1934), p. 9, 8:3.

*"Hindemith's *Mathis der Maler*." *Modern Music* 12 (November 1934): 13–17.

*"Heinrich Schenker's Contribution." *Modern Music* 12 (May 1935): 170–78.

*"America Moves to the Avant-Scene." *American Musicological Society Papers* (1937): 108–19.

*"The New Musical Horizon." *Modern Music* 14 (January 1937): 59–66.

*"Hindemith on Theory." *Modern Music* 15 (November 1937): 57–63.

*"Exposition by Křenek." *Modern Music* 15 (January 1938): 123–28.

*"Escape by Theory." *Modern Music* 15 (March 1938): 192–97.

*"To Revitalize Opera." *Modern Music* 15 (March 1938): 145–52.

*"Vienna—*Vale, Ave*." *Modern Music* 15 (May 1938): 203–8.

*"The Function of Theory." *Modern Music* 16 (May 1938): 257–68.

*"On the American Future." *Modern Music* 17 (January 1940): 71–75.

*"American Music and the Crisis." *Modern Music* 18 (May 1941): 211–17.

"Musicology and the Composer." *Bulletin of the American Musicological Society* 5 (August 1941): 5–7.

*"The Composer and His Message." *The Intent of the Artist*. Ed. by Augusto Centano, 101–34. Princeton: Princeton University Press, 1941.

*"Artists and This War." *Modern Music* 20 (November 1942): 3–7.

*"No More Business-as-Usual." *Modern Music* 19 (March 1942): 156–62.

"How Far Will We Go with Popularization." *Saturday Review of Literature* 27 (22 January 1944): 25–26.

Letter citing Summer Music Institute, Black Mountain College. *New York Times* (24 September 1944), p. 2, 4:5.

"Alfred Einstein's Study of Mozart." *New York Times* (18 February 1945), pp. 3, 18, 20 [book review].

"Sir Donald Tovey: Musical Articles from the *Encyclopedia Britannica* and *Essays in Musical Analysis: Chamber Music*." *Kenyon Review* (Summer 1945): 504–7.

*"Europe Comes to America." 1945.

*"Music in a Business Economy." *Berkeley: A Journal of Modern Culture* (July 1948): 1–2, 7–8.

*"Schönberg in den U.S.A." *Stimmen* 16 (1949): 440–43. Rev. repr. in "Schönberg in the United States." *Tempo* 103 (December 1972): 8–17.

Einstein, Alfred. *The Italian Madrigal*. 3 vols. Trans. by Alexander H. Krappe, Roger H. Sessions, and Oliver Strunk. Princeton, N.J.: Princeton University Press, 1949.

*"The Composer and the University." 1949.

*"How a 'Difficult' Composer Gets That Way." *New York Times* (8 January 1950), p. 2, 9:5.

The Musical Experience of Composer, Performer, Listener. Princeton, N.J.: Princeton University Press, 1950. New York: Antheneum, 1962.

Harmonic Practice. New York: Harcourt, Brace & World, Inc., 1951.

*"Some Notes on Schönberg and the 'Method of Composing with Twelve Tones.' " *Score* 6 (May 1952): 7–10.

*"Music and the Crisis of the Arts." *Frontiers of Knowledge* (1954): 32–39.

Reflections of the Music Life in the United States. New York: Merlin Press, 1956.

*"Song and Pattern in Music Today." *Score* 17 (September 1956): 73–84.

"Contemporary Music in Our Concert Halls." *Newsletter* of the American Symphony Orchestra League (Charleston, W. Va.) 8, no. 6 (1957): 15.

*"Thoughts on Stravinsky." *Score* 20 (June 1957): 32–37.

*"Art, Freedom, and the Individual." *Sewanee Review* 66 (1958): 282–96.

"To the Editor." *Score* 23 (July 1958): 58–64.

*"Problems and Issues Facing the Composer Today." *The Musical Quarterly* 46 (April 1960): 159–71. Repr. in *Problems of Modern Music.* Ed. by Paul Henry Lang, 21–33. New York: W. W. Norton & Co., 1962.

*"Style and 'Styles' in Music." 1961.

"The Classical Tradition in Music." *From Sophocles to Picasso.* Ed. by Whitney J. Oates. Indiana: Indiana University Press, 1962.

"Brickbats and a Bouquet for Sir John." *Musical America* 84 (September 1964): 4.

*"To the Editor." *Perspectives of New Music* 5 (Spring–Summer 1967): 81–97. Also in Boretz and Cone, *Perspectives on American Composers,* 108–24. Repr. in *Roger Sessions on Music; Collected Essays* under the title "What Can Be Taught?"

Questions About Music. Cambridge, Mass.: Harvard University Press, 1970. New York: W. W. Norton & Co., 1971.

Roger Sessions on Music; Collected Essays. Princeton: Princeton University Press, 1979.

*Republished in *Roger Sessions on Music; Collected Essays.*

Reviews of Roger Sessions's Writings

"The Composer and His Message"

Engel, Carl. "Views and Reviews." *The Musical Quarterly* 27 (October 1941): 527–38.

Harmonic Practice

Bauman, Alvin. *American Musicological Society Journal* 5 (Fall 1952): 265–68.

Piston, Walter. *The Musical Quarterly* 38 (July 1952): 457–68.

Tischler, Hans. *Notes* 9 (June 1952): 409–10.

The Musical Experience of Composer, Performer, Listener

Barzun, Jacques. "Not Art for Art's Sake Alone." *Saturday Review of Literature* 34 (28 July 1951): 18–19.

Capell, Richard. *Music and Letters* 33 (October 1952): 360–61.

Epperson, Gordon. *The Musical Symbol; A Study of the Philosophic Theory of Music.* Ames, Iowa: Iowa State University Press, 1967.

Questions About Music

Cone, Edward T. *Perspectives of New Music* 10 (Spring–Summer 1972): 164–70.

Evett, R. "Music," *The New Republic* 162 (9 May 1970): 40–42.

Johnson, Robert S. *Music and Letters* 52 (January 1971): 71–72.

Raynor, Henry. *The Music Review* 32 (February 1971): 73–74.

Turok, Paul. *Music Journal* 28 (July 1970): 96.

Roger Sessions on Music; Collected Essays

Brody, Martin. "Book review." *Journal of Music Theory* 27, no. 1 (Spring 1983), pp. 111–20.
Dickinson, Peter. "Against the tide." *Musical Times* 122 (October 1981), p. 674.
Kivy, Peter. *The Journal of Aesthetics and Art Criticism* 38 no. 3 (Spring 1980), pp. 346–47.
Olmstead, Andrea. *Perspectives of New Music* (Spring–Fall 1981): 491–500.
Salzman, Eric. "An American International," *New York Times Book Review* (18 March 1979), p. 9.
Whittall, Arnold. "Book reviews." *The Music Review* 43, no. 1 (1982), pp. 68–72.

Books Discussing Sessions Among Others

Austin, William. *Music in the 20th Century,* 437–39, *passim.* New York: W. W. Norton & Co., 1966.
Boretz, Benjamin and Edward T. Cone, eds. *Perspectives on American Composers.* New York: W. W. Norton & Co., 1971.
Chase, Gilbert. *America's Music,* 525–30. New York: McGraw-Hill, 1955.
Copland, Aaron. "Sessions and Piston." *Our New Music,* 176–86. New York: McGraw-Hill, 1941. Revised and enlarged in *The New Music 1900–1960,* 127–34. New York: W. W. Norton & Co. 1968.
Copland, Aaron and Vivian Perlis. *Copland/1900–1942.* New York: St. Martin's/Marek, 1984.
Deri, Otto. *Exploring Twentieth-Century Music,* 479–81. New York: Holt, Rinehart & Winston, Inc., 1968.
Ewen, David. *The Complete Book of 20th Century Music,* 365–66. New York: Prentice-Hall, Inc. 1952.
_____. *Composers Since 1900,* 519–22. New York: The H. W. Wilson Co., 1969.
Goss, Madeleine. *Modern Music Makers,* 253–65. New York: E. P. Dutton & Co., 1952.
Hamm, Charles. *Music in the New World,* 555–61. New York: W. W. Norton & Co., 1983.
Hansen, Peter S. *An Introduction to Twentieth Century Music,* 325–28. Boston: Allyn & Bacon, Inc., 1961.
Howard, John Tasker. *Our Contemporary Composers.* New York: Thomas Y. Crowell Co., 1941.
_____. *Our American Music.* 4th ed. New York: Thomas Y. Crowell Co., 1965, *passim.*
Howard, John Tasker and George Kent Bellows. *A Short History of Music in America,* 293–95, *passim.* New York: Thomas Y. Crowell Co., 1957.
Huntington, James Lincoln. *Forty Acres: the Story of the Bishop Huntington House.* New York: Hastings House, 1949.
Machlis, Joseph. *Introduction to Contemporary Music.* 2nd ed., 398–407. New York: W. W. Norton & Co., 1979.
Rosenfeld, Paul. "Roger Sessions." *Port of New York,* 145–52. New York: Harcourt & Brace, 1924.
Sessions, Ruth Huntington. *Sixty-Odd; A Personal History.* Brattleboro, Vt.: Stephen Daye Press, 1936.
Sessions, Francis Charles. *Materials for a History of the Sessions Family in America.* Albany, N.Y.: J. Munsell's Sons, 1890.
Slonimsky, Nicolas. "Roger Sessions." *American Composers on American Music.* Ed. by Henry Cowell, 75–81. Palo Alto, Cal.: Stanford University Press, 1933.
_____. *Music Since 1900.* New York: Charles Scribners Sons, 1971.

Articles on Sessions

Abruzzo, James and Henry Weinberg. "Roger Sessions." *The New Grove Dictionary of Music and Musicians.* 20 vols. Ed. by Stanley Sadie. Vol. 17, 194–97. London: Macmillan Publishers Ltd., 1980.
Berger, Arthur. "Enduring Sessions." *Saturday Review of Literature* 33 (August 1950): 53.
Boretz, Benjamin. "Sessions Festival." *Musical America* 81 (March 1961): 25–26.
_____. "Current Chronicle." *The Musical Quarterly* 27 (July 1961): 386–96.
Broder, Nathan. "Roger Sessions." *Die Musik in Geschichte und Gegenwart.* 14 vols. Ed. by Friedrich Blume. Vol. 12, cols. 590–91. Kassel: Bärenreiter, 1965.

Brunswick, Mark. "American Composers, X: Roger Huntington Sessions." *Modern Music* 10 (May 1933): 182–87.

Cone, Edward T. "Conversations with Roger Sessions." *Perspectives of New Music* 4 (Spring 1966): 29–46. Repr. in Boretz and Cone, *Perspectives on American Composers*, 90–107.

_____. "In Honor of Roger Sessions." *Perspectives of New Music* 10 (Spring–Summer 1972): 130–41.

_____. "In Defense of Song: The Contribution of Roger Sessions." *Critical Inquiry* 2, no. 1 (Autumn 1975): 93–112.

Copland, Aaron, "The American Composer Gets a Break." *American Mercury* 34 (April 1935): 490–91.

_____. "America's Young Men of Promise." *Modern Music* 3 (March 1926): 13–20.

Daniel, Oliver. "Roger Sessions," *Ovation* (March 1984): 12–15, 48.

Epstein, D. M. "Sessions at 60—An Appraisal of His Work." *Musical America* 77 (September 1957): 28.

Ferro, E. F. "Los Conciertos." *Buenos Aires Musical* 20, no. 331 (1965): 2–3.

Harbison, John and Andrea Olmstead. "Roger Sessions." *The New Grove Dictionary of Music in the United States*. Ed. by H. Wiley Hitchcock. New York: Macmillan Publishers Ltd., forthcoming.

Henahan, Donal. "Roger Sessions." *New York Times* (14 April 1968), p. 2, 17:1.

Henderson, Ronald D. *Tonality in the Pre-Serial Instrumental Music of Roger Sessions*. Ph.D. diss.: The Eastman School of Music, 1974.

Imbrie, Andrew. "Roger Sessions: In Honor of His Sixty-fifth Birthday." *Perspectives of New Music* 1 (Fall 1962): 117–47. Repr. in Boretz and Cone, *Perspectives on American Composers*, 59–89.

_____. "The Symphonies of Roger Sessions." *Tempo* 103 (1972): 24–32.

Kastendieck, M. "Roger Sessions." *Broadcast Music Incorporated* (February 1968): 9.

Keats, Shiela. "Reference Articles on American Composers: An Index." *Juilliard Review* 1 (Fall 1954): 32–33.

"Moments Musicaux. Roger Sessions: Celebration of his 80 Years." *Perspectives of New Music* 16 no. 1 (1978): 85–154. [music by Imbrie, Helps, Lansky, Diamond, Gamer, Babbitt, Randall, Gideon, Kirchner, Cone, Boretz, Fine, Swift, Lewin, Westergaard, Weisgull, Spies].

Oja, Carol. "The Copland-Sessions Concerts." *The Musical Quarterly* 65 (April 1979): 212–29.

Olmstead, Andrea. "Roger Sessions: A Personal Portrait." *Tempo* 127 (December 1978): 10–16.

Petrobelli, Pierluigi and Henry Weinberg. "Roger Sessions e la musica americana." *Nuova Rivista Musicale Italiana* 5 (March–April 1971): 249–63.

Rockwell, John. "Roger Sessions, Nearing 85, Is Still a Maverick Composer." *New York Times* (22 March 1981), pp. 17–18.

Romano, J. "Musicos de hoy: Roger Sessions." *Buenos Aires Musical* 20, no. 332 (1965): 5–6.

_____. "Retratos de musicos americanos: Roger Sessions." *Buenos Aires Musical* 24, no. 400 (1969): 3.

Rosenfeld, Paul. "The Newest American Composers." *Modern Music* 15 (March–April 1938): 153–59.

Schubart, Mark A. "Roger Sessions: Portrait of an American Composer." *The Musical Quarterly* 32 (April 1946): 196–214.

"Roger Sessions." BMI pamphlet. New York: Broadcast Music Inc., 1965.

Slonimsky, Nicholas. "Composers of New England." *Modern Music* 7 (February 1930): 24–27.

_____. "The Six of American Music." *Christian Science Monitor Weekly Magazine* (17 March 1937): 8–9.

Vinton, John, ed. "Roger Sessions." *Dictionary of Contemporary Music*, 675. New York: E. P. Dutton, 1974.

Articles on Individual Works Arranged Chronologically

Incidental Music and Orchestral Suite from *The Black Maskers* (1923 and 1928)

"Black Maskers by Roger Sessions Is Introduced to Philadelphians." *Musical America* 10 (November 1933).

Henderson, Ronald. *Tonality in the Pre-Serial Instrumental Music of Roger Sessions*, 31–108. Ph.D. diss.: The Eastman School of Music, 1974.

Trimble, Lester. "Black Maskers Suite." *New York Herald Tribune* (13 February 1955).

Rosenfeld, Paul. "Roger Sessions." *Port of New York*, 145–52. New York: Harcourt & Brace, 1924.

Three Chorale Preludes for Organ (1924 and 1926)

Henderson, Ronald. *Tonality in the Pre-Serial Instrumental Music of Roger Sessions*, 18–31. Ph.D. diss.: The Eastman School of Music, 1974.

Symphony No. 1 (1927)

Carter, Elliott. "The Rhythmic Basis of American Music." *Score* 12 (June 1955): 29.

Cowell, Henry. "Current Chronicle: New York." *The Musical Quarterly* 36 (January 1950): 94–98.

Hale, Philip. "First Performance of Roger Sessions' Symphony in E Minor." *New York Times* (1 May 1927), p. 8, 7:2.

Henderson, Ronald. *Tonality in the Pre-Serial Instrumental Music of Roger Sessions*, 108–65. Ph.D. diss.: The Eastman School of Music, 1974.

Imbrie, Andrew. "The Symphonies of Roger Sessions." *Tempo* 103 (1972): 24–32.

Lopatnikoff, N. "America in Berlin." *Modern Music* 9 (January 1932): 90–91.

Mooser, A. "Geneva—Another Disappointment." *Modern Music* 6 (May 1929): 12.

"Roger Sessions' Symphony No. 1 Hissed at First Philadelphia Performance." *New York Times* (21 December 1935), p. 10:8.

Eric Salzman. *New York Times* (19 June 1960).

Sessions, Roger. "Symphony No. 1." Boston Symphony Programs, 1926–1927, 1874–78.

Welch, Roy D. "A Symphony Introduces Roger Sessions." *Modern Music* 4 (May 1927): 27–30.

On the Beach at Fontana (1930)

Blitzstein, Mark. "Mid-Season in New York." *Modern Music* 11 (January 1934): 101.

Cogan, Robert. "Toward a Theory of Timbre: Verbal Timbre and Musical Line in Purcell, Sessions, and Stravinsky." *Perspectives of New Music* 8 (Fall 1969): 75–81.

The Joyce Book, 36–41 [music]. London, 1933.

Piano Sonata No. 1 (1930)

Boys, H. "America in London." *Modern Music* 9 (January 1932): 93.

Campbell, Michael Ian. *The Piano Sonatas of Roger Sessions: Sequel to a Tradition*, 74–112. DMA diss.: Peabody Institute, 1982. Unpublished.

Copland, Aaron. "Contemporaries at Oxford, 1931." *Modern Music* 9 (November 1931): 22–23.

Hill, Edward B. "The Young Composers' Movement." *Modern Music* 5 (May–June 1928): 32–33.

Sessions, Roger. *The Musical Experience of Composer, Performer, Listener*, 52ff. Princeton, N.J.: Princeton University Press, 1950.

Slonimsky, Nicholas. *Music Since 1900*, 534, 549. New York: Charles Scribners Sons, 1971.

Thompson, R. "Forecast and Review—Jacobi's Quartet and Sessions' Sonata." *Modern Music* 12 (March 1935): 137–38.

Concerto for Violin and Orchestra (1935)

Abruzzo, James and Henry Weinberg. "Roger Sessions." *The New Grove Dictionary of Music and*

Musicians. 20 vols. Ed. by Stanley Sadie. Vol. 17, 194–97. New York: Macmillan Publishers Ltd., 1980.

Biancolli, Louis, "Sessions Concerto has N.Y. Debut." *New York Herald Tribune* (16 February 1959).

Carter, Elliott. "Current Chronicle—New York." *The Musical Quarterly* 45 (July 1959): 375–381.

"Composer R. Sessions Speaks on Violin Concerto." *New York Times* (20 February 1959), p. 18:5.

Dyer, Richard. "Sessions Work Handled Well." *The Boston Globe* (20 April 1981): 43.

Hamilton, David. "The New Craft of the Contemporary Concerto: Carter and Sessions." *High Fidelity/Musical America* 18 (May 1968): 67–68.

Henahan, Donal. "Reviews of Records." *The Musical Quarterly* 54 (July 1968): 385–86.

Henderson, Ronald. *Tonality in the Pre-Serial Instrumental Music of Roger Sessions,* 170–237. Ph.D. diss.: The Eastman School of Music, 1974.

Imbrie, Andrew. "Roger Sessions: In Honor of His Sixty-fifth Birthday." *Perspectives of New Music* 1 (Fall 1962): 117–47.

Kolodin, Irving. "Music to My Ears." *Saturday Review* 42 (7 March 1959): 30.

Lerdahl, Fred. "Communications." *Perspectives of New Music* 10 (1972): 175.

Machlis, Joseph. *Introduction to Contemporary Music.* 2nd ed., 398–407. New York: W. W. Norton & Co., 1979.

Petrobelli, Pierluigi and Henry Weinberg. "Roger Sessions e la musica americana." *Nuova Rivista Musicale Italiana* 5 (March–April 1971): 249–63.

Taubman, Howard. "Sessions Violin Concerto." *New York Times* (21 February 1959), p. 24:2.

Trimble, Lester. "N.Y. Premiere of Concerto for Violin and Orchestra." *The Nation* 188 (7 March 1959): 216.

"Premieres." *Broadcast Music Inc.,* January 1972.

String Quartet No. 1 (1936)

Carter, Elliott. "Spring Fancies, 1937." *Modern Music* 14 (May 1937): 216.

Cone, Edward T. "Roger Sessions' String Quartet." *Modern Music* 18 (March 1941): 159–63.

Downes, Olin. "Festival of Music Closes in Capital." *New York Times* (12 April 1937), p. 14:3.

Henderson, Ronald. *Tonality in the Pre-Serial Instrumental Music of Roger Sessions,* 237–96. Ph.D. diss.: The Eastman School of Music, 1974.

Pages from a Diary (1940)

Cone, Edward T. "Analysis Today." *The Musical Quarterly* (April 1960): 172–88.

Fine, Irving. "Reviews of Records." *The Musical Quarterly* 38 (July 1952): 480–81.

Forte, Allen. *Contemporary Tone Structures,* 48–62. New York: Bureau of Publications of the Teachers College, Columbia University, 1955.

Duo for Violin and Piano (1942)

Schubart, Mark. "Roger Sessions: Portrait of an American Composer." *The Musical Quarterly* 32 (April 1946): 196–214.

Sessions, Roger. "Duo for Violin and Piano." Liner notes. *Columbia* ML 2169.

"Three Contemporary Sonatas." *International Musician* 49 (September 1950): 14.

Turn, O Libertad (1944)

Cooper, David S. *"Turn, O Libertad."* *Notes* 10 (June 1953): 494.

Symphony No. 2 (1946)

Cogan, Robert and P. Escot. "Roger Sessions." *Boletino Interamericano de Musica* 33 (January 1963): 3–10.

Cook, J. D. "The Composer Tells How." *Saturday Review* 37 (26 June 1954): 51.

Cowell, Henry. "Current Chronicle: New York." *The Musical Quarterly* 36 (April 1950): 268–70.

Danchenka, Gary Robert. *Quantitative Measurement of Information Content via Recurring Associations in Three Movements of Symphony No. 2 by Roger Sessions.* Ph.D. diss.: University of Miami, 1981, 148 pp. Unpublished.

Diamond, David. "Roger Sessions: Symphony No. 2." *Notes* 7 (June 1950): 438–39.

Downes, Olin. "Corigliano Soloist for Philharmonic." *New York Times* (13 January 1950), p. 19:3.

Fisher, Marjory M. "Sessions Symphony Has Premiere." *Musical America* (25 January 1947).

Henderson, Ronald. *Tonality in the Pre-Serial Instrumental Music of Roger Sessions,* 316–81. Ph.D. diss.: The Eastman School of Music, 1974.

Kerman Joseph. *Hudson Review* (Spring 1951).

Korn, Peter. *The Symphony in America.* In *The Symphony.* Ed. by Roger Simpson, 260–61. Baltimore: Penguin Books, II, 1967.

Kress, Steven Morton. *Roger Sessions, Composer and Teacher: a Comparative Analysis of Roger Sessions' Philosophy of Educating Composers and his Approach to Composition in Symphonies no. 2 and 8.* Ph.D. diss.: University of Florida, 1982, 178 pp. Unpublished.

Porter, Andrew. "Musical Events." *The New Yorker* 58 (31 January 1983), pp. 94ff.

Taubman, Howard. "Records: Sessions' Second Symphony Played by Philharmonic under Mitropoulos." *New York Times* (2 July 1950), p. 2, 99:6.

Piano Sonata No. 2 (1946)

Burge, David "Contemporary Piano: Piano Music of Roger Sessions." *Contemporary Keyboard* (October 1980), p. 61.

Campbell, Michael Ian. *The Piano Sonatas of Roger Sessions: Sequel to a Tradition,* 113–63. DMA diss.: Peabody Institute, 1982. Unpublished.

Cone, Edward T. "Analysis Today." *The Musical Quarterly* (April 1960): 172–88.

Foldes, Andor. "Roger Sessions: Second Sonata for Piano Solo." *Notes* 7 (March 1950): 312–13.

Henderson, Ronald. *Tonality in the Pre-Serial Instrumental Music of Roger Sessions,* 381–426. Ph.D. diss.: The Eastman School, 1974.

Lowens, Irving. "Recent Music—The Piano." *Musicology* 2 (July 1949): 429.

The Trial of Lucullus (1947)

Boretz, Benjamin. "Current Chronicle." *The Musical Quarterly* 47 (July 1961): 393–96.

Drew, David. "Out of Limbo." *New Statesman* (24 June 1966): 937.

Ericson, Raymond. "Operatic Ghosts and Shades." *New York Times,* 15 May 1966.

Kolodin, Irving. "Murder, to Music, at the Juilliard." *Saturday Review* 49 (4 June 1966): 38.

"Lucullan Feast." *Time* 65 (9 May 1955): 69.

"Opera." *Broadcast Music Inc.* (October 1966): 4.

Steinberg, Michael. "Sessions' 'Lucullas' [sic] Impresses at Juilliard." *The Boston Globe,* 26 May 1966.

Zoff, O. "Auf dem Wege zur amerikanischen Oper." *Melos* 24 (May 1957): 137.

————. "Neue Chorwerke in New York." *Melos* 23 (February 1956): 54.

String Quartet No. 2 (1951)

Cone, Edward T. "Sessions: Second String Quartet." *The Musical Quarterly* 43 (January 1957): 140–41.

Ericson, Raymond. "A Sessions Retrospect." *New York Times*, 24 March 1977.
Joachim, H. "Current Chronicle." *The Musical Quarterly* 41 (January 1955): 94.
Livingston, Herbert. "Roger Sessions: Second String Quartet." *Notes* 13 (June 1956): 523-24.
Schubart, Mark. "Bay Area Diary—New Music Is News." *Opera and Concert* 16 (July 1951): 26-28.
Schweitzer, Eugene. *Generation in String Quartets of Carter, Sessions, Kirchner, and Schuller.* Ph.D. diss.: The Eastman School of Music, 1965. Unpublished.

Sonata for Violin Solo (1953)

Drew, David. "Alwyn and Sessions." *Musical Times* 97 (December 1956): p. 656.
Greissle, Felix and Lester Trimble. "Current Chronicle." *The Musical Quarterly* 43 (April 1957): 236-40.

Idyll of Theocritus (1954)

Dahl, Ingolf. "Roger Sessions: *Idyll of Theocritus.*" *Notes* 15 (September 1958): 656.
Jacobs, A. "B.B.C.—I.C.A. Concert." *Musical Times* 98 (March 1957): 157.
Keller, H. "XXXth I.S.C.M. Festival at Stockholm, 3rd-10th June." *Music Review* 17 (August 1956): 248.
"Masterpiece in Louisville?" *Time* 67 (30 January 1956): 58.

Mass (1955)

Lowens, Irving. "Roger Sessions: *Mass.*" *Notes* 16 (December 1958): 151-52.
Stevens, Denis. "New York." *Musical Times* 97 (May 1956): 268-69.
_____. "Roger Sessions *Mass.*" *Musical Times* 102 (November 1961): 696-97.
Tortolano, W. "Melody in 20th Century Masses." *Diapason* 60 (April 1969): 18-19.

Piano Concerto (1956)

Boretz, Benjamin. "Current Chronicle." *The Musical Quarterly* 47 (July 1961): 388-91.
Lang, Paul Henry. "Sessions Piano Concerto." *New York Herald Tribune*, 12 February 1956.
Porter, Andrew. "Musical Events: Line and Color." *The New Yorker* (12 November 1984): 174.
Taubman, Howard. "Juilliard Orchestra." *New York Times* (11 February 1956), p. 13:2.
Zoff, O. "Festwochen amerikanischer Musik," *Melos* 23 (May 1956): 150.

Symphony No. 3 (1957)

Chanler, Theodore. "Current Chronicle." *The Musical Quarterly* 44 (April 1958): 228-30.
Downes, E. "Sessions' Third." *New York Times* (8 December 1957), p. 2, 13:8.
Sargeant, Winthrop. "Musical Events: Really Atonal and Otherwise." *The New Yorker* 33 (21 December 1957): 91.
Sessions, Roger. "Entr'acte—A New Symphony." Boston Symphony Orchestra Programs (6 December 1957): 476-82.
Taubman, Howard. "Sessions' Third Symphony." *New York Times* (12 December 1957), p. 34:2.

String Quintet (1958)

Abruzzo, James and Henry Weinberg. "Roger Sessions." *The New Grove Dictionary of Music and Musicians.* 20 vols. Ed. by Stanley Sadie. Vol. 17, 194-97. New York: Macmillan Publishers, Ltd., 1980.

Goldman, Richard F. "Current Chronicle." *The Musical Quarterly* 46 (January 1960): 71–73.

Imbrie, Andrew. "Current Chronicle." *The Musical Quarterly* 44 (July 1958): 370–71.

_____. "Roger Sessions: In Honor of His Sixty-fifth Birthday." *Perspectives of New Music* 1 (Fall 1962): 117–47.

Lang, Paul Henry. "Modern Chamber Music." *New York Herald Tribune*, 24 November 1959.

Sessions, Roger, "Quintet for Two Violins, Two Violas and Violoncello," Program Notes for the Juilliard String Quartet, 21 October 1980.

Taubman, Howard. "Premiere of Sessions' Quintet." *New York Times* (24 November 1959), p. 46:1.

_____. "Testing Ground." *New York Times* (6 December 1959), p. 2, 13:1.

Weinberg, Henry and Pierluigi Petrobelli. "Roger Sessions e la Musica americana." *Nuova Revista Musicale Italiana* (March–April 1971): 249–63.

Wheeler, Scott. *Harmonic Motion in the Music of Roger Sessions: An Examination of the Quintet, first movement*. Ph.D. diss.: Brandeis University, 1984. Unpublished.

Symphony No. 4 (1958)

Boretz, Benjamin. "Current Chronicle." *The Musical Quarterly* 47 (July 1961): 391–93.

Slominsky Nicholas. *Music Since 1900*, 1078, 1088. New York: Charles Scribners Sons, 1971.

Divertimento for Orchestra (1959)

"Premieres." *Broadcast Music Inc.* (April 1965): 10–11.

Montezuma **(1963)**

"The Bland Giant." *Time* 83 (8 May 1964): 50.

Bender, William. "Three for the Opera." *Time* (12 April 1976): 84.

Bollert, W. "Roger Sessions: *Montezuma*." *Musica* 18 (July–August 1964): 206.

Davies, Peter Maxwell. "Montezuma." *New York Times* (21 April 1964), p. 43:1.

_____. " '*Montezuma*' Creates a Stir in Berlin." *New York Times* (3 May 1964), p. 2, 11:3.

Davis, Peter G. "Montezuma's Revenge." *New York Magazine* (8 March 1982): 89–90.

Dyer, Richard. "Momentous 'Montezuma' Impressive yet Baffling." *Boston Sunday Globe*, 11 April 1976.

Eckert, Thor. " 'Montezuma'—Sarah Caldwell's Personal Triumph." *The Christian Science Monitor*, 5 April 1976.

Freeman, J. W. *Opera News* 46 (17 April 1982), 38ff.

Harbison, John. "Roger Sessions and Montezuma." *New Boston Review*, June 1976. Repr. in *Tempo* 121 (June 1977): 2–5.

Hoelterhoff, M. "Four Odd Operas get a Hearing." *Wall Street Journal* 62 (5 March 1982): 19.

Joachim, H. "Germany/*Montezuma* and the *Messiah*." *Musical America* 84 (May 1964): 20–21.

Kerner, Leighton. "A Great American Opera is Opening out of Town." *The Village Voice*, 26 January 1976.

_____. "An American Opera Comes Home." *The Village Voice*, April 1976.

_____. "Candidates for the Repertory." *The Village Voice* (9 March 1982), p. 72.

Kolodin Irving. "Opera and the Power that Corrupts." *Saturday Review*, 15 May 1976.

Laufer, Edward C. "Roger Sessions: *Montezuma*." *Perspectives of New Music* 4 (Fall 1965): 95–108.

Lüdicke, H. "Roger Sessions' *Montezuma*—Aztekentragödie als Oper." *Musik und Gesellschaft* 14 (October 1964): 623–24.

Mason, Charles Norman. *A Comprehensive Analysis of Roger Sessions's Opera "Montezuma."* DMA diss.: University of Illinois, Urbana-Champaign, 1982, 179 pp. Unpublished.

Moor, Paul. "American Opera's Premiere in Berlin." *New York Herald Tribune*, 21 April 1964.

Oehlmann, W. "*Montezuma* Untergang: Roger-Sessions-Uraufführung in der deutschen Oper." *Neue Zeitschrift für Musik* 125, no. 6 (1964): 265-67.

Olmstead, Andrea. "The Plum'd Serpent: Antonio Borgese's and Roger Sessions's *Montezuma.*" *Tempo* 152, March 1985.

Oppens, Kurt. *Opernwelt* 23 n. 6 (1982), p. 54.

Parmenter, Ross. "The World of Music." *New York Times* 15 (December 1963), p. 113:13.

Peyser, Joan. " 'Montezuma' Reaches New York—At Last." *New York Times* (14 February 1982), p. D-21.

Porter, Andrew. "The Matter of Mexico." *The New Yorker*, 19 April 1976.

———. "A Magnificent Epic." *The New Yorker* (March 1982): 128-37.

"Premieres." *Broadcast Music Inc.* (November 1966): 18.

Rich, Alan. "Noble Savage, Noble Failure." *New York Magazine,* 1976.

Rockwell, John. "Sessions's 'Montezuma' Comes to the U.S. "*New York Times,* 2 April 1976.

Smith, Patrick J. *High Fidelity/Musical America* 32 (June 1982), p. 21.

Steinberg, Michael. "Enter Montezuma." *Opera News,* 3 April 1976.

Stuckenschmidt, Hans H. "Der weisse Gott Cortez in Montezumas Aztekenreich." *Melos* 31 (June 1964): 192-94.

Sutcliffe, J. H. "New Hall for Montezuma." *Opera News* 33 (17 May 1969): 6-7.

"World Premiere of *Montezuma.*" *New York Times* (30 April 1964), p. 32:2.

Psalm 140 **(1963)**

Rogers, Harold. "Sessions' Psalm 140." *The Christian Science Monitor*, 12 February 1966.

Sessions, Roger. "Psalm 140 for Soprano and Orchestra." Boston Symphony Orchestra Programs (11 February 1966): 982-85.

Slonimsky, Nicholas. *Music Since 1900*, 1214. New York: Charles Scribners Sons, 1971.

Symphony No. 5 (1964)

Gruen, John. "A New Sessions' Symphony Played." *New York Herald Tribune,* 19 February 1964.

Hitchcock, H. Wiley. "Current Chronicle." *The Musical Quarterly* 50 (July 1964): 381-82.

Imbrie, Andrew. "The Symphonies of Roger Sessions." *Tempo* 103 (1972): 24-32.

Parmenter, Ross. "Symphony No. 5." *New York Times* (19 February 1964), p. 35:1.

Piano Sonata No. 3 (1965)

Burge, David. "Contemporary Piano: Piano Music of Roger Sessions." *Contemporary Keyboard* (October 1980): 61.

Campbell, Michael Ian. *The Piano Sonatas of Roger Sessions: Sequel to a Tradition,* 164-215. DMA diss.: Peabody Institute, 1982. Unpublished.

Cone, Edward T. "In Defense of Song: The Contribution of Roger Sessions." *Critical Inquiry* 2, no. 1 (Autumn 1975): 93-112.

Daniel, Oliver. "The Fruits of Industry, or What AR Hath Wrought." *The Saturday Review* 53 (26 December 1970): 47.

Duffin, Diana Ruth. *The Interpretation of Accent Signs in Roger Sessions's Third Piano Sonata.* DMA diss.: Ohio State University, 1979. Unpublished.

Fanfare 4, no. 3 (1981): 59 [record review].

Hughes, Allen. "New York City Premieres of Helps' Quartet for Piano and Sessions' Piano Sonata No. 3." *New York Times* (3 May 1971), p. 51.

Merryman, Marjorie Jane. *Aspects of Phrasing and Pitch Usage in Roger Sessions's Piano Sonata No. 3.* Ph.D. diss.: Brandeis University, 1981. Unpublished.

Zenge, M. "Sonata No. 3 for Piano Solo." *Notes* 26 (December 1969): 362–63.

Symphony No. 6 (1966)

Ericson, Raymond. "Concert: Symphony by Sessions." *New York Times*, 6 March 1977.
Felton, James. "New Sessions Work Has World Premiere." *The Evening Bulletin*, 21 November 1966.
Henahan, Donal. "For Roger Sessions, a Tribute and a Premiere at 80." *New York Times*, 4 March 1977.
Moor, Paul. "Homage to Roger Sessions." *Musical America* (March 1984): 31, 39.
"Premieres." *Broadcast Music Inc.* (March 1966): 2
"Premieres." *Broadcast Music Inc.* (February 1967): 6.
Strongin, Theodore. "New Jersey Symphony Plays First Two Movements of Unfinished Work." *New York Times* (20 January 1966), p. 28:6.

Six Pieces for Violoncello (1966)

Henahan, Donal. "N.Y. Premiere of Sessions's *Six Pieces for Violoncello.*" *New York Times* (1 April 1968), p. 56:5.
Neuman, K. "6 Pieces for Violoncello." *Notes* 25 (March 1969): 599–600.
The Village Voice, 18 April 1968.

Symphony No. 7 (1967)

Parsons, Arrand. "Symphony No. 7." Chicago Symphony Orchestra Programs, 5 October 1967, 13–21.
"Premieres." *Broadcast Music Inc.* (December 1967): 8–9.

Symphony No. 8 (1968)

"Estrenos." *Boletino Interamericano de Musica* 69–70 (January–March 1969): 72.
Johnson, Harriet. *New York Post*, 3 May 1968.
Kress, Steven Morton. *Roger Sessions, Composer and Teacher: a Comparative Analysis of Roger Sessions's Philosophy of Educating Composers and his Approach to Composition in Symphonies No. 2 and 8.* Ph.D. diss.: University of Florida, 1982, unpublished.
"Premieres." *Broadcast Music Inc.* (July 1968): 26.
Sargeant, Winthrop. "Musical Events: Is Music Dead?" *The New Yorker* 44 (11 May 1968): 140.
Schonberg, Harold. "Music: Steinberg Leads Philharmonic in New Sessions Work." *New York Times* (3 May 1968), p. 41:4.
Sessions, Roger. "Symphony No. 8." The Philharmonic–Symphony Society of New York Programs, 2 May 1968, B-D. Liner notes *Argo* ZRG 702.

Rhapsody for Orchestra (1970)

Hughes, Allen. "Moderns Arrive from Baltimore." *New York Times*, 23 March 1970.
Kerner, Leighton. "Music: *Lilacs* in bloom. *The Village Voice* (28 January 1981): 66.
Sessions, Roger. "Rhapsody for Orchestra." Liner notes *Argo* ZRG 702.

When Lilacs Last in the Dooryard Bloom'd (1971)

Hamilton, David. "Music." *The Nation*, 19 April 1975.

Henahan, Donal. "A Soothing Sessions Leads off Contemporaries at Tanglewood." *New York Times*, 15 August 1977.

Kaplan, Justin. "Whitman and Music." *New World Records* 296.

Kerner, Leighton. "Sessions Blooms in Chicago." *The Village Voice*, 16 February 1976.

Porter, Andrew. "Sessions' Passionate and Profound *Lilacs*." *High Fidelity Magazine*. February 1978): 70–71.

———. "An American Requiem." *The New Yorker*, April 1977.

Powers, Harold S. "Current Chronicle." *The Musical Quarterly* 58 (April 1972): 297–307.

Steinberg, Michael. "Roger Sessions: *When Lilacs Last in the Dooryard Bloom'd*." Tanglewood 1977 Program notes, 18–21. Repr. in *New World Records* 296 liner notes.

Swan, Annalyn. "Sessions: *When Lilacs Last in the Dooryard Bloom'd*." *Time*, 26 June 1978.

Tempo. Record review of *Lilacs*. 125 (June 1978): 35–37.

Whitman, Walt. *Leaves of Grass*. Including a facsimile autobiography, variorum readings of the poems, and a department of gathered leaves. Philadelphia: David McKay, 1900 [edition used by Sessions].

Concerto for Violin, Violoncello, and Orchestra (1971)

Hughes, Allen. "Juilliard and Manhattan Present New Sessions and Haieff Works." *New York Times* (7 November 1971), p. 83:2.

Sessions, Roger. "Concerto for Violin, Cello, and Orchestra." Program notes, Aspen Conference on Contemporary Music, 1972.

Canons (1971)

Henahan, Donal. *New York Times* (9 February 1973): 32.

Sessions, Roger. "Canons." *Tempo* 98, March 1972 [music].

Concertino for Chamber Orchestra (1972)

Cone, Edward T. "Sessions's Concertino." *Tempo* 115 (December 1975): 2–10.

Three Choruses on Biblical Texts (1972)

Mishin, Henry G. "The Genesis of a Commission: Roger Sessions, Three Choruses on Biblical Texts." Published by The Friends of Amherst College Music on the occasion of the Amherst College Sesquicentennial Celebration, Spring 1974.

Five Pieces for Piano (1975)

Olmstead, Andrea. "In Honor of Beveridge Webster and Roger Sessions." League of Composers-ISCM Program notes, Carnegie Recital Hall, 17 March 1978. Repr. for ISCM World Music Days, Athens, 1979.

Symphony No. 9 (1978)

George, Earl. "Symphony's World Premiere Impresses." *Syracuse Herald Journal*, 19 January 1980.

Kenyon, Nicholas, "Challenges." *The New Yorker*, 7 April 1980.

Kerner, Leighton. "Music: A contrast of symphonies." *The Village Voice* 25 (14 April 1980), p. 68.

Olmstead, Andrea. "Roger Sessions's Symphony No. 9." The Syracuse Symphony Program notes, 17–19 January 1980. Repr. in Carnegie Hall Program notes, 22 March 1980.

_____. "Roger Sessions's Ninth Symphony." *Tempo* 133 (December 1980): 79–81.

Concerto for Orchestra (1981)

Daniel, Oliver. "Roger Sessions—Pulitzer Recognition Again." *BMI: The Many Worlds of Music*, no. 2 (1982): 4.

Kerner, Leighton. "Music: Boston Symphony Orchestra—going on 101." *The Village Voice* 26 (28 October 1981), p. 76.

_____. "Music: Sessions of lyrical, witty sound." *The Village Voice* 26 (11 November 1981), p. 68.

Kihss, Peter. "A Composer, 85, and a Dead Poet Among Winners of Pulitzer Prizes." *New York Times* (13 April 1982): 1.

Porter, Andrew. "Celebration." *The New Yorker* (9 November 1981): 164–67.

_____. "Musical Events." *The New Yorker* 58 (31 January 1983), pp. 94ff.

Rockwell, John. "Concert: Boston Symphony Opens at Tanglewood." *New York Times* (11 July 1982), p. 39.

Sessions, Roger. "Concerto for Orchestra." Boston Symphony Orchestra Program notes, 21 October 1981.

"World Premieres." *Symphony Magazine* 32 no. 6 (1981), p. 46.

Works Index

Subject Index